Chasing

Summer

Chasing

Start: November 1, 2000

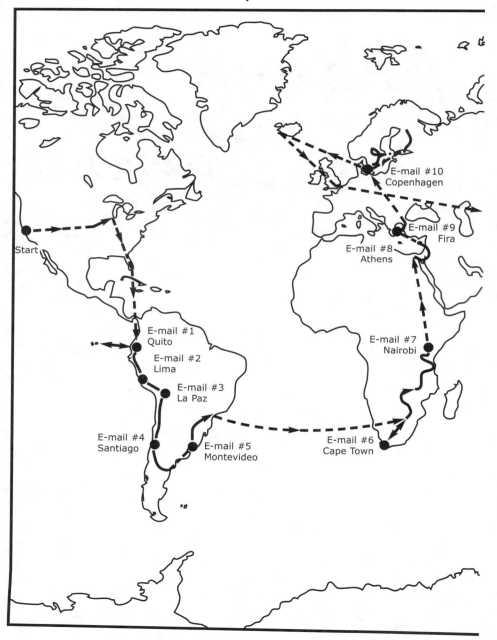

Start

E-mail #1
Quito

E-mail #2
Lima

E-mail #3
La Paz

E-mail #4
Santiago

E-mail #5
Montevideo

E-mail #6
Cape Town

E-mail #7
Nairobi

E-mail #8
Athens

E-mail #9
Fira

E-mail #10
Copenhagen

Summer

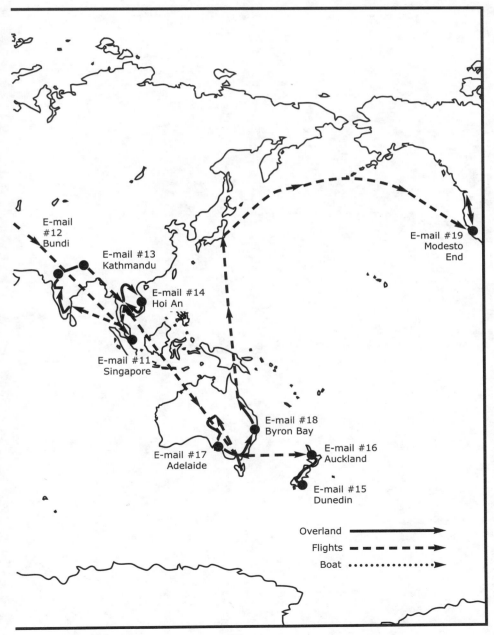

Chasing Summer

Exploring the world on an 18-month honeymoon

Jennifer & Erik Niemann

JSL Publishing • St. Louis, Missouri

ISBN, print ed. 0-9728643-4-2

LCCN 2003090588

Cover and interior photos by Erik Niemann

Front cover photo: Sunset on Uyuni Salt Flats, Bolivia

Edited by Hollie Keith

Published by: JSL Publishing, St. Louis, Missouri
                   www.jslpublishing.com

Printed in the United States

To everyone who eagerly
read our grand adventure
e-mails and vicariously
circled the globe with us.

Contents

Prologue

What makes a successful lawyer and architect quit their jobs and embark on an eighteen-month honeymoon to explore the world? Our grand adventure started with a chance remark. We were engaged for less than one month when Erik suggested we travel the world after we married. Jennifer loves to travel, so it sounded great to her. Before we knew it, we had circled the globe and visited thirty-five countries on six continents.

Between November 2000 and May 2002, we chased summer and zigzagged between the northern and southern hemispheres. We spent one-third of our time traveling on tours and the rest traveling independently. We traveled by local bus, train, overland camping safari, felucca, car, campervan, ferry and plane. Both of us had previously traveled extensively in Europe, so we chose to concentrate on other parts of the world.

We did not intend to write a book chronicling our adventures when we left the United States. To keep in touch with friends and family during our trip, we sent monthly e-mails describing our travels, the sights we saw, and the cultures we visited. Our e-mails were enthusiastically received and we eventually realized many people would enjoy reading about our experiences.

How did we make our grand adventure happen? Jennifer owned a house in Oakland, California that doubled in value in four years. The house would be small for the two of us, so we decided to sell it before getting married. We realized we could either purchase another house at the height of a declining real estate market or invest the proceeds, travel the world with part of the funds and decide what to do and where to settle when we returned to the United States. It took us about two seconds to choose the second alternative.

We took six months to organize and arrange our lives for this adventure. First, we set a date for quitting our jobs (eight days before our wedding) and told our employers of our radical plans. Next, we set a schedule for preparing and selling the house. The house sold in a slightly longer time frame than originally anticipated, but the closing papers were signed a few days before the wedding and possession transferred four days after. Third, we planned a small wedding in Yosemite National Park for October 28, 2000. Because our wedding was small and we wanted to say good-bye to numerous friends and family, we had four open-house receptions across the United States. The first was the day after our wedding in Oakland, California and the other three occurred over the next two weekends in Kansas, Illinois and Michigan. Fourth, we sketched out our around-the-world itinerary and set up our initial travel to South America.

We searched the Internet and found an eighty-four-day tour from Quito, Ecuador to Rio de Janeiro, Brazil starting a month after our wedding. We booked it thinking a tour would ease us into traveling and also booked a week-long cruise of the Galapagos Islands. Finally, we madly sorted, threw away, gave away and stored our things, and organized what to take on our trip.

We decided to travel light. We purchased two large backpacks with straps that could be hidden so the bags looked like large soft-sided luggage and we each had a small day pack. We downloaded lists from the Internet and canvassed friends to determine essential travel needs.

We left California four days after getting married in Yosemite and flew to Kansas City and later to Chicago. We left Chicago on Tuesday, November 14 for Key West, Florida. We enjoyed five days and four nights in Key West on a "traditional" honeymoon before the "around-the-world" honeymoon.

Thanks to the suggestion of one of Erik's friends, we started our travels with a wonderful outdoor dinner midway through the Keys at a restaurant called Milemarker 88. We sat outside in balmy 80°F (27°C) weather on a wooden deck overlooking dimly lit ponds. We sampled conch chowder and Jennifer (a self-proclaimed food aficionado) had a delicious, grilled yellowtail snapper topped with a sweet basil and tomato *concasse* and grilled bananas. In Key West, we toured the city by bus, visited Ernest Hemingway's home, and cruised the coral reef in a glass bottom boat at sunset. We enjoyed the wonderful, unique restaurants and the warm, tropical air. We also finished writing our wedding thank you notes, got haircuts and shipped our remaining unwanted items to California for storage. On November 19, 2000, we left Key West, purchased guidebooks for Ecuador and Brazil on our way to the airport and began our overseas adventures.

First we flew to Quito, Ecuador and the Galapagos Islands. On November 30, 2000, we joined an eighty-four-day tour of South America. On March 1, 2001, we flew to South Africa and then joined a thirty-day overland expedition from Johannesburg to Nairobi, Kenya. From there, we traveled in the Middle East, Greece, Turkey and Scandinavia. In mid-August 2001, we flew to Southeast Asia for four and one-half months.

We rang in 2002 in New Zealand. For six weeks we extensively toured that country in a campervan starting in the south and heading north. Afterward, we visited Australia for two and one-half months before returning to the United States approximately eighteen months from when we left.

This book is an expansion of our monthly grand adventure e-mails sent to family and friends during our travels. We hope you enjoy chasing summer as much as we did on our around-the-world trip.

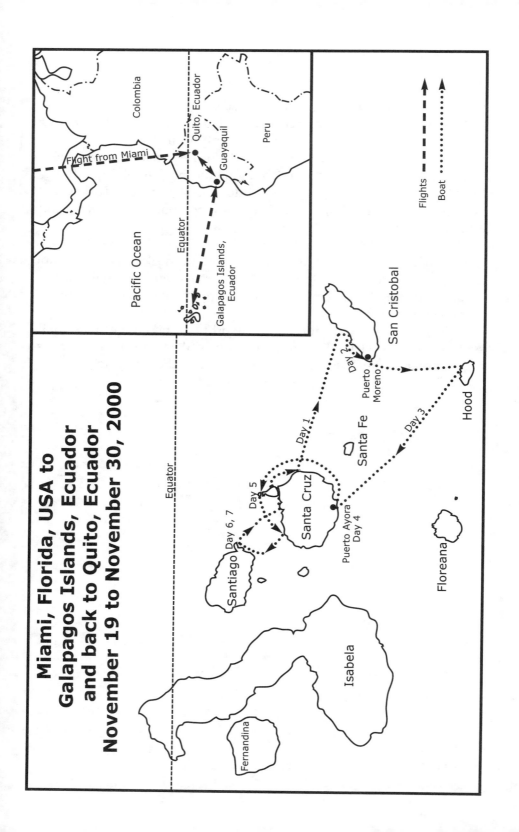

Miami, Florida, USA to
Galapagos Islands, Ecuador
and back to Quito, Ecuador
November 19 to November 30, 2000

1

Quito, Ecuador
Thursday, November 30, 2000

Dear friends and family,

   On November 19, we left Miami for Quito, Ecuador and a week-long cruise in the Galapagos Islands. Ecuador is slightly smaller than Nevada with a population of 13.2 million people. The capital, Quito, is located 10 miles (16 kilometers) south of the equator. Ecuador eased us into our international travels. We did not need to convert any money upon our arrival since Ecuador recently stopped using sucres and adopted the U.S. dollar as its official currency. Also, many locals understand some English since Quito is a popular place for Westerners to attend Spanish immersion classes. On the flight from Miami, we sat next to an Ecuadorian woman who taught English at one of the numerous language schools in Quito. We showed her a small photo album of our wedding pictures and she taught us many useful Spanish words.

   Our arrival in Quito assured us we had left the United States. We disembarked into the night air down steps rolled to the door of the plane and crossed the tarmac to immigration. Erik immediately noticed the thin air. Quito sits in the middle of mountains at an eleva-tion of 9,350 feet (2,850 meters). The high altitude affected Erik—he found it hard to sleep the first night. Soldiers in camouflage fatigues carrying automatic weapons patrolled the immigration area. We quickly passed through immigration and waited for our checked bags to arrive.

   Being in our first "third world" country, Erik was anxious about pickpockets and bag snatchers. Our bags arrived safely on the luggage carousel and we braved the dense crowd of locals standing immedi-ately outside the terminal. We trusted an apparent taxi driver with our belongings, walked down to the taxi area and hopped in his cab. Once in the cab, Erik relaxed and trusted everything would be okay.

We departed for the Galapagos Islands early the next morning. We flew first to the coastal city of Guayaquil before continuing on to the islands. The Galapagos Islands are a group of thirteen large and six smaller islands that straddle the equator approximately 600 miles (1,000 kilometers) west of mainland Ecuador. The volcanic islands were created by the separation of three tectonic plates—the Pacific, Cocos and Nazca Plates—under the Pacific Ocean. We landed at the airport, a former World War II U.S. military field on Baltra Island in the middle of the archipelago.

After each paying our US $100 national park entry fee, we boarded a bus from the airport to our sixteen-passenger cruise yacht, the *Cruz del Sur* (Cross of the South). A crew of eight manned the yacht, including the captain and our naturalist guide. Our guide was very funny with a quiet demeanor and quite knowledgeable about the flora, fauna and geology of the Galapagos Islands. We traveled with fourteen other passengers from America, Britain, Australia, Holland and Italy.

The Galapagos Islands are a popular vacation destination, so many cruise ships simultaneously sail the waters. Each boat is assigned a certain route for the year and must tour the islands in the prescribed order and hike the islands at certain times. This system limits the number of tourists on an island at any given time, and protects this natural wonder while permitting many tourists to see it.

Our itinerary was jam packed. After lunch the first day, we swam and snorkeled (our first snorkeling experience) and then hiked for two hours on South Plaza Island where we walked right next to sea lions, bright red crabs, large yellow land iguanas, small lava lizards and swallow-tailed gulls. The island, like most of the Galapagos Islands, was very arid. The soil was thin and the flora consisted mostly of cacti and low, red-leaved, scrubby plants growing among the rocks.

From South Plaza Island, we cruised all night toward the southeast edge of the archipelago. Because the Galapagos Islands straddle the equator, the sun rises promptly at 6 AM and sets at 6 PM. The first morning of our cruise we awoke at 5:30 AM to see the sun rising behind a spectacular rock formation called "Kicker Rock" looming beside us. This rock formation is narrow and tall, resembling an American football ready to be kicked. We walked up to the bar area of the boat, made ourselves cups of hot tea, then went outside on one of the decks to soak in the glorious sunrise.

After breakfast, we boarded two dinghies and motored around the rocky coastline of San Cristobal Island. We saw pelicans and blue-

Kicker Rock, Galapagos Islands,
Ecuador.

footed boobies (a white bird with dark gray wings and baby blue feet)
dive-bombing into the water for fish. We passed through a rock arch
with many small crabs crawling on the rocks and stopped on a sandy,
white beach to snorkel before heading back to the ship for lunch. The
waves knocked us around as we put on our flippers, but the snorkeling was great! Jennifer wore a life vest and found it easy to stay afloat.
We saw numerous fish and Erik swam over a 4-foot (1.2-meter) sleeping stingray camouflaged in the sand which startled him.

After lunch, we sailed west to Puerto Baqueizo Moreno on another
part of San Cristobal Island. We boarded a bus at the port and drove
to a beach of black rocks—the remains of ancient lava flows. We
watched black marine iguanas sunning themselves. Male marine iguanas measure about 2 feet (60 centimeters) in length with a pug face and
a line of small spikes running down their back to the end of their tails.
Their tails are as long as their bodies. Marine iguanas are the only
lizards in the world that swim in the ocean for their food. These rep-

tiles spend most of the day lying in the sun on the black rocks warming up so they can swim for algae found near the shore. They rid their bodies of excess salt from their ocean swimming through small holes in their heads. Every now and then, a marine iguana shoots a white salt liquid out of these holes.

On another part of the beach we watched a baby sea lion and his mother yelp until they found one another in the large mass of sleeping sea lions. The best part of the Galapagos Islands is that humans do not scare the animals, so you can get within 2 feet (60 centimeters) of most wildlife. After viewing the wildlife, we visited the new Galapagos Cultural Center. Erik appreciated the innovative architecture of the Center, but was even more excited and surprised when he found an Internet cafe in Puerto Moreno. He sent an e-mail to our immediate family letting them know we had arrived safely in South America.

Over the next three days, we explored Hood and Santa Cruz Islands. On Hood Island we saw more marine iguanas, blue-footed boobies, crabs, local finches, and a waved albatross. While hiking on Hood Island, our guide cautioned us to hide our water bottles because it is so dry the local finches will land on your water bottle wanting a drink. (These may be the same type of finches Darwin studied when he visited the islands in the 1830s.) Erik did not appreciate the extent these birds seek water until he went to the bathroom behind a bush and the finches drank the puddle of urine before it seeped into the ground! Snorkeling near the island we saw two white-tipped reef sharks in the abundant marine life. From Hood Island we sailed northwest to Santa Cruz Island and Puerto Ayora, the largest town in the Galapagos Islands.

The fourth day of our week-long cruise, Thanksgiving Day in America, we drove around Santa Cruz Island in a small bus. We walked through a farm to see about twenty giant land tortoises. These magnificent creatures live to be approximately one hundred fifty years old. Their size is hard to fathom. Their shell is almost 5 feet (1.5 meters) long and they move slowly on huge feet and feed or drink water with tiny heads. We especially enjoyed watching four giant tortoises move around in a shallow, muddy pond.

After lunch we toured the Charles Darwin Research Center where scientists raise giant tortoises for five years before releasing them back into the wild. Originally the Galapagos Islands had fifteen species of giant tortoises because almost every island had its own species. When whalers and others came to the islands more than one hundred years ago, the islands housed over one hundred thousand giant tortoises. Whalers discovered these tortoises could survive in the hull of a ship for a full year without food or water and hunted the giant tortoises nearly to extinction to provide fresh meat for their long voyages. Due to the actions of man, four species are extinct.

At the Research Center, examples of each of the eleven remaining species roam inside an enclosed area. We walked among these giant tortoises, just as we did the other wildlife on our hikes. The shape of their shells varies widely because each species adapted to the unique environment of its island. On islands where rainfall and grasses are plentiful, the giant tortoises have dome-shaped shells. On islands where vegetation is sparse and the tortoises eat leaves from plants, they have shells that curve up at the neck allowing the animal to reach food high off the ground. These latter animals gave the islands their name, as *galapagos* means "saddle" in Spanish, referring to the shape of their shells.

After some free time in Puerto Ayora and a visit to another Internet cafe, we re-boarded our yacht and sailed north past Baltra Island to North Seymour Island. On most of our hiking excursions, we boarded two dinghies from the back of our yacht and rode these to the shore. Sometimes we had docks to disembark at; other times we pulled close to the sandy beach and climbed out of the boat in the water. At North Seymour Island, rough seas caused the tide to drop about 6 feet (1.8 meters) in a matter of a couple of seconds and it took several tries for the dinghy to dock on the rocks so we could disembark.

After we landed, we hiked for two hours and saw tons of frigate-birds and blue-footed boobies. Both birds breed on this island, so we observed the birds mating and nurturing their young. Male frigate-birds were building nests to attract females. These large, black birds have a pink throat pouch that turns red during mating season. After a frigatebird builds a nest, he inflates his red pouch, flaps his black wings, and calls loudly to the females to inspect his nest. If a female likes the nest, the pair mates. The blue-footed boobies had already hatched their young and we watched the white downy chicks wandering near their nests testing out their fuzzy wings.

Over the next few days we hiked several more times. We watched small, red Sally light-foot crabs navigate the surf and scuttle sideways on the beach and three pink flamingos search for shrimp in the mud. Flamingos eat by turning their heads almost upside-down in the water with their bills facing their legs because their black bill is shaped so the top part moves and the bottom part is stationary. We also saw where sea turtles dug holes in the sand at night to lay their eggs. We saw two sea turtles swimming in the ocean near the sandy beach waiting for nightfall so they could crawl up the beach and lay their eggs. We watched two large yellow male land iguanas fighting for a nearby female iguana. We also saw many prickly pear cacti. These cacti stand about 6 feet (1.8 meters) high with a thick trunk and large, round, flat green "leaves" to store water. We saw a cactus finch picking the seeds out of a beautiful yellow flower on one of the cacti. Many cacti had these yellow flowers in bud or in bloom, as the plants were preparing to reproduce before the wet season starts in January.

On the last full day of our cruise, we spent the morning hiking on Santiago Island. We hiked for two hours over "fresh" lava (meaning from the volcanic eruption in 1897). The ground was rock hard and mostly gray in color. We saw "rope" lava and lava tubes everywhere. Rope lava looks like pieces of rope laying one next to the other. It happens when the surface lava cools before that underneath it and the hotter lava drags the cooled lava with it. Lava tubes are places where the outside lava cooled before the inside lava, but the outside lava stayed stationary. After the inside lava stopped flowing, the interior remained empty. After a hundred years, the outside of the tubes has eroded and broken in several places, so you can see the hollowed out interior of the lava tubes.

On our last afternoon in the Galapagos Islands, we snorkeled near Pinnacle Rock and saw our first Galapagos penguin. These birds stand 16 to 18 inches (40 to 45 centimeters) high with the usual penguin markings and live the furthest north in the world. After snorkeling we rode in the dinghy looking for more penguins and saw several in the water and standing on the rocks.

We capped off our fabulous Galapagos Island adventure with an early morning dinghy ride before heading back to the airport. We boarded the dinghies at 6 AM and explored Black Turtle Cove near Santa Cruz Island. The calm cove is an area where fish relax. The crew turned the engines off and glided through the water using poles so we would not disturb the wildlife. Several rays swam by the boat. We also saw eight white-tipped reef sharks resting in the shallow water and several sea turtles, including a pair that was copulating! All in all, it was a magical finale to our cruise.

Once in Quito we had three days to explore the town before our eighty-four-day South America tour departed. We first ran many errands. We bought more film using our rudimentary Spanish, shopped for Christmas gifts online at the Internet cafe, visited the woman we met on the plane from Miami, and cashed in traveler's checks at the bank. The pair of armed guards standing outside every bank astounded us. Our first evening, we met a friend of Erik's sister at a small jazz cafe. We had traditional Ecuadorian food, listened to jazz and marveled at the candles with open flames burning on every table. A candle without glass around the flame is virtually unheard of in a Californian restaurant!

Yesterday evening we toured Old Town Quito with a former co-worker of Erik's father. Erik and his family lived in Quito for the first two years of Erik's life and remained in contact with our host. What a treat! Old Town Quito is very different from the newer area where we stayed and had spent all of our time. Old Town has narrow streets, Spanish colonial architecture, and a myriad of churches and plazas. We parked the car and walked by the presidential palace, visited San Francisco Church and stopped inside the church where our host was baptized. We then visited his house and ate a wonderful home-cooked Ecuadorian meal at the typical dinner hour of 9:30 PM. Because it was the eve of the ten days of festivities to celebrate the founding of Quito, we danced in the living room after dinner.

Today we returned to Old Town Quito. First we visited the history museum of Quito housed in the oldest hospital in South America. Then we saw a huge parade celebrating the Viva Quito festival near the San Francisco Plaza. Marching bands, clowns, dancers and merry-makers packed the narrow street. When we arrived at the square, the plaza resembled a political rally with huge crowds, banners, a platform and a loud speaker. We soaked up the festive atmosphere before walking around more of Old Town.

Later this evening we join our group for the eighty-four-day tour from Quito to Rio de Janeiro. We will spend the next six weeks traveling to other parts of Ecuador, Peru and Bolivia. Then we travel to Chile, Argentina, Uruguay, Paraguay and Brazil. We will write again in Peru.

Love, Jennifer & Erik

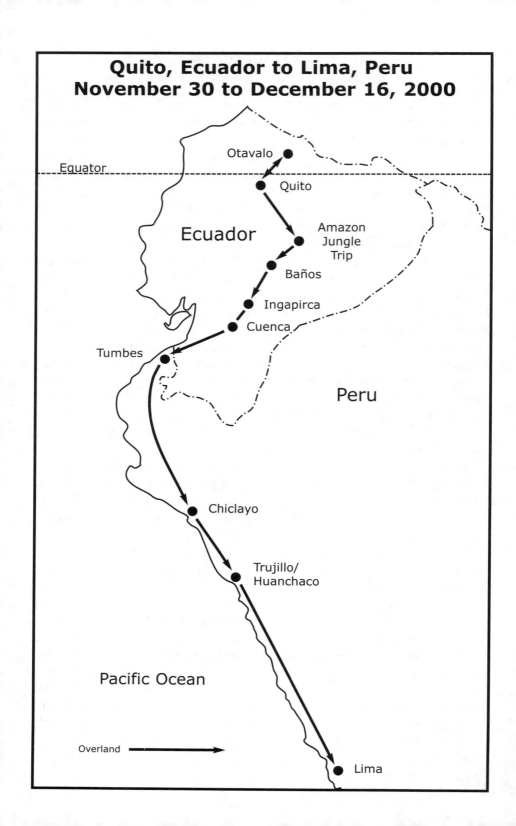

Quito, Ecuador to Lima, Peru
November 30 to December 16, 2000

Equator

Otavalo

Quito

Ecuador

Amazon
Jungle
Trip

Baños

Ingapirca

Cuenca

Tumbes

Peru

Chiclayo

Trujillo/
Huanchaco

Pacific Ocean

Overland

Lima

2

Lima, Peru
Saturday, December 16, 2000

Dear friends and family,

We joined our South America tour group on November 30. Four of us travel for the entire eighty-four days and ten others will travel as far as La Paz, Bolivia. We are the only Americans. The rest come from England, Australia, New Zealand and Canada. Our guide is a twenty-four-year-old native of Lima, Peru. He has guided similar tours for the past eighteen months.

We are having a ball! First we traveled to Otavalo, 75 miles (120 kilometers) north of Quito. At the hotel in Quito, we all hopped in unmarked taxis for the ride to the main bus station in Quito. We had traveled less than two blocks when a motorcycle policeman pulled the whole convoy over. Apparently our use of non-official taxis for the journey upset the regular taxi drivers and they called the police. Our guide used his diplomacy to have us continue in the same taxis, and twenty minutes later we were again on the road.

The bus ride to Otavalo was very scenic. The only not-so-pleasant part of it was driving through a long tunnel in Quito. Normally tunnels are not so terrible, but the air pollution in this tunnel was especially bad since all the bus windows were open! A fellow traveler, who sat in the front of the bus, vowed upon her arrival in Otavalo to "never again" ride in the front due to the bus constantly overtaking other vehicles on narrow mountain roads.

After settling in our rooms in Otavalo and eating lunch, we drove for forty minutes to Laguna de Cuicocha, a lake in an inactive volcano. We took a boat ride and saw bubbles in the water where the thermal energy from inside the earth escapes. We also went to a small nearby village specializing in leather goods. Our guide told us we would go crazy looking at about twenty leather stores in a row. He was right; our heads were spinning after the fifth identical leather shop.

Back in Otavalo, we happened upon a twilight parade. Groups of young schoolchildren marched carrying 3-foot- (1-meter-) tall wooden poles topped with a lit candle set in a box of blue, red, or green transparent plastic film. These groups were separated by decorated pick-up trucks carrying four-year-old children wearing fancy white dress. We never learned what the parade was for, but we enjoyed the festivities. At dinner, Otavalo Indian children wearing traditional dress of solid color ponchos and bowler-type hats performed traditional dances. Jennifer even danced with them!

The next day we enjoyed the Otavalo Market, the most renowned Indian market in South America. Every Saturday, Otavalo Indians converge on this picturesque town framed by the Cotacachi volcano to sell their animals, produce, textiles, and other wares. Early in the morning we walked the streets of town to the animal market. The main market spills over from the square down various side streets, so we saw people setting up market stalls on every street. At the weekly animal market, dozens of pigs, piglets, sheep, goats and cows were individually tied up and available for sale. People would bargain with the owner for a price then pay and take the animal away. Other people prepared and sold breakfast to those at the animal market at a makeshift area with tables.

Since we had no pressing need for a piglet or a goat that day, we wandered back to the main market where everything else under the sun was for sale. Vendors wearing traditional garb displayed hats, ponchos, linens and knickknacks. We found the market for chickens, chicks, rabbits and guinea pigs, and wandered through the local fruit and vegetable market. Money exchanged hands fastest at these markets. While wandering around this visual and aromatic spectacle, we met two of our companions from the Galapagos Island cruise at a rooftop cafe. It was great seeing familiar people from a week ago in such an obscure place; but since Otavalo is on the tourist trail, it is fairly common to run into other tourists you know.

We returned to Quito for the night before heading for the jungle. Since it was still Viva Quito days, every fifteen to twenty minutes a vehicle full of revelers drove by the restaurant where we ate dinner. Each bus or truck had a band onboard and dancing merrymakers. Large music stages were also set up along main thoroughfares for additional partying well into daylight hours the next day!

From Quito we headed southwest by local bus over a high mountain pass and through lush green mountains to the mist and waterfalls of the Ecuadorian jungle. Erik pointed out to Jennifer the snow-capped mountain peaks camouflaged among the clouds. Local Ecuadorians rode the bus as well as tourists. An Ecuadorian mother with two children (one holding a live white rabbit) sat behind us. As we ate banana chips we purchased at the bus station before leaving, the woman gestured to us if we could share some of our food with her children. We were happy to do so; it reminded us how lucky we are that we can buy food at a bus station with little financial consideration.

As we traveled further into the jungle we came to a road block with armed soldiers. We had arrived at the entrance to a national forest and we had to get out of the bus with our passports in hand. We then went one by one to an outside desk to register ourselves. Erik was a bit nervous since this was our first roadblock with soldiers carrying guns in the middle of nowhere. After a few more of these later on in the trip, it became old hat and Erik calmed down considerably!

Our first stop was a lovely hotel at the base of the Rio Napo, one of the tributaries to the Amazon River. We boarded two long dugout canoes for the ten-minute journey to the hotel. Once in the canoe we frantically applied insect repellant. If we only knew that in fifteen minutes we would be swimming in a beautifully tiled swimming pool, we would not have stunk up our clothing with the repellant. Now we only apply repellant when insects actually bother us!

The swimming pool was a godsend after a six-hour trip in rural Ecuador. Erik never wanted a swim so badly in his life. Soon most of the group was cooling off in the pool with a beer in hand. We stayed in bungalow huts outfitted with mosquito netting and ate in a lovely outdoor-covered dining area complete with sofas and a pool table. To start dinner we enjoyed Ecuadorian soup served with popcorn that floated on top. After dinner most of us went to an area with hammocks circling a fire where we chatted well into the night.

The next morning we rode ninety minutes in dugout canoes to our jungle camp where we stayed in small wooden huts for the next two evenings. After arriving we went for a three-hour hike in the jungle and learned how the natives use the different plants. Jennifer had her face painted with berries and we both tried lemon ants—crunchy and very lemony! We had a brief rain shower, but the vegetation was so dense we hardly got wet. We got quite muddy climbing down a vertical 12-foot (3.7-meter) drop. Fortunately we had many tree roots and a sturdy vine to hold onto during our descent. We got very wet when our hike took us through a creek. Erik ended up wading through

Jennifer receiving red berry paint on her face, Ecuador jungle.

waist-deep water; Jennifer took the drier shore route which involved walking carefully on a small cliff-face.

Our meals in the jungle were cooked on three portable burners in a kitchen without running water that measured 8 feet by 15 feet (2.4 meters by 4.6 meters). The meals were wonderful. After lunch we tubed down the Rio Napo. Not having much tubing experience, Jennifer was soon hopelessly spinning in circles near the riverbank. One of the local guides swam out and pulled her back into the flow of the river. We tubed for a few hours, and when it was getting late, we grabbed onto the side of the motorized long canoe which pulled us quickly down the river!

That evening one of the local guides took a live tarantula down from the ceiling of our dining room to show us its characteristics. One of the teenagers from Australia was quite excited about this eight-legged find. Both of us touched the spider's sticky legs! The next day we saw a demonstration of traditional hunting tools and tried our hands at blowing darts through a blowgun. Let's just say that if we needed to hunt via blowgun, we would definitely let Erik do the hunting, and even then we would probably starve!

From the jungle we headed back into the Andes on a harrowing bus ride, complete with a large mudslide in front of us that delayed us for two hours and a very narrow mountainous road that required the bus to back up in certain places to allow other traffic through. We were very happy to arrive in Baños, a small town famous for its hot springs at the base of Tungurahua, an active volcano. This town was recently reoccupied after the volcano forced an evacuation in October 1999. We hiked up a trail to overlook the town, but turned around when the trail became almost vertical. After hiking, Erik enjoyed the very hot thermal baths directly beneath a beautiful waterfall!

We saw many strolling musicians in Baños. In Ecuador and Peru, if tourists are nearby, so are three to four musicians dressed in Andean Indian dress playing pan-pipe music. These musicians wander from restaurant to restaurant playing for tips. The first couple of times we enjoyed it; after the thirtieth time it became somewhat grating.

Local buses are our main mode of transportation. Riding these buses is quite an experience. The bus looks like it has survived several wars and you wonder how it runs. Most of our rides last about three hours. As we travel we pick up and drop off passengers. Many people usually stand in the aisle. Luggage is carried on the roof of the bus in a rack and you can forget about a toilet! We ride on these types of buses about two-thirds of the time. The nicer buses we sometimes ride may or may not have a toilet, and luggage is stored tightly underneath. During the ride, loud Spanish rock music or traditional pan-pipe music plays over the speakers of the bus.

Private cooperatives run the buses in Ecuador and Peru. As a bus leaves its starting point, it picks up as many passengers as possible while creeping out of town. A teenage boy stands half way out the door yelling at the top of his lungs the destination of the bus to all the pedestrians. If we are headed to Quito, for example, you will hear "A Quito! A Quito! A Quito!" Also while the bus creeps out of town at about 5 miles (8 kilometers) per hour, different food vendors board the bus walking up and down the aisle selling everything from ice cream, local foods, candy, small cheap plastic toys, to fruit juice in a sandwich bag with a straw! Apparently no child labor laws exist, as many vendors are boys and girls five to fourteen years old. In Baños, Erik went to an Internet cafe tended by a five-year-old boy!

From Baños we headed into the Andean highlands to the Inca ruins at Ingapirca, a town nestled in the Andes at a height of 9,600 feet (2,925 meters) above sea level. We drove through mountains rising 6,000 feet (1,830 meters). Agricultural fields almost vertical in topography are interspersed with small villages and little towns. The fertile fields of volcanic ash are farmed without the aid of machines—only the cow, plow and farmer. The farming communities assist each other to harvest their crops.

The Inca ruins at Ingapirca are the best preserved in Ecuador. We had a wonderful guided tour and learned about the Cañari Indians that occupied the area before the Incas. The Cañari people built a temple to the moon and a small settlement; only the foundations of both remain. We saw a replica of the typical Cañari house with trapezoidal niches and front door to stabilize the house during earthquakes. We watched llamas graze on the terraced agricultural fields of the Cañaris and toured the remains of the temple of the sun built by the Incas. Inca buildings are made of stones carved so the blocks of stone fit together exactly and do not need mortar. We look forward to seeing more Inca ruins in Peru, especially along the Inca Trail.

From Ingapirca, we headed three hours southwest to Cuenca, Ecuador's third largest town. We arrived late Saturday and left early Monday, so most of the town and the museums were closed. The closed shops had metal, garage-like security doors covering the storefronts, so we could not tell what kind of shops they were. The street in front of our hotel looked completely different Monday driving out of town when all the shops were open for business.

The nearby supermarket was open on Sunday and we stopped to buy snacks for our Monday bus ride. Jennifer loves to browse supermarkets and was wandering around the store while Erik shopped. Suddenly Jennifer spotted a skinned guinea pig with claws on a Styrofoam meat tray wrapped in saran wrap sitting in the meat section. After an initial reaction of disgust, this unique sight reminded us that we can learn a lot about a country running errands.

We visited the "Original Panama Hat" factory on our way out of town and saw how the hats are woven, soaked in water and shaped in various styles. From Cuenca we traveled southwest descending through amazing canyons to the flatlands of western Ecuador. Bonita and Dole bananas grow in plantations everywhere in the flatlands and we saw the large purple flower that grows into a bunch of bananas.

We entered Peru that afternoon. Peru has 27.8 million people and is slightly smaller than Alaska. It was the center of the Inca and Spanish empires. We stopped to have our passports stamped out of Ecuador and into Peru. To cross the border, we carried our four bags and walked over the international bridge that spans a dry creek bed. The two towns on either side of the border bustled with people, cars and markets selling anything and everything. It was a feast for the eyes!

We took taxis into Tumbes, Peru where we hung out for six hours waiting for our night bus to Chiclayo. The nine-hour bus ride was very crowded with some people sitting in the aisle and we had a live turkey in the luggage storage under the bus. We stopped twice for the various check points and again at 4:30 AM for breakfast. We arrived in Chiclayo at 5:30 AM, and headed to the hotel for a few hours of sleep. We experienced culture shock in Chiclayo because this large city with paved roads had no traffic lights or stop signs. To drive through an intersection, the driver honks his horn as he approaches then proceeds through the intersection without slowing down or stopping. This driving method works surprisingly well and we saw no crashes.

That afternoon we drove through fields of sugar cane to the Lord of Sipan archaeological site, three worn-down "pyramids" resembling large mounds of dirt due to the El Niño effects over the centuries. We saw the Lord of Sipan himself, a skeleton decked out in a reproduction of his original burial garments of gold, silver, copper and bronze. The Lord was a warrior of the Moche people, a pre-Inca civilization that pre-dated the Chan Chan people whose ruined mud city we saw later outside Huanchaco.

From Chiclayo we headed south once again to Trujillo, Peru's third largest city. We stayed at the beach resort of Huanchaco for two nights. As we passed through villages near the west coast of Peru, we noticed reinforcing bars sticking up in the air from the four corners of the house. It looked like people were preparing to build a second floor, but every house? Our guide told us people build their homes this way so when they can afford to build a second floor, the reinforcing bars can secure the new floor to the rest of the house.

Throughout Peru we noticed political graffiti—the logo or candidate names of particular political parties—painted on the sides of mud or brick buildings. Large "Xs" were painted over the names of the candidates. At first we thought it was political rivals defacing their opponents' names. As it turns out, Peruvians vote by placing an "X" over the candidate's name, so the graffiti indicates which candidate to vote for.

In Huanchaco, the local men fish from one-man reed boats. We watched two men build a reed boat on the side of the road near the beach. Two bundles of reeds form each boat. The men wrapped rope around each bundle of reeds then tied both bundles to each other to form the boat. After they finished the boat, one of them took it out on the ocean for a test run. Reed boats usually last for four or five months. Sunset at the beach is the time for the local fish market. The fishermen

Reed boats beached for the night, Huanchaco, Peru.

ride the surf back to shore after having fished all day. When the men return, their families help unload the crabs and fish, set up buckets at the edge of the beach, and sell the seafood to passersby for dinner.

One of our favorite sights was Chan Chan, ruins of the biggest mud city in the world, between Trujillo and Huanchaco. Chan Chan dates from 950 to 1440 AD and was the capital of the Chimu civilization. The Chimu people were the dominant civilization in Peru before they fell to the Incas. In its heyday, Chan Chan was the largest city in the Americas and one of the earliest examples of urban planning. We toured one of the nine palaces. Each palace, built by a different king, housed the king and aristocracy. The primarily adobe buildings deteriorate quickly, so many have been restored. Narrow mazelike corridors linked large open areas used for religious ceremonies. The palace walls were carved with a variety of patterns, including fish caught in nets and other things.

We also visited Pyramid of the Moon, an ancient pyramid from the same period several miles away. Extensive archaeological activity continues at the site. The interior of the pyramid sports colorful murals of stylized warriors painted in red, yellow and blue and 2-foot (60-centimeter) tall stylized faces separated by a 1-foot (30-centimeter) wide border of solid red or a yellow and black uniform pattern. The archaeological excavations reveal the pyramid was built by an incline system that allowed materials for the next level to be transported alongside the existing structure.

We arrived in Lima yesterday on a fabulous nine-hour daytime ride on a half-full air-conditioned bus with a working toilet. We watched two movies and no one boarded the bus to sell us things. What a treat! Just a short stay here; tomorrow we leave for Pisco.

Today we shared an authentic meal at the home of our Peruvian tour guide. The main course was *ceviche,* a traditional Peruvian dish of raw fish marinated in lime, salt and onions. Yummy! We met our guide's extended family and spent time in their home. After lunch we toured the catacombs of a Franciscan monastery and visited the Museum of the Spanish Inquisition.

The Spanish Inquisition spanned a period of 356 years (1478-1834) when the Roman Catholic Church questioned and punished heretics. The church set up the court in Lima to protect the areas of Peru, Chile, Argentina, Bolivia, Paraguay and Uruguay. The museum is small, but very well presented. The new museum surrounds numerous archaeo-logical remains and the old building. The torture room with 3-foot (1-meter) thick walls was the most interesting. Inquisitors considered tor-ture an appropriate method to question heretic suspects. Certain rules insured the torture did not kill the suspect, but damaging the body by water torture, a stretching machine, a choking machine and a pulley system were perfectly acceptable. Most accused heretics were not exe-cuted and had lesser sentences or were released.

That's all for now. We wish you all happy holidays! We hike the Inca Trail on December 24, 25, 26, and 27. On the 27th we arrive at Machu Picchu, the lost Inca city!

Love, Jennifer & Erik

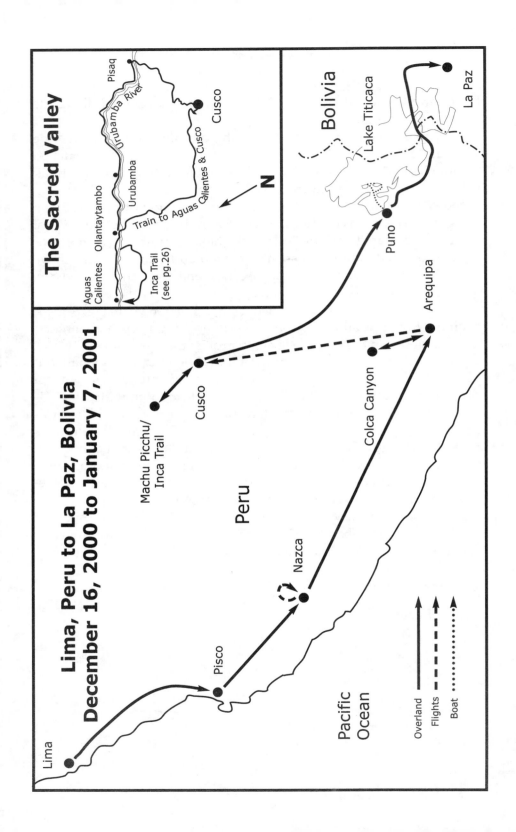

The Sacred Valley

Pisaq

Urubamba River

Cusco

Urubamba

Ollantaytambo

Train to Aguas Calientes & Cusco

N

Aguas
Calientes

Inca Trail
(see pg.26)

Lima, Peru to La Paz, Bolivia
December 16, 2000 to January 7, 2001

Lima

Pisco

Nazca

Machu Picchu/
Inca Trail

Cusco

Peru

Colca Canyon

Arequipa

Puno

Lake Titicaca

Bolivia

La Paz

Pacific
Ocean

Overland

Flights

Boat

3

La Paz, Bolivia
Sunday, January 7, 2001

Dear friends and family,

Wow! Much has happened in the three weeks since we last wrote. First of all, we wish all of you a prosperous, happy and healthy 2001!

From Lima we traveled south to Pisco, home of the Pisco Sour, a drink made from eggs, lime juice, sugar, ice and a liquor of fermented grapes. Pisco sours are really good, after the initial reaction to the sour taste! At a museum near Pisco, we saw several bizarre elongated skulls of a pre-Inca civilization. This civilization considered elongated heads beautiful, so they deformed the heads of the babies so the back of the head jutted upward and back. Due to this deformation, the skulls in the museum show approximately fifty percent of the people had skull surgery during their life.

We next stopped in Nazca to view the famous Nazca lines, large figures etched into the desert over five hundred years ago. Most of the figures represent animals, plants and shapes, but a few represent man. The figures are so large you can only see them from the air. We flew in a small, six-seated plane to view the lines. The flight was quite turbulent as the plane constantly tipped to the side and veered back and forth to allow passengers on both sides of the plane to view the lines. Jennifer was fortunate to have the co-pilot seat; Erik had a seat in the middle of the plane and suffered severe motion sickness as a result!

We also visited the nearby pre-Inca civilization cemetery of Chauchilla. Farmers previously looted this area, so the remaining mummies and artifacts have been replaced in the excavated tombs. The cemetery sits in a desert, at the edge of irrigated land. Surprising to us, the whole coast of Peru is a desert due to the Humbolt current coming up from Antarctica. In order to feed themselves, the pre-Inca civilizations built underground channels from the mountains through the desert to irrigate a small strip of desert with snow melt. Farmers still use those channels today.

From Nazca we rode a very comfortable night bus to Arequipa (although we did have a ninety-minute delay at 5 AM when the bus ran out of fuel), the second largest city in Peru. We enjoyed visiting a museum housing a frozen mummy found on one of the nearby volcanoes. The mummy, a young girl, was sacrificed by the Incas and buried in the top of the volcano just after death with all sorts of belongings. Because of her frozen state, scientists have learned much about the Incas, including the food given to sacrifice victims.

We also toured parts of a former convent shut off from the rest of the world until 1970. This city within a city stretches for several city blocks and has its own streets, cemetery, washing area and church. The streets are labyrinth-like with buildings painted in bright, beautiful colors. Prior to the mid-1800s, wealthy Spanish families sent their second-born daughters to this convent so the nuns' rooms are elaborately decorated. Each nun had an area to do her own cooking and an area for her servants to sleep. In the mid-1800s, the Pope, upset with the excess, reformed the convent, created a common cooking area, and released the servants, permitting them to become nuns themselves.

From Arequipa we drove to Colca Canyon, one of the deepest canyons in the world and nearly twice as deep as the Grand Canyon. During the drive we saw numerous llamas, alpacas and vicunas. These three animals are from the camel family and live in the South American mountains. Llamas, the largest of these animals, are used as beasts of burden to carry heavy loads in the mountains. Alpacas, slightly smaller than llamas, have a more fleece-like coat than the llama. Alpaca wool is very soft and warm. We both bought alpaca sweaters for our Inca Trail hike. Vicunas, the smallest of the three animals, are wild. They are cinnamon in color with a white chest. We drove over a high mountain pass that sits over 16,000 feet (4,900 meters) above sea level. We joined in the local tradition of chewing coca leaves to combat altitude sickness. At that altitude breathing is very difficult and you feel nauseous because your internal organs expand with the pressure and press against each other. Fortunately, we descended to an altitude of only 11,000 feet (3,350 meters) above sea level for the night.

In the canyon, we hiked between two small towns in the valley, admiring the picturesque terraces and the river below. The Peruvians farm the sides of the valley leading into the canyon in terraces more than two thousand years old. The farmers grow mostly potatoes at that altitude. Potatoes originated in the Andes Mountains of Peru and Bolivia; Europe did not have potatoes until the Spanish conquest of South America in the mid-1500s. Modern scientists once collected 3,500 varieties of native potatoes in the Peruvian Andes. These potatoes are a variety of sizes and colors, including purple, yellow, orange and brown. Farmers plant half of the terraces at a time, allowing the other half to recover from the prior planting. Farmers plant cacti along the tops of the stone walls that create the terraces to keep grazing animals from eating the crops.

After an overnight return trip to Arequipa, we flew to Cusco, center of the former Inca empire, to hike the Inca Trail. We began hiking the Inca Trail on Christmas Eve and finished on December 27 at Machu Picchu, the lost Inca city discovered in 1911 by an American working for National Geographic. In total we hiked approximately 28 miles (45 kilometers). The Inca Trail was built at the same time as Machu Picchu and was designed to be very difficult and out of the way, so Machu Picchu could never be conquered.

We left Cusco, Peru at 6:30 AM and started hiking around 11 AM. Twelve of us hiked the full trail and we picked up twelve porters on our drive to the trailhead. These men (aged from sixteen to thirty) carried the tents, equipment, duffle bags with our clothes, sleeping bags, food and cooking supplies. Each carried about a hundred pounds (45.4 kilograms) on their backs! We would not want to be a porter, even for one hour! Every time we set out to hike, the porters put away all the food and other cooking utensils and broke down a large dining tent that seated twenty people, then raced ahead of us to set up for the next meal! We hiked during the rainy season of Peru, so every few hours we put on ponchos to protect us from the downpours. The porters, however, did not have rain ponchos. They typically wore sandals made of used tires, a tee-shirt, sweatpants, and maybe a sweater.

The first day of the hike was relatively easy. We hiked for two hours before stopping for a hot lunch of soup, meatballs and vegetables prepared by the cook and his assistant. We ate our fill then proceeded to hike straight uphill for fifteen minutes to overlook the Inca ruins of Llactapata, foundations of various small, uniform buildings that sit atop a terraced hillside. It is believed this ruin represents an agricultural station and the terraced hillside was farmed to provide food for Machu Picchu. From the lookout we descended into the valley and hiked along the Urubamba River. We passed numerous small houses

Inca Trail
December 24 to December 27, 2000

Dead Woman's Pass
13,780 ft/4,200 m

Night 1 Camp
9,843 ft/3,000 m

Night 2 Camp-Paqaymayu
11,811 ft/3,600 m

Runkurakay

Sayaqmarka

Llactapata

Urubamba River

Train to Cusco

Night 3 Camp-Winay Wayna
8,858 ft/2,700 m

Sun
Gate

Km. 82
Start
9,022 ft/2750 m

N

Train to Cusco

Machu Picchu
7,874 ft/2,400 m

Aguas Calientes
End

and saw many farm animals and hummingbirds. When we arrived at our campsite, our tents were already in place and all we had to do was relax. We watched the sunset over the Andes Mountains and enjoyed another wonderful meal, topped off with bananas flambé for our Christmas Eve dinner!

Day two of the hike was the hardest. We climbed from 9,843 feet (3,000 meters) above sea level to 13,780 feet (4,200 meters) before lunch. Thirty minutes before we reached the top of Dead Woman's Pass, it started to hail and we were soon trudging through a downpour of pellet-sized hail. In addition to the hail, 30 mile (50 kilometer) per hour winds buffeted us at the top of the pass—not a pleasant experience since we were already wet and cold and wearing shorts. We were both freezing! Luckily, the warm lunch tent was only ten minutes down the other side of the pass. We arrived at the tent and our cook warmed up towels to put on Jennifer's legs and neck. We warmed up quickly, ate lunch and headed straight downhill to our second night camp at Paqaymayu. Fortunately the sun came out, and we enjoyed the beautiful flora of the area and saw more hummingbirds during our pleasant afternoon descent. The second night's camp was very muddy and cold. We were so tired we napped in our tent for a couple of hours before Christmas dinner of marinated steak and champagne.

Day three was the longest day of hiking. We hiked uphill again for a grueling forty-five minutes to the ruins of Runkurakay. All along the Inca Trail, the Incas set up outposts about every 3 miles (5 kilometers) with strategic views of the trail to see any adversaries coming. Runkurakay was a semi-circle-shaped outpost and a place for Inca pilgrims to stay on their way to Machu Picchu. After Runkurakay, we climbed a little further to the third pass at 12,700 feet (3,900 meters). After that we visited the ruins of Sayaqmarka, an important cleansing stop for the Inca pilgrims. We forced ourselves to climb up to explore the terraced ruins of lodgings and three ritual baths where pilgrims purified themselves.

After Sayaqmarka, we hiked for the next ninety minutes on a lovely flat piece of trail that wrapped around a couple of small mountains and through a cave. Unfortunately clouds obscured the view of the mountain ranges around us. We could however see a large waterfall in the distance. We ate a huge lunch, and then walked down an endless number of stone steps, descending about 3,500 feet (1,100 meters) to our third night's camp at Winay Wayna. One of our guides made us two bamboo walking sticks for which we were very grateful. The downhill lasted about three hours—all but thirty minutes of that in pouring rain. Our knees took a beating! We just wanted to collapse when we arrived at the camp, but the ruins of Winay Wayna were only five minutes away, so we decided to tough it out and see them. The ruins were incredible. These beautiful ruins terrace steeply down the mountainside in narrow fields and a series of fifteen ritual baths one below another.

Five members of our tour who stayed in Cusco over Christmas hiked half a day to our third night camp and we had a fun meal together. Our porters dressed in their traditional garb of multi-colored woven ponchos and traditional hats and we presented them with our cash tips. The camps during the first two nights were relatively sparse of tents, but at Winay Wayna, tents were everywhere! For the first time the camp site had a lodge with working bathrooms. We could shower at very inflated prices, but we had come this far without a shower, so what was another fifteen hours?

Jennifer and Erik with Machu Picchu, Peru in the background.

We arrived at the fabled Machu Picchu on the fourth day. We started hiking at 5 AM to reach Machu Picchu before the bus loads of tourists. We arrived at the Sun Gate at 6:30 AM which gave us our first glimpse of the lost Inca city, a forty-five-minute walk downhill. The sun still had not come out even though it was very light out. At the Sun Gate during the summer solstice (December 21 in the southern hemisphere), the sun shines though a series of stone monoliths and illuminates Machu Picchu.

We toured Machu Picchu for two hours starting at 8 AM. Our Peruvian guide was an expert about the different aspects of Machu Picchu. The city sits on a hillside and is divided into five different sectors for the various activities of agriculture, spiritual worship, housing for the Inca nobles and priests, and other domestic activities. The site is almost entirely terraced as a means to farm the steep mountain terrain and also to prevent erosion. Some stone buildings have been reconstructed. We saw the ritual cleansing baths, the aqueduct system and the rooms where the head Inca stayed.

Machu Picchu is believed to be the principal religious site of the Inca civilization. We visited a water temple, a sun and moon temple, and the temple of the sun located at the highest point in Machu Picchu. The altar of the sun temple is a large granite rock said to radiate energy. The rock feels warm when you place your hand about an inch (2.5 centimeters) from the surface, but is actually cold when you touch the surface. Theories are the Incas quickly abandoned Machu Picchu around the time the Spanish conquered the Incas in the 1530s. The Spanish never found Machu Picchu since it was so well hidden. The western world did not learn of its existence until 1911.

We left Machu Picchu right when hundreds of tourists poured in. We nearly laughed out loud when we passed a video-camera toting tourist expressing relief at having "finally arrived" at Machu Picchu. Their early morning train ride and bus to the base of the site seemed trivial compared with our four-day hike!

We rode the bus down the switchback road to Aguas Calientes, the town at the end of the railroad line from Cusco, and headed straight for the hot springs to relax our aching muscles and bathe for the first time in four days. What a treat! After a couple hours there, we could move easier. We slowly ventured back into the main street of town for lunch. The main street runs for three blocks along either side of the railroad tracks that terminate the line from Cusco. We ate lunch with part of our group, visited the Internet cafe, and then sat on the porch of the cafe watching a downpour of rain and being extremely grateful we were no longer hiking the Inca Trail. At 4 PM, we walked on the muddy streets to the train station for our trip back to Cusco.

The next day we toured more ruins around Cusco in the "Sacred Valley of the Incas." This valley along the Urubamba River leads to the area where we started our Inca Trail hike. We visited Inca ruins nestled above the town of Pisaq and then the market in Pisaq. We had a traditional Peruvian lunch of *lomo saltado*, a dish of sautéed beef, onions, and red pepper on top of French fries with a side of rice. On our way to the next Inca ruin, we stopped at a local "pub" (men sitting on wooden benches in a dark room drinking beer) and tried Inca *chicha* beer, a local home-brew made from fermented corn. We both enjoyed the unusual tasting beer and tried our hand at a game where you throw gold coins into slots to score points. Our last stop was the ruins of Ollantaytambo. This former fortress temple sits atop the near vertical walls of the river valley. We enjoyed exploring the ruins, but the steep temple steps nearly did in our tired bodies!

Over the next few days we explored Cusco and enjoyed several meals on a restaurant balcony overlooking the main plaza. Cusco was the heart of the Inca empire. When the Spanish came, they destroyed much of Cusco and the temples near there. The Spanish built on top of destroyed buildings and Inca stonework is evident in the foundations of many large buildings in Cusco. The Spanish built the local cathedral entirely from stones of an Inca temple. Inca stonework is simply beyond words. Most stones are the size of a large television and some even five times larger than that. When put together, the angled sides of the stones fit perfectly to other stones without mortar. You cannot even get a needle in between the stones.

We spent New Year's Eve in Cusco. What an amazing experience! A friend of our tour leader invited us to annual celebrations at his family home. The party lasted from 10 AM until 4 PM, and then from 8 PM until 2 AM. The party started with a local shaman performing the *Pachimama* ceremony, an ancient ritual that prepares a "meal" for mother earth. At the end of each year, the locals give back to the earth some of the wealth of the previous year. This fascinating ceremony combined pre-Inca, Inca and Roman Catholic elements. The shaman prayed over a cloth filled with all sorts of items, wrapped the items in the cloth, and then buried the cloth in the ground in the garden.

During the *Pachimama* ceremony, the family prepared our lunch. They heated rocks on a metal grate over a fire in a large pit for a couple of hours. When the rocks were hot, they put half of the hot rocks at the bottom of the pit, threw in whole potatoes and covered them with cabbage leaves. They added four sides of a marinated pig (along with two pig heads) and interspersed hot stones with the food. More cabbage leaves, quarters of marinated chicken, ears of corn, pods of lima beans, and herbs were added, interspersed with hot rocks. They then covered the whole pile of food with large sheets of paper and burlap bags, shoveled dirt over the top and let it cook for two and one-half hours. The food was delicious! They also had an oven where they baked homemade bread and roasted guinea pig (a Peruvian delicacy). We both tried the guinea pig; Jennifer ate much more of it than Erik!

In the evening, we danced the night away wearing yellow party favors for good luck, including yellow underwear on the outside of our pants! After toasting in 2001 with champagne spraying from all directions, we followed a marching band down the narrow streets and around the main square of Cusco filled with thousands of partiers. Fireworks exploded all around us. We returned to the house behind the band and partook in a midnight feast.

On New Year's Day we drove to Puno, Peru, on the shores of Lake Titicaca. Lake Titicaca is the highest navigable lake in the world at 12,500 feet (3,800 meters). It covers approximately 3,200 square miles (8,300 square kilometers), with sixty percent in Peru, and forty percent in Bolivia. If you ask a Bolivian, they would say that sixty percent of the lake is in Bolivia!

On January 2, we took a three and one-half hour boat ride out to Amantani Island where everyone in our group spent the night with local families. On the way we stopped at two floating islands made from reeds piled approximately 3 feet (1 meter) thick to create a living space. When you walk around these islands, you cannot stay in one place for too long or you start to sink. Several families live on these artificial islands and continually add layers of reeds as the island sinks. Most huts were small, one room affairs with cooking facilities over a burner located in a covered area next to the hut. A couple of huts had solar panels and televisions. We boarded a reed boat with a large reed dragon head at the bow and taxied to another reed island.

On Amantani Island, we stayed with a woman who had a separate one-room building for guests. The island has no running water or electricity. Some houses had solar panels for power at night. The island families eat mainly local produce of potatoes, corn and beans. They only travel to Puno once a month, so it is customary for guests to bring gifts. We brought bananas, papayas, rice, noodles, two notebooks of paper and two pens. After settling in, we walked across the courtyard and watched our hostess's cousin cook our lunch in the small 5 foot by 10 foot (1.5 meter by 3 meter) dark, smoky kitchen. The cousin used

Reed island on Lake Titicaca, Peru.

eucalyptus wood to fuel the fire that heated the pots for the soup and rice and the skillet. For lunch we had rice, thick french fries cooked with eggs, and quinoa soup. It was very delicious! We learned the family owned ten sheep and one chicken and had a large field of potatoes. They also planted onions for their use. That evening a local pan-pipe band played and we danced for ninety minutes with the local women. During our entire visit we did not see many men; they were at another town on the island playing soccer.

The next day we took a boat to the nearby Taquile Island. Like Amantani Island, Taquile Island is rocky and steep. We climbed up five hundred steps from the shore to the main village. The stone buildings of the town border narrow, stone-paved paths, since the island has no cars, only donkeys. On Taquile Island, the men do all the knitting and the women weave. All the boys on the island learn how to knit when they are five or six and are quite proficient when they reach their teenage years. Everyone on the island wears traditional clothing that indicates whether they are single or married.

We took the boat back to Puno, and the next day, January 4, we crossed into Bolivia. Bolivia is a country three times the size of Montana with a population of 8.4 million people. It is a large landlocked country and relatively poor, although it has many natural resources. We took a bus to the Bolivian border; walked across the border and re-boarded our bus on the other side. We transferred buses in Copacabana and loaded our luggage on top. A forty-five-minute ride later we arrived at the Tiquina Strait where we got off the bus and boarded a rickety ferry to the other side. We wondered why we did not ferry across in the bus. When we watched the bus ferry bob back and forth precariously, we were relieved we crossed as we did. When the bus arrived at the other side, we had a further forty-five-minute delay while new brake pads were installed!

Two hours later we arrived in La Paz. La Paz sits in a valley about 1,000 feet (300 meters) below the flat Bolivian plain (called the Altiplano) near Lake Titicaca. La Paz is a modern bustling city of two million people structured differently than most cities in terms of its layout. In La Paz, the poor live on the upper part of the city and the wealthy live down in the valley. We were surprised to see people selling things everywhere! The sidewalks look like one huge flea market. You can buy just as many goods on the streets as in the stores—everything including film, pens, calculators, deodorant and disposable diapers! You can even buy 2-foot- (60-centimeter-) tall dried out llama fetuses in one area of town for good luck!

We have seen much of La Paz since we needed to get our visas for Brazil at the Brazilian Embassy here. As required, we photocopied our credit card, blacked out the account number, and took a taxi to the embassy. That embassy had moved, so we went to the new address. Once there, we learned we had to pay our visa fee at the Brazilian bank in La Paz and return with a receipt. After another taxi ride to the bank, we left our passports to be picked up before 5 PM. We returned to our hotel, dropped off laundry and ran other errands before picking up our passports with the new Brazilian visas.

Yesterday we found the NFL (American football) on television, and watched the playoffs. We also saw our first theater movie in South America. The movie, "Charlie's Angels," cost US $1.50 each — the right price because the film broke and started to melt in the middle of the showing! Before the film we ate at the local Burger King. Erik found he can only eat six weeks of local food before an old favorite is needed. He was also very excited to find Internet computers inside Burger King and checked e-mail while Jennifer finished eating with the rest of our group!

We have found Internet access readily available in South America and a fabulous way to stay in communication while traveling. In addition to sending these mass e-mails, we purchased our Christmas gifts, resolved loose ends regarding health insurance and finances, read news from home and researched our next travel destinations. Right now we are finalizing plans in Brazil after our tour ends and setting up a thirty-day overland safari in Africa. While the connections can be unreliable, the price (around one U.S. dollar an hour) is right.

Seven members of our group ended their tour here in La Paz. Seven of us continue on into the heart of Bolivia tomorrow, and six of us then continue into Chile next week. We will write from there. We hope 2001 will be incredible for all of you!

Love, Jennifer & Erik

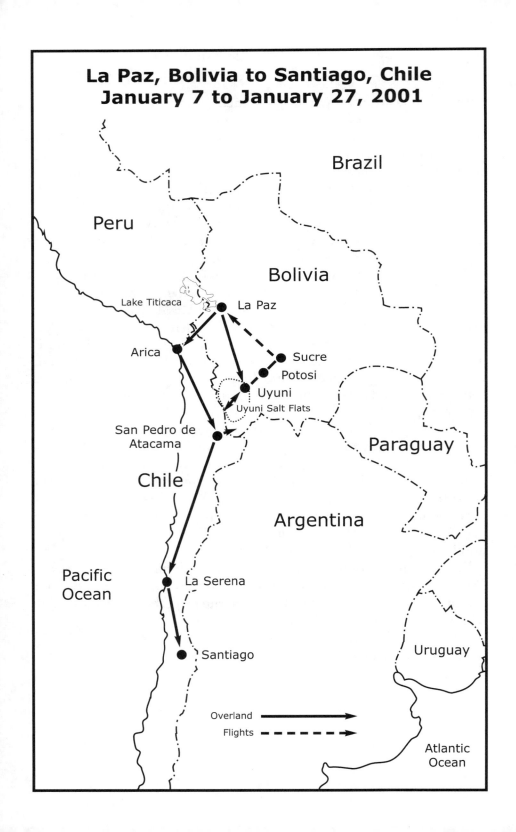

La Paz, Bolivia to Santiago, Chile
January 7 to January 27, 2001

Brazil

Peru

Bolivia

Lake Titicaca

La Paz

Arica

Sucre

Potosi

Uyuni

Uyuni Salt Flats

San Pedro de
Atacama

Paraguay

Chile

Argentina

Pacific
Ocean

La Serena

Uruguay

Santiago

Overland

Flights

Atlantic
Ocean

4

Santiago, Chile
Saturday, January 27, 2001

Dear friends and family,

We left La Paz on Monday, January 8 for the Uyuni salt flats. We bussed to Oruro where we boarded a train to Uyuni. From the train we saw many llamas and alpacas in the desert-like landscape. A range of low mountains were visible in the distance. We watched lightening near the mountains while we ate in the dining car and celebrated the birthday of one of our fellow travelers. Once in Uyuni, we hopped in a Toyota Land Cruiser for a three-day trip to the largest salt flats in the world. We stayed the first night at the Salt Hotel located on the edge of the flats. The hotel was made of salt blocks about the shape and size of regular bricks used to build houses in America. Inside the hotel all of the furniture—beds, chairs, and tables—was made from salt blocks or carved from salt. A half inch (1.3 centimeters) of salt grains covered the floor. Red and blue pillows, brown and tan fur seat covers, bedspreads and tablecloths decorated the white furniture. That night at dinner we joked around asking "please pass the salt" and someone would pinch some from the table top and hand it over!

The next morning, we drove the Land Cruiser out on the salt flats for an eight-hour trip to the other side. The salt flats are usually dry and very white. This time of year, however, 2 inches (5 centimeters) of water covered the flats. We only drove about 25 miles (40 kilometers) per hour to minimize the amount of salt water hitting the underside of the vehicle. The scenery was amazing. Everything was simply white as far as the eye could see with no horizon. We could not determine how far we had traveled during the day. At one point we had a flat tire, so we walked barefooted on the warm and shallow flats while the driver fixed the tire. Five- and six-sided interlocking geometric designs measuring about 20 inches (51 centimeters) across on average covered the flats. Apparently, these natural designs resemble the shape of a salt molecule. We ate a picnic lunch at Fisherman's Island, so named because with the reflection in the water, the island looks like a fish. This island is made of sharp volcanic rock with amazing tall cacti all over the place. Erik must have taken a whole roll of film just at this one location! We hiked to the top for a three-hundred-sixty-degree view of the salt flats. In the distance we counted ten other Land Cruisers either coming or going. They looked like little ants crawling across the salt flats with a v-shaped wake behind them.

After lunch, we drove to Jirira, a small village at the base of the Tunupa volcano. Many of the adobe homes in the village are vacant because the younger generation prefers to live in larger towns like Uyuni. This farming village grows mainly *quinoa* (pronounced "keen-wa"), a hearty grain grown high in the Andes full of vitamins and protein and often served in soup. The next morning, while most of the group hiked the volcano, we walked past the *quinoa* fields to the edge of the salt flats. We watched flocks of flamingos eating in the small ponds at the edge of the salt flats and taking flight as we approached their feeding grounds.

On our trip back to Uyuni we stopped at a small village to see the salt manufacturing process. Salt manufacturing is truly a cottage industry. Workers gather and dry the salt on the flats before transporting it to the village. The salt is further dried in the village outside and inside the homes. At the cottage we visited, the family was repairing the straw roof that had caught fire accidentally during the drying process. Once dry, the salt is ground up, combined with iodine, and bagged for use as table salt.

We also stopped at the train cemetery just outside of Uyuni. Here trains in use just ten years ago now sit rusted, ruined, and slowly deteriorating. Most of the trains operated from the 1930s to the 1980s. A huge thunderstorm heading toward us gave us some great photos, but we did not linger.

From Uyuni we drove seven hours by bus northeast to Potosi, a town with a population of 150,000 located 13,400 feet (3,960 meters) above sea level, the highest town we stayed in. The town's livelihood depends on the large silver mine on the edge of town. The mine, inside a large mountain, has been in use since the 1500s. The Spanish discovered silver here in 1545 and used the indigenous people as slaves or forced labor in the mines. One of the wealthiest cities in South America in 1610, Potosi is today one of the poorest. Widows work outside the mine sorting through a large pile of scrap stones for leftover silver.

Erik and Bolivian woman miner, Potosi, Bolivia.

One woman had worked there for forty-five years! Their salary ranges from 2 to 10 Bolivianos per day, about US $.35 to US $1.50.

Jennifer toured inside the mine; Erik stayed behind and read in the truck. Jennifer wore a helmet, a long yellow rubber jacket, knee-high rubber boots, and carried an open flame lantern for light. She ducked through tunnels about one-third of the time, climbed up and down ladders, and met many miners. The lack of oxygen and the dust made breathing difficult underground. Most of the group held handker-chiefs to their noses. Miners who work for more than ten years sub-stantially reduce their life span due to toxins in their lungs. Our guide worked in the mines for eight years. Jennifer met one miner who had worked in the mine for thirty years. One miner had worked double shifts and had been underground for twenty-four hours. The miners do not eat while in the mines; they chew coca leaves for their energy. Tourists visiting the mine customarily bring gifts for the miners: Coca-Cola, coca leaves, and cigarettes. Senior miners earn around 50 Bolivianos a day (a little over US $8.00). A few miners were fifteen years old. Most of the ore is shipped to Chile, and then Germany to be crushed and refined.

From Potosi we visited Sucre, the official capital of Bolivia. Most of the Bolivian government is located in La Paz, but the judicial branch is still located in Sucre. Sucre looks different from other parts of Bolivia we visited. The streets are generally paved (unlike many parts of Potosi) and colonial and nineteenth century architecture dominate. We toured the Presidential Cemetery, where most of the deceased Bolivian presidents rest and Castle Gloria, the late nineteenth-century home of a wealthy Bolivian mine owner. While Jennifer rested in bed recovering from a bout of food poisoning, Erik and the rest of the group toured recently discovered dinosaur footprints. These footprints, located on an ancient lake bed, were pushed up over time and now sit upright at an eighty-five-degree angle. They are said to be one of the best examples of multiple dinosaur footprints in the world.

We flew from Sucre back to La Paz for one final day before heading to Chile. We spent about two hours at the Chilean/Bolivian border. The Chilean authorities, very concerned with what comes into their country, thoroughly search all buses crossing their border. We had our bags x-rayed and partially searched. After crossing the border, we drove through the Lauca National Park on our way to the Atacama Desert, descending over 15,000 feet (4,500 meters) in three hours. We traveled from lush meadows with grazing vicuna, through a lovely river valley, past cacti shaped like candelabra, to a fertile valley (only a few miles wide) surrounded by barren sand dunes rising 4,000 feet (1,200 meters) high.

Chile is two-thirds the size of Bolivia and has almost 15.5 million people. It is the most modern country we have visited in South America. In 1973, a highly controversial military coup overthrew the three-year-old Chilean communist government. At that time, Chile was on the brink of bankruptcy. Since then Chile has experienced rapid economic growth and many social advances, like universal healthcare. Thirty-five percent of the world's copper comes from Chile. Chile typically enjoys economic growth of about eight percent a year and Chile's economic prosperity depends heavily on the market price of copper. We have noticed this prosperity in various ways: Chile has a large, thriving middle class we did not see in Ecuador, Bolivia or Peru; people sell things at various tourist spots out of their cars instead of carrying the goods on their backs; Chileans camp and tour their own country; Chilean farmers use tractors and wagons; we pass more industry on the outskirts of the various cities; and many Chileans use cell phones. While Chile reminds us of the United States, certain things remind us that we are in South America. For example, stores close from 2 PM to 5 PM for siestas, we go out for dinner at 9 PM, and the bars start to fill at 1 AM and stay full until 5 AM!

We traveled first to Arica, the northernmost city in Chile. Arica once belonged to Peru, but after a war in the 1880s, Chile seized control of this area. One evening, our group enjoyed a wine and cheese sunset party atop a large cliff overlooking the town. A huge Chilean flag purposely flies in tribute to the taking of Peruvian land. Arica is a seaside resort town packed with Chileans enjoying their summer holidays, as January and February are the peak vacation months. We enjoyed the beaches and boogie-boarded on the waves. Erik experienced some nausea from "reverse" altitude sickness as we were at sea-level for the first time in over a month. On the architectural front, we visited a church and brick office building designed by Gustav Eiffel, the architect who designed the Eiffel Tower in Paris. Both buildings were designed and assembled in France, then shipped in pieces to Chile.

From Arica, we rode a night bus to San Pedro de Atacama, a small tourist town close to the Bolivian and Argentinean borders and in the driest desert on earth, the Atacama Desert. During our three days here, we explored the sights. We toured the "Valley of the Moon," a barren, arid wasteland filled with craggy rocks and sand. We hiked up sand dunes, walked through salt caves, and cheered on our fellow group members as they mountain biked on the desert roads past our tourist van. Another day we visited the nearby geysers and a hot spring. We left San Pedro at 4 AM (passing full bars) to arrive at the geysers just before sunrise. We saw dozens of hot bubbling pools of water steam the cold morning air. The primary geyser rose about 15 feet (4.6 meters) into the air—no "Old Faithful," but impressive nonetheless. We ate hard boiled eggs cooked inside one of the geyser pockets for breakfast and later soaked in a shallow hot spring. When we returned to town, we rode three hours on horseback into "Death Valley." We passed through the outskirts of town to the narrow canyons of rock and sand, and finally rode up and down the sand dunes. It took Erik about five days to fully recover from the ride, as his saddle was too small for him!

Our final day in San Pedro we drove a short distance back into Bolivia to see Lago Verde, a lake that changes color twice a day. When we arrived, the lake was brown and reflected the nearby volcano. Then, on the far end of the lake, we noticed an area of aqua-colored water. In no more than fifteen minutes, this aqua-colored area spread over the entire lake, changing the lake to an aqua-green color that no longer reflected the volcano. Lago Verde is a glacier-fed lake with a high amount of glacier sediment. Apparently, as the wind picks up in the morning, it stirs up the sediment, changing the brown water to aqua. It was quite a sight! We also enjoyed seeing hundreds of flamingos eating in a nearby lake.

The next day, we drove twelve hours south to La Serena, a coastal town with one of the most popular beaches in Chile. This quaint colonial town bustled with Chileans enjoying the summer. Chileans appear more European than the citizens of the other South American countries we have traveled in. The Spanish conquistadors used Chile primarily as a farming colony to provide food for the colonies of Ecuador, Peru and Bolivia. When the Spanish conquered Chile, the indigenous people resisted fiercely and the Spanish killed nearly all of them. Only pockets of indigenous people remain in Chile. Most Chileans trace their heritage to the Germans, Irish, Danes and Czechoslovakians that settled their country.

We joined several Chileans on a minibus tour of the Elqui Valley, a valley full of vineyards that reminded us of California's Napa Valley. Because Chileans travel within their country, most tours in Chile are in Spanish. In Ecuador, Peru and Bolivia, most of our tours were in English. For the Elqui Valley tour, our guide spoke some English, so we understood some of the information. We also practiced our limited Spanish conversing with the Chileans on our tour. We stopped first at a Pisco factory. Pisco is an alcoholic drink made of grapes, much stronger than wine. We enjoyed a lovely lunch under a weeping willow tree. The Chileans sang "Happy Birthday" to Jennifer as it was her 37th birthday. After lunch we visited the burial site for Gabriela Mistral, the winner of the 1945 Nobel Prize for literature. We later visited a museum in her honor. Gabriela Mistral, a renowned poet in her time, is a very famous Chilean. Early in her adult life, she spent two years in Mexico transforming their educational system; later she was a prominent diplomat and consul for Chile in several countries around the world.

From La Serena, we drove to Santiago, a five-hour drive further south. Santiago is as far south of the equator as San Diego, California is north of it. The landscapes and vegetation along the drive from La Serena to Santiago reminded us of California. Santiago might as well be a large city in America; we could hardly tell the difference with its skyscrapers and modern appearance. We traveled to different parts of the city on a modern subway system. Santiago also has familiar fast food like Pizza Hut, Burger King, McDonald's, Taco Bell, Dunkin' Donuts, and KFC. These restaurants opened in Chile only in the last ten years to the health detriment of Chile. More and more Chileans are gaining weight, which is very unusual for them historically.

We have enjoyed sightseeing in Santiago. We visited American relatives who have lived here for thirteen of the last twenty years. They drove us all around and gave us an inside perspective about life here. We visited a vast supermarket with fifty-nine checkout counters and a former monastery that now houses small art shops. With our group we rode a gondola up a small mountain in the middle of town to overlook the entire city. Santiago reminded us of Los Angeles, with the mountains ringing a city sprawling in every direction. Yesterday we visited the Cousiño-Macul Winery, the oldest family-owned winery in Chile. The wine cellar was built in the French tradition with long vaulted brick storerooms divided by a multi-arched wall. We entered the cellar down stone stairs lit by red candles sitting on iron holders fastened to the wall. Tomorrow we head further south to Pucon, Chile, and then over into Argentina and Uruguay. Until then!

Love, Jennifer & Erik

Santiago, Chile to Montevideo, Uruguay
January 27 to February 10, 2001

Uruguay

Santiago

Buenos Aires

Chile

Argentina

Montevideo

Pucon

Bariloche

Esquel

Puerto Madryn

Atlantic Ocean

Overland ⟶
Flights ⟶
Boat ⟶

5

Montevideo, Uruguay
Saturday, February 10, 2001

Dear friends and family,

Greetings from the capital of Uruguay! We traveled through three countries since we last wrote and have traveled through six countries since leaving the United States.

We departed Santiago and headed southeast to Pucon, a beautiful town on the shores of Lake Villarica. During the first hour on the bus to Pucon, we played along with the bingo game run by the bus attendant. It was fun to know our Spanish could keep up with the fast clip of the numbers being announced. Pucon sits at the base of Villarica Volcano, a huge, snow-capped, active volcano. A picturesque view of the lightly smoking volcano greeted us upon our arrival. The landscape around Pucon reminded us of Wisconsin or parts of Oregon — rolling hills and lots of trees. We enjoyed walking on very popular lake beaches and swimming in the frigid water. We hiked around some waterfalls and watched local boys dive into a deep blue pool of water from a 20-foot (6-meter) cliff. We also enjoyed some incredible hot springs! The springs were landscaped with natural rocks to create three pools of differing temperatures. We moved between the three pools and enjoyed pink clouds at sunset, the rising moon, and the appearance of Venus in the sky. The American sporting institution, the Super Bowl, was happening while we relaxed in the hot springs, but we did not mind missing it because our hotel room had no television.

The next day, Jennifer and the rest of the group climbed the volcano. Outfitted with cold-weather gear and ice axes, they climbed for three hours in the snow, snaking along single-file and stepping in the well-worn footprints of prior climbers. Clouds covered the top seventy percent of the volcano on the day of their climb and caused incredibly strong winds at the top. The winds slowed Jennifer down since she had to adjust to them to maintain her balance while hiking up the nearly vertical slope. Those who made it to the very top could not stay long due to the strong sulfur fumes coming from the magma deep inside the volcano. The trip down was much faster than the trip up. To descend the mountain, everyone slid on their bottoms and used their ice axe to slow themselves down. At one point, Jennifer spun around and was sliding down the mountain head first on her back with the ice axe outstretched above her head!

From Pucon, we entered Argentina. Argentina is just under three-tenths the size of the United States with a population of 37.8 million. Nearly half live in Buenos Aires. Argentina is the home of tango dancing, a sensual dance of complicated steps popular in the United States and Europe in the early twentieth century. We most enjoyed Argentina's beautiful scenery and national parks.

Our first stop was Bariloche, a town also situated on the edge of a very large lake surrounded by mountains. The town was built by Swiss immigrants with alpine architecture. No wonder it reminded us of being in Switzerland or parts of Germany. They specialize in making chocolate, so we did some chocolate tasting! The days were very sunny, but windy and chilly. We cruised Lake Nahuel Huapi in a catamaran. Most of the passengers on the boat were Argentinean. Like Chileans, Argentines travel quite a bit in their country during the summer. We stopped and hiked around on two islands. On the first island, we walked through a grove of Arraynes trees. These trees have cinnamon-colored trunks with many branches extending from the base of the tree. On the other island, we rode a chair lift to a lookout point and then hiked back down.

From Bariloche, we drove nine hours via the Seven Lakes Highway to Esquel, a Welsh immigrant town. The mountain and lake scenery was spectacular. The next day, we sailed and hiked in the Los Alerces National Park. We cruised in two different boats on three different lakes and a river. Snow-capped mountains surrounded each lake and we even cruised past a very large glacier! We hiked for two hours through a grove of Alerces trees. These trees are one of the longest living organisms on earth. The oldest tree we saw is approximately two thousand six hundred years old, but the trees can live to be four thousand years old. These very tall trees reminded us of the redwood and sequoia trees in California. These trees grow in a very damp forest with an undergrowth of solid bamboo plants. Water dripped off moss-covered rock walls and the trail overlooked another mountain lake and followed an emerald green river with rapids and waterfalls. Our guide stopped every five to ten minutes along the trail and spoke for five to ten minutes in Spanish. We only understood *muy importante* ("very important"), so we amused ourselves looking at the "very important" scenery around us.

From Esquel we traveled to Puerto Madryn on the Atlantic coast of Argentina. We rode for nine hours through some very desolate and dry areas on our way to the coast. Puerto Madryn is located next to the Valdes Peninsula, a wildlife preserve and popular area for whale watching. We happened to visit in the non-whale watching months, so we drove to various points on the peninsula and saw sea lions, elephant seals and penguins. We also saw guanacos, Argentina's version of the llama.

The next day, we drove south to Punta Tombes to visit a huge colony of penguins. The colony encompasses approximately 250 acres (1 square kilometer). The penguins nest in the dirt under bushes and in shallow holes in the ground. We saw hundreds and hundreds of penguins, many walking around us, just like in the Galapagos Islands. At this time of year, the penguins are finishing raising their young and waiting for their feathers to be replaced before traveling to south Brazil to spend the winter months. (Penguins shed their feathers once a year.) A few nests had young penguins waiting for their downy feathers to change to adult feathers. The penguins waiting to molt looked fat with a brown coat. When not molting, penguins spend three days in the water to feed. They swim for about a day to reach the feeding grounds, eat for a day, and then return to the penguin colony, where they spend about three days before repeating the process. When we reached the colony, most penguins were lying in their nests or casually walking around on the pathways. After an hour, however, the penguin parade began! Suddenly dozens and dozens of penguins left their nests and waddled to the water to begin their feeding. It was quite a sight!

From Puerto Madryn we opted to forgo a twenty-five-hour bus ride to Buenos Aires and, for an extra fee, flew ninety minutes instead. Buenos Aires is a fantastic, modern, bustling city with a European feel. Pockets of colonial and nineteenth century architecture interrupt the tall urban feel. On our first day, we walked all over the city and visited the Egyptian embassy to apply for our Egyptian visas. We were pleased to learn we knew enough Spanish (more than just our numbers) to complete the visa form written in Spanish and successfully communicate with the personnel who did not speak English. Another day we took a city tour and visited the Casa Rosada. *Casa Rosada*, a nickname meaning "Pink House" because the building is painted pink, is almost the equivalent of our White House, except the Argentine President only works at the Casa Rosada and lives in a house 6 miles (9.6 kilometers) away. The tour of the Casa Rosada was in Spanish, so we mostly gawked at the colonial architecture and interiors.

One evening we saw a tango show at the oldest tango house in Buenos Aires. The dancing was just incredible! We marveled at the intricate foot work and how they danced so close without kicking each other. The dancers changed outfits four times, with singing and Peruvian pan-pipe music between the acts. We laughed when the pan-pipes came out, because we had not heard a band like that for nearly a month. We never imagined a traditional Andean pan-pipe band at a Buenos Aires tango show!

From Buenos Aires we ferried to Montevideo, Uruguay. The Rio Plata, a very large river, separates Argentina and Uruguay. At the point that we crossed, the river is approximately 30 miles (48 km) wide. The river flows into the Atlantic Ocean, so most of the southern coast of Uruguay is an estuary and you can see the color change where the fresh water of the river meets the salt water of the ocean. The ferry was very big with a large area for vehicles on the bottom deck and an enclosed seating area on top. The seats looked like those in airplanes, complete with tray tables. Because the ferry is very wide, each row has twenty seats. Sitting in the seats was disconcerting because instead of having a back to front motion, like on an airplane, the seats rocked from side to side because we were on a boat!

Uruguay is a small nation, slightly smaller than the state of Washington. The population is three million, with half of them living in Montevideo and the surrounding area. Montevideo was originally a slave port, so it has a large African community. Last night we saw their Carnival parade. It was wonderful! We watched from a well-lit vantage point where the television cameras were set up. (We found out how great the lights were when they went out for five minutes during the parade and it was quite dark!) We stood five deep from the front of the spectators with several rows of people behind us! Many groups of people paraded past us. In each group, people waved huge flags with bright colors, girls and women in sequined costumes and feathers danced the samba, men twirled long batons, and men in costume drummed an African beat in unison. As we walked to our vantage point, we passed the drummers heating the head of their drums over fires to tune them. We watched for ninety minutes, until the heat (it was a very muggy 84°F (29°C)) and the shoulder-to-shoulder crowds caused us to retreat to our hotel. Once in our hotel, however, we found the parade on television and watched for another two hours!

Yesterday, we also took an all-day trip to Punta del Este, one of the largest and most popular beach resort towns in South America and one of the main gambling destinations for Brazilians. Our favorite part of the trip was our stop at the home of Uruguayan painter and sculptor Carlos Paez Vilaro, painter of the fresco in the main gallery of the United Nations building in New York. His self-designed house looks like something out of a "Dr. Seuss book." The nine-story house with round windows and domed sections terraces down the hill to a rocky beach. Tiled terraces and some blue trim color the white exterior. We saw two swimming pools from our vantage point: one at the very bottom of the house (complete with a painting of the sun by Carlos Vilaro); and the other on the second level from the top. A couple of hot tubs also sat among the terraces. To finance renovations for this forty-year-old house, Carlos Vilaro has converted half of it into a hotel and opened part of his gallery to the public. The remaining part of the house remains his private residence. The African community of Montevideo inspired many of his paintings. As a side note, his son survived a plane crash in the Chilean mountains in the early 1970s. That crash inspired the book and movie "Alive."

One observation about Argentineans and Uruguayans is they drink *mate* tea all of the time. This tea, made from a mixture of leaves, tastes very bitter. Everywhere we went—on boat rides, day tours, buses, and in outdoor cafes—people held wooden cups shaped like gourds with a fancy wood straw with a metal mouthpiece sticking out of it and a thermos full of hot water. People place the mate mixture in the bottom of their cup, fill the cup from the ever-present thermos, and sip the tea through the wooden stick. The wooden stick strains the tea through a filter at the bottom of it.

Today we take an all-day bus through Uruguay back to Argentina and an all-night one through Argentina to an area where Argentina, Paraguay and Brazil meet. Fortunately, the buses in Argentina and Uruguay are rather nice, so the ride should be pleasant. Then it is on to Brazil and Carnival!

Love, Jennifer & Erik

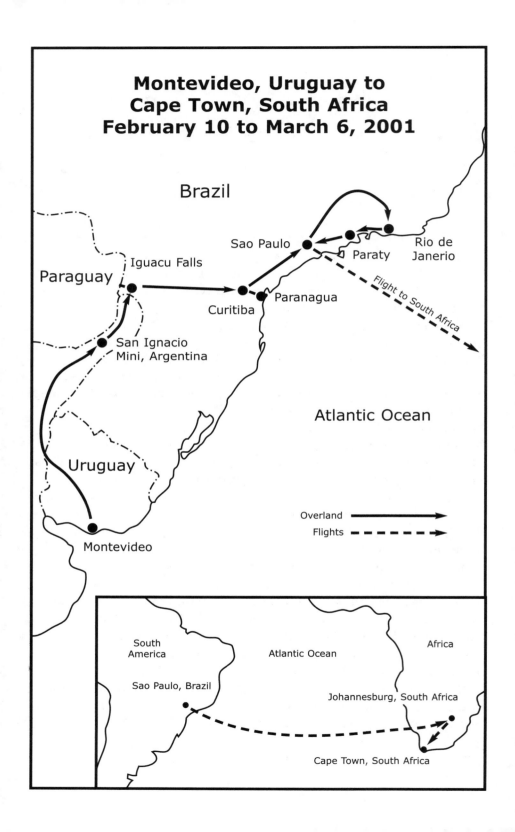

Montevideo, Uruguay to Cape Town, South Africa
February 10 to March 6, 2001

Brazil

Sao Paulo

Iguacu Falls

Paraguay

Curitiba

Paranagua

Paraty

Rio de Janerio

Flight to South Africa

San Ignacio Mini, Argentina

Atlantic Ocean

Uruguay

Montevideo

Overland
Flights

South America

Sao Paulo, Brazil

Atlantic Ocean

Africa

Johannesburg, South Africa

Cape Town, South Africa

6

Cape Town, South Africa
Tuesday, March 6, 2001

Dear friends and family,

Wow! We covered much ground since we last wrote. We completed our tour of South America, traveled to Africa, and tomorrow we embark on a thirty-day overland camping safari from Johannesburg, South Africa to Nairobi, Kenya.

From Montevideo, Uruguay, we rode four buses and traveled for twenty-one hours to a small town in northern Argentina, San Ignacio Mini. One thing we noticed on our bus trip is the easy border crossings between Uruguay and Argentina. Entering Uruguay, we cleared customs at the ferry dock. We had our passports stamped to exit Argentina, and stepped 2 feet (60 centimeters) along the counter to be stamped into Uruguay. The same thing happened when leaving Uruguay—we had our passports stamped to exit Uruguay and walked 10 feet (3 meters) in the same building to have them stamped to enter Argentina. Quite a change from the 3 miles (5 kilometers) of "no-man's" land between the Bolivia and Chile border stations!

In San Ignacio Mini, we visited the Jesuit mission ruins that are the basis for the 1986 movie "The Mission." When the Jesuit missionaries came to South America, they permitted the indigenous people to maintain their social structure and language. The natives lived in small houses connected five in a row, and ten on a street. The Jesuits educated them in their native language, as well as Spanish, and taught them skills such as stone carving. The Jesuits governed the mission with input from the natives. As a result, when the Jesuits abandoned the mission in the 1700s (after operating it for approximately one hundred fifty years), the natives still spoke their own language and retained their traditions. In other parts of South America, the Spanish did not preserve the culture of the indigenous people and many traditions were lost.

From San Ignacio, we traveled to the border of Argentina, Brazil and Paraguay. Brazil is slightly smaller than the United States (including Alaska and Hawaii) and has 170 million people. Settled by the Portuguese, Brazil has a different feel from the other South American countries we visited. First, Portuguese is spoken instead of Spanish. Also, the Portuguese used African slaves as their colonial labor force, so Brazil has more of an African influence than the western part of South America.

Our first stop was the stunning Iguacu Falls. Unlike the uniformity of Niagara Falls, the Iguacu Falls consist of more than two hundred seventy-five separate falls spanning approximately 1.5 miles (2.4 kilometers). The water tumbles approximately 180 feet (55 meters) over the falls in huge white sheets, hitting the rocks and causing tons of spray. In a few areas, the water falls the full length uninterrupted, but in most areas it tumbles over in two tiers divided by large rock formations covered with trees. Walkways on both the Argentine and Brazilian sides allow you to view the falls from above and below—and get very wet. We took a speedboat ride under the falls and emerged totally soaked! It was a welcome respite from the humid heat.

While near the falls, we visited Paraguay for an afternoon of duty-free shopping. Paraguay is slightly smaller than California with a population of 5.8 million people. The Friendship Bridge linking Brazil

Iguacu Falls, Brazil

with Paraguay was quite crowded with Brazilians and Paraguayans bringing goods back and forth between the two countries to be sold. Cars and vans were backed up for miles on both sides and thousands of people walk the half-mile- (800-meter-) long bridge every day. The border is quite relaxed as the border officers rarely stop cars and about ninety percent of the people pass freely. We had a productive four hours in Paraguay purchasing many rolls of duty-free film for our Africa trip.

We also visited the largest hydroelectric dam in the world, Itaipu Dam, which produces twelve million kilowatts of power. We normally do not consider dams interesting places, but this one certainly was. Built between 1975 and 1991, it straddles the border between Paraguay and Brazil. The two countries built the dam and share the power fifty-fifty. However, because Paraguay only uses five percent of the electricity that it owns, it sells the remaining forty-five percent to Brazil. This power plant produces twenty-five percent of the electricity for the entire country of Brazil. The pace of dam construction equated to building a twenty-story building every fifty seconds. The amount of steel used in the dam equaled almost four hundred Eiffel Towers and the amount of concrete used exceeded that for two hundred large Olympic-size stadiums. The dam is as tall as a sixty-five-story building. Only one of the four spillways was open when we visited. The dam created a huge reservoir and many environmental and reforestation programs operate in connection with the dam.

We also visited a fabulous bird park just outside of the Brazil entrance to the Iguacu Falls. We loved seeing all the different types of South American birds. South American birds are very colorful, especially the parrots and toucans. We walked through numerous aviaries with rainforest-type vegetation and the birds flying all around us. We also saw flamingos, ostriches, crocodiles, butterflies and turtles. At the end of our visit, a park keeper was putting a very large parrot on people's shoulders for a photo opportunity. Jennifer knew as soon as Erik saw this he would want the bird to sit on her for a photo. So, Erik asked that the bird be put on Jennifer's head! We have a great photo, but the bird really dug its claws into Jennifer's scalp!

From the Iguacu Falls, we headed to Curitiba, a large city in southern Brazil. Curitiba was named one of the three cleanest cities in Latin America. We rode a four-hour scenic train from Curitiba to the Atlantic coast, said to be the most spectacular train journey in Brazil. The 65-mile (105-kilometer) track opened in 1885 after five years of construction. The train traveled through lush jungle-type vegetation (typical of all the parts of Brazil we saw), in between two mountain ranges and along deep gorges and waterfalls. Unfortunately, the day we rode was overcast, so clouds obscured the mountains. Upon arriving at the coastal town of Paranagua, we walked along the picturesque beach. It is a good thing we walked when we did because after lunch the skies opened up and it rained about 3 inches (7.6 centimeters) in one hour! We sought refuge under an awning next to an automatic teller machine and eventually took a taxi across flooded streets to catch our bus back to Curitiba.

In Brazil, we ate many meals in their typical buffet style. Breakfast buffets typically included fresh fruit, dessert-like cakes, cheese, ham, bread, fresh squeezed fruit juices, sliced hot dogs cooked with sautéed onions and tomatoes (Erik's favorite), and occasionally eggs. During bus trips and for lunch, we typically ate at self-service buffet bars. These buffets had a table full of salads and cooked vegetables (which Jennifer liked) and a table of meats, beans, rice and pasta (which Erik liked). Once you filled your plate, you took your plate to be weighed, and were charged by the kilo. It is a great system because you can eat well in a short period of time (usually one-half hour) and can have a variety of food.

From Curitiba, we drove to Sao Paulo, the largest city in South America. Sao Paulo is responsible for the majority of Brazil's economy and is not a touristy town. We visited a "snake farm," a private foundation that studies poisonous animals and produces many types of venoms for bites and other illnesses. We also went to the Memorial da America Latina designed by the famous Brazilian architect, Oscar Niemeyer, and built in 1989. This museum houses handicrafts from all over Latin America and a large three-dimensional cartoonish relief map of Latin America underneath a glass floor displaying all the major sites and capital cities in Central and South America.

In Sao Paulo we reconnected with the cousin of a classmate of Jennifer's from the University of Illinois. The cousin stayed with Jennifer nearly twenty years ago when she visited the University of Illinois. Our hostess studied architecture, so she took us to visit the largest park in town also designed by Oscar Niemeyer. We also saw an architectural exhibit on the work of James Cutler, the architect that designed Bill Gates' residence in the state of Washington. When we arrived at the exhibit, it was closed for a private wine and cheese party, but our hostess talked the security into letting us view the exhibit anyway. We had a wonderful visit with her, her husband and son, and enjoyed our first home-cooked meal in a long, long time. What a treat!

We arrived in Rio de Janeiro on February 20. Rio is famous for its beaches, landscape, and the Carnaval (as spelled in Portuguese) events that happen during the four days before Ash Wednesday. Carnaval is celebrated all over in Brazil, but the most famous and popular for foreign tourists is the celebration in Rio. Many Brazilians travel to other cities in Brazil for Carnaval. A three-day samba school competition highlights Carnaval activities in Rio. Samba schools are social clubs that gather throughout the year. The participants sing, play instruments or dance. They practice for the samba school competition starting in August.

In the competition, each school presents 3,000 to 5,000 participants, divided into various wings. These wings include the people who clear the way for the parade, singers, the elected "king and queen" of the school, samba dancers, percussionists, older women performing a coordinated dance, and young girls dancing the samba. Each samba school chooses a theme, composes a song, choreographs a samba, and designs elaborate costumes and floats to fit the theme. Each school competes for sixty to eighty minutes. They parade the length of the Sambadromo (just over one-third of a mile (540 meters)) and are judged on various components of their procession. The samba school competition starts around 7 PM and ends at 7 AM, to make use of the coolest part of the day—the night! The competition is televised nationally and internationally.

Because we were not in Rio for Carnaval, we attended a samba show at the Plataforma. The show covered five hundred years of Brazilian history and was full of samba dancing with a cornucopia of amazing costumes. The costumes had feathers, sequins and elaborate headdresses. We sat no more than 10 feet (3 meters) from the dancers; closer than if we went to the Sambadromo. We also saw the practice parade (no costumes) of Imperatriz Leopoldinense, the samba school that won the Rio samba school competition this year and the year before. We enjoyed the drums and the samba dancing. Erik even recognized one of our taxi drivers banging on a drum. Many fewer members participated in the practice than competed, but we had a taste of being in the action.

When we arrived in Rio we first dropped off our laundry. Laundry service is very common in South America and very inexpensive. In fact, we found no place where we could do our own laundry. We are quite spoiled as a result. Rather than doing hand laundry in the sink, we simply drop off the laundry, go off for some sightseeing, and pick up the laundry when we return. A few places even returned our laundry directly to the hotel!

After dropping off our laundry, we took a taxi up 2,300 feet (700 meters) to the "Christ the Redeemer" statue. This is perhaps the most famous postcard view of Rio—the Christ statue overlooking the city with Sugar Loaf Mountain in the distance. The statue faces downtown Rio, but on many postcards the statue is rotated one hundred eighty degrees so the front of the statue can be seen along with the city! Even though it was a hot sunny day, small, fog-like clouds (reminding us of San Francisco) kept things cool up near the statue. The clouds moved past the huge statue (it stands 125 feet (38 meters) atop the mountain) making for some very unique pictures. A couple of days later we visited Sugar Loaf Mountain, a huge rock formation 1,300 feet (400 meters) tall. We rode a cable tram to the top to overlook Rio. We also visited Copacabana beach, one of the most famous beaches in the world. The beach curves like a crescent moon, with tall apartment buildings and hotels lining the entire beach, giving it one of the highest population densities in the world. During the day locals and tourists crowd the beach and at night the main street and restaurants bustle with street vendors selling anything and everything in the outdoor restaurant seating areas.

One of the most interesting tours we took in South America was a *favela* tour. *Favelas*, the slum areas of Brazilian cities, are high-density, make-shift housing with no apparent sense of order. The largest *favela* in Rio has 150,000 people. We toured Vila Canoas *favela* where 2,000 people live in 500 apartments. A sixteen-year-old lifelong resident of Vila Canoas led our tour. He spoke English very well and was one of the nicest tour guides we have encountered. The company that provides the tours is training him to become a professional tour guide. We visited his home and he showed us his room with posters of his favorite soccer team and his computer. We met his mother and chatted in their living room while cooling off next to a portable fan. The people living in this *favela* decided to form a type of homeowners association four years ago with an elected president and council to work with the city government to improve their living conditions. Most houses in the *favela* have cable hook-up, running water and electricity. Wiring and plumbing cover the exterior of the dwellings. Narrow, maze-like passageways run up and down inside the *favela*. From the outside street, however, the *favela* did not look that complex.

On Friday, February 23, we left Rio and headed to the small historical resort village of Paraty, halfway between Rio and Sao Paulo on the Atlantic coast. This was the first time since November we were not with a tour group, so the dynamic of traveling was more relaxed; yet we had to be more responsible as we now had to find our own hotels and transportation. We decided this would be a nice five-day break between Rio and Cape Town. In the 1600s, Paraty was the second most important port in Brazil and the main port for the exportation of gold. By the early eighteenth century, coffee exportation replaced gold, but the completion of a railroad connecting Sao Paulo and Rio caused Paraty's population to drop from sixteen thousand to just six hundred. For the next hundred years, Paraty stayed isolated until a new coastal highway built in the mid-1970s made it a very popular destination for those living in Sao Paulo and Rio. Walking through the historical center is like stepping back in time three hundred years. The building exteriors date from the sixteenth and seventeenth centuries and large cobblestones pave all the streets. Consistent with colonial social structures, the town has four churches: one built for the wealthy whites; one for the middle and lower class whites; one for the free blacks; and one for the black slaves. The streets in the historical center of town are closed to traffic, so we enjoyed wandering around the area soaking up the ambience.

Former colonial buildings in the historical center, Paraty, Brazil.

Paraty had a wonderful Carnaval atmosphere. From 11 PM until dawn, this town absolutely bustled with street vendors and one-man variety shows. We usually returned from a day tour around 6:30 PM, swam and/or napped until 10 PM, showered, then headed out to eat dinner and watch the mass of people wildly celebrating. Brazilians party basically non-stop during the four days of Carnaval, the equivalent of a victory celebration for a Super Bowl or World Cup every night. On Saturday afternoon, we watched a Paraty Carnaval tradition—around 1,000 mud-covered people ran through the streets screaming like pre-historic creatures! Many shook Erik's hand as they passed, so he was not spared from the mud. Horses completely covered in mud and screaming kids (not covered in mud) running away from those covered in mud added to the fun. Most of the mud-covered people jumped from a bridge into a river below to remove the mud after a good thirty to sixty minutes of fun.

We also toured various sights around Paraty. We took a ten-minute boat ride to Kon Tiki, a private island where we swam on a private beach and ate lunch gazing at Paraty. Jennifer thoroughly enjoyed the food there and at all the restaurants we ate at in and around Paraty. It was quite the culinary experience! We also visited Trindade, a small fishing town to the south of Paraty with spectacular beaches. We hiked to a rocky cove area that formed a natural, calm swimming pool. Typically, only a handful of people would be at the pool, but due to Carnaval, around 300 people, including vendors selling drinks and food out of Styrofoam coolers, crowded the area. The ease with which some young Brazilians left trash and cigarette butts floating on the water shocked us.

Another day we visited several local waterfalls and a former sugar estate. We hiked in the humid heat for over an hour to the first falls and cooled our overheated bodies in the ice cold pool at the base of the falls. We ate lunch at the former seventeenth century sugar estate then visited a large sloped rock formation with water falling over it. Here young men and women slid down the 60-foot (18-meter) rock, using it as a natural water slide. Some of the more daring ones slid down the slope standing up! Paraty has numerous islands along its coast and our last full day we relaxed on a schooner tour of these islands. We joined approximately eighty other passengers laying on the deck of the schooner and enjoying the scenery. The boat stopped at three different beach/swimming areas where we jumped off the large schooner and swam in the water as others rode rafts to the beaches.

Just for fun, we thought we would let you know some of the statistics of our one hundred three days of travel in South America. From November 19, 2000 through March 1, 2001, we traveled in eight countries; stayed in forty hotels; took twenty-eight day-tours; rode in seven planes, ninety taxis, seventeen boats, forty-three long-haul buses, twenty-three trains and subways; and used ninety-one rolls of film without developing any of them!

On March 1, we returned to Sao Paulo for a day. We visited the Sao Paulo Museum of Art and took care of some e-mail loose ends before our six-hour night flight to Johannesburg, South Africa. South African Airways was our air carrier over the Atlantic Ocean to our second continent—Africa! When we first researched flights from South America to Africa, we did not initially find direct ones. It turns out direct flights are only two days per week. We chose to fly on a day with a direct flight, and the trip was short and easy over the South Atlantic Ocean.

South Africa is slightly less than twice the size of Texas with a population of 43.6 million people. AIDS is at an epidemic proportion here. An estimated ten to twenty-five percent of South Africans have HIV. Other countries in sub-Saharan Africa have similar statistics. Many myths such as you can be cured by having sex with a virgin and HIV does not cause AIDS permeate the thinking. Most people who have AIDS think they have tuberculosis or other diseases, not AIDS. A social stigma is associated with AIDS and women who contract AIDS are usually banished from their families.

In Johannesburg, we experienced a bit of culture shock since we heard and spoke Spanish and Portuguese for the past three and one-half months and could now communicate in English. It took a couple of minutes for this to sink in! We flew immediately to Cape Town and spent three nights with a lovely retired couple we met by joining an international peace organization, Servas. Servas connects international travelers with host families, typically for a two-night stay. It is a chance for people to share with each other different aspects of their culture, city and personal beliefs, thereby promoting world peace. Part of the fun of travel is meeting people in the various countries we visit so we definitely enjoyed connecting with native South Africans.

Our host family lived near the world famous Kirstenbosch Botanical Gardens, so we recuperated from jet lag in these beautiful gardens. The Cape Town region is the smallest of the world's six floral kingdoms and its most diverse. More than one thousand three hundred species of plants can be found in this 3,800 square mile (10,000 square kilometer) area. Our hosts treated us to a picnic dinner while watching the sun set over Cape Town. At dusk a fox joined us on the grass—our first wild animal in Africa!

Continuing in the nature track, we also visited Table Mountain, a large, flat mountain that looms on the edge of downtown and is Cape Town's most well-known physical landmark. We rode a cable car up to the top and overlooked the city. While we visited Cape Town, various parts of the mountain suffered recurrent brush fires. From the top we watched one fire start and then grow and grow. Soon the fire trucks and helicopter arrived to douse it out. Yesterday, the fires still burned near some residential areas of downtown.

Last Saturday we toured Robben Island, the prison island where Nelson Mandela, the former President of South Africa, spent the majority of his twenty-six years of political imprisonment. We found this three-and-one-half-hour trip very interesting and quite moving. We ferried from the trendy waterfront shopping area to the island 4.3 miles (7 kilometers) away, toured the island by bus, then toured the prison that housed all of South Africa's black and colored (a common term used in South Africa to describe someone other than black or white) male political prisoners from 1961-1991. On January 1, 1997, the island officially became a museum and is no longer a prison. In 1999, Robben Island became a United Nations World Heritage Site, so everything from the stones in the road to the shipwrecks up to one-half mile (1 kilometer) off the coast is protected.

We learned about Nelson Mandela's life and admired the integrity of his actions in living his belief of non-discrimination. For instance, while in prison, the black prisoners received less food than the colored prisoners. Mandela and his fellow black prisoners, objecting to this discrimination, caused the prisoners to combine all the food and distribute it evenly among all the prisoners before eating. Also, in the 1970s, Mandela suffered back problems caused by sleeping on the floor every night. The prison wardens offered him a bed, but he refused until all prisoners received proper beds.

Last Sunday, we toured some Cape Town townships and saw first-hand the impact of Apartheid on South Africa. Apartheid was a system of laws created by the Nationalist Party starting in 1949 to segregate the races of South Africa. This regime lasted until 1994 when South Africa held democratic elections and the Nationalists were ousted from power. Internal and worldwide pressure helped eliminate the racist policies of this government. Our tour guide, a colored woman, shared her personal experiences under Apartheid with us. Today, almost ten years after the end of Apartheid, she is still nervous about entering downtown hotels and other formerly "white only" areas. During Apartheid, the government used a "pencil test" to determine a person's racial category. An official would stick a pencil in the hair, above the forehead. If the pencil fell out, that person was deemed white; if not, they were deemed colored. Some people would be "officially" white while their brother or sister was "officially" colored.

Our tour started in a Muslim section of town where all the colored families were forced out during Apartheid, even though their families had lived in those homes for generations. We also saw an area of town known as District Six, a fully integrated, vibrant neighborhood before Apartheid. In 1966, the government declared the district a "slum neighborhood" and bulldozed all the homes and businesses. Only the churches and mosques were left standing. This destruction lasted until 1982 and forced tens of thousands of people to flee. Today, this area of town remains as largely undeveloped dirt fields with an occasional church or mosque. You can even see some old sidewalks and curbs that used to be part of a thriving community. Some former residents are now trying to recover their land and eventually move back.

We visited three townships on our tour. Townships result directly from the segregation of Apartheid; it is the area next to a South African town where the blacks and/or coloreds live. As we flew from Johannesburg to Cape Town, each town we saw from the plane, even the smallest towns, had two living areas. The one where the whites lived had wide streets and trees. The township next to the town had no grass or trees, dirt roads and extremely crowded housing.

We stopped first at Guguletu Township. We attended a Baptist church service while there; it was a wonderful experience. The congregation of the church uses a large classroom of a technical college for their service. The pastor chatted with us before the service about a vacant lot for sale at a good price that might be the site of their new church. We were the only whites at the service. We felt very welcomed and comfortable in the presence of their joy and celebration.

We then went to one of the newest townships, Khayelitsha, Cape Town's largest. Over one million people live here in what most people would consider desperate conditions. Township houses typically measure 15 feet by 15 feet (4.6 meters by 4.6 meters) and appear to be put together with whatever materials were available at the time. They all have flat metal roofs. Township roads are usually unpaved and

Vicky's B&B in Khayelitsha Township, Cape Town, South Africa.

electricity is obtained by tapping into the utility poles. Numerous wires hang in all directions from these poles.

We visited Vicky's Bed & Breakfast located in Khayelitsha. Vicky lives in a three-bedroom house on a site that she shares with another family. Their house is behind Vicky's. Vicky and her neighbors share a working toilet between their houses and have running water outside their homes. Vicky opened her home as a B&B to allow tourists from all over the world to experience township life first hand. Numerous international television stations and newspapers have published articles on her. We also visited the neighborhood pub across the street and met some of the local young men playing pool. They were glad to see us and wanted to know where we were from. We saw many small children around five years old running around and playing. One young boy showed us his karate moves, and all the kids had big smiles as they waved to us when we drove by.

We finished our tour by driving through Langa Township, the oldest in Cape Town and a sharp contrast to Khayelitsha. Here housing units are more varied. One room homes built in the 1930s for the migrant workers with indoor utilities are next to free-standing multi-bedroom homes with small yards and block apartments being converted from three-family to one-family units.

Cape Town has been quite an eye-opening experience for us. Many blacks consider Cape Town the "better" part of the country, so they move here from the east and other African countries to the north. The white population slowly continues to move out of South Africa. Violent robberies have increased dramatically since 1997. We noticed the difference in safety ourselves. We were comfortable walking around downtown Cape Town during the weekdays, but were uncomfortable walking around early on the weekend. At night we took a taxi six blocks because walking that short distance (something we did all over in South America) we risked encountering street children who unfortunately mug and injure their victims.

Today we fly back to Johannesburg to meet our new tour group from Drifters Adventure Tours. Tomorrow we start a thirty-day overland safari from Johannesburg to Nairobi, Kenya. We will travel through Zimbabwe, Zambia, Malawi, Tanzania and Kenya and arrive in Nairobi on April 4. We will update you in Kenya in early April. Until then!

Love, Jennifer & Erik

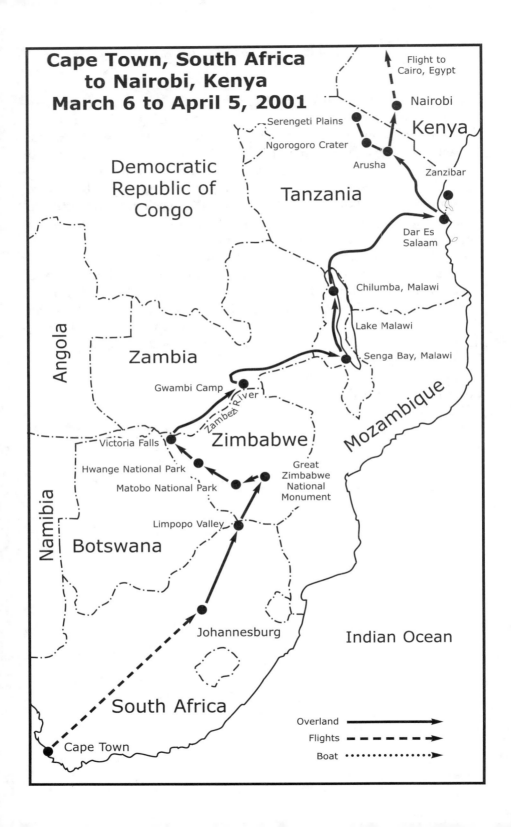

Cape Town, South Africa to Nairobi, Kenya
March 6 to April 5, 2001

Flight to Cairo, Egypt

Nairobi

Kenya

Serengeti Plains

Ngorogoro Crater

Arusha

Zanzibar

Democratic Republic of Congo

Tanzania

Dar Es Salaam

Chilumba, Malawi

Lake Malawi

Senga Bay, Malawi

Zambia

Gwambi Camp

Zambezi River

Victoria Falls

Hwange National Park

Matobo National Park

Zimbabwe

Great Zimbabwe National Monument

Mozambique

Angola

Namibia

Limpopo Valley

Botswana

Johannesburg

Indian Ocean

South Africa

Cape Town

Overland

Flights

Boat

7

Nairobi, Kenya
Thursday, April 5, 2001

Dear friends and family,

What a wonderful adventure Africa has been! We loved seeing the wild animals in the game parks and meeting the friendly African people. We have felt very safe traveling through Africa and highly encourage everyone to visit! We recommend coming during June or July if you want to avoid the rains and the heat, and see lots of wildlife.

After sending out our last e-mail, we flew back to Jo'burg (Johannesburg) to meet our new tour group with Drifters Adventure Tours. Thirteen of us traveled together on our thirty-day overland camping safari. We traveled with our South African guide/driver and his brother, two women from Australia, a woman from Denmark, two men from the Netherlands, a couple from Austria, a woman from Switzerland, and a man from Canada (who has lived in the U.S. for four of the past six years). Another guide who is from Malawi but now lives in Dar es Salaam, Tanzania, joined us for the last ten days of the trip. A few of the travelers had been on Drifters' safaris before and came back to do the most popular and longest trek, Jo'burg to Nairobi. Drifters started safaris back in 1983 and now has fourteen different routes in the whole of southern Africa. We were lucky to travel with one of the best overland companies in the business.

We traveled in a specially-designed six-wheel converted Mercedes diesel 170 HP truck. It reminded us of a big forest green Swiss army knife—very self-contained. The truck had a tank for 80 gallons (300 liters) of fresh water and an extra gas tank for long hauls through remote parts of Africa. The floor of the truck sat about 5 feet (1.5 meters) above ground level with 6-foot- (1.8-meter-) tall windows for excellent views. Inside were airplane-like seats for sixteen people, a library of books on Africa, and three cooler boxes for our drinks and meat storage. We each had a large storage locker in the back of the truck for our backpacks and sleeping bags. We entered the truck via a ladder that came down and extended out like on a lunar mission! A long ladder in the back near the lockers allowed for more access. Front opening windows provided excellent forward vision and access to four roof seats we used during slow game drives. Outside the truck numerous doors accessed the on-board gas stove, washing sink, storage areas for kitchen utensils, dry food, tents, mattresses, tool boxes, folding canvas chairs, and so on. Old metal grenade boxes from the South African army held most of our eating equipment. A 16-foot- (5-meter-) wide shade awning rolled along the length of the left side of the truck provided shelter when cooking and eating in the rain. Drifters has twenty-one of these large trucks and also many smaller 4x4 vehicles that hold fewer people.

We left on Wednesday, March 7 and headed north from Jo'burg toward the Zimbabwe border. We stopped for the night just inside the northern border of South Africa and Zimbabwe at a private bush camp in the Limpopo Valley. We arrived in the afternoon and familiarized ourselves with the truck and equipment and learned how to set up our dark khaki domed tents. We took a short walk to see some excellent examples of two thousand-year-old rock paintings of local animals the native people painted after being in a trance. We even saw small paintings of different insects, said to be the only known example of insect rock paintings in the world. We enjoyed the sunset and the stunning views north to Botswana and Zimbabwe, both visible from our location. We ate a delicious barbecue that first night and most of us took turns with kitchen duties, like set-up, cooking, and washing and drying the dishes. One of the Dutch men was a former professional chef. He offered to do most of the cooking on our trip, and we were glad to eat such delicious meals!

The next day, we crossed into Zimbabwe. Zimbabwe is slightly larger than Montana with a population of 11.3 million people. We purchased our visas at the border and stopped for lunch on the side of the road next to a huge Baobab tree. Baobabs are not actually trees, but rather large succulents. They grow in ever-wider circles for hundreds of years. Some tree trunks are 9 feet (2.8 meters) in diameter! The tree tops have the same structure as the roots, so in the dry season when they have no leaves, the trees look as if they are planted in the ground upside-down.

After lunch we visited the Great Zimbabwe Ruins. *Zimbabwe* means "stone house" and the country is named for these ruins. Built between

1200 and 1500 AD, the ruins consist of the large circular remains of a community run by the sister of the king where young women of the Shosana people came to live and learned how to be "good wives." Many white and gray monkeys ran through the tall, wet grass to greet us. We visited a small, modern village next to the ruins and watched a few locals sing and dance. Local artisans sold "curios" (souvenirs) nearby and we bought a very nice 9-inch- (23-centimeter-) tall stone sculpture. We walked to the top of a nearby hill with more ruins where the king lived and where the Shosana people held their spiritual ceremonies. From the top of the ruins we watched an amazing sunset and beautiful moonrise!

That night we stayed at a local lodge. Erik and a couple of others stayed up late chatting and drinking beer with the owner of the lodge about the political situation in Zimbabwe. The President of Zimbabwe has called white Zimbabweans "enemies of the state" and asserted all white-owned farms and lands be taken and given to the black people of Zimbabwe. About ten white farmers have been murdered in recent years as the pressure grows to kick them out. The political turmoil has severely impacted the country. Tourism has dropped by eighty percent. The large commercial farms owned by whites that produce the vast majority of Zimbabwe's agriculture no longer function at full capacity. In the weeks before we arrived, Zimbabwe's President started deporting western journalists. In our experience, the Zimbabweans are incredibly friendly, especially toward tourists. We never saw or experienced the negatives highlighted by the western media. We only noticed the lack of economic activity (no construction and little truck traffic) and tourism compared to other African countries we visited.

On the third day, we boarded a twelve-person, open-air, off-road vehicle for our first game drive. We drove for four hours through the Matobo National Park, with the largest concentration of white rhinos on earth. Moments after entering the park we saw a rhino just off the side of the road!

Africa has two types of rhinos—black and white. Both species are grey in color, so the name does not indicate their color; rather they differ in the shape of their heads. The white rhino eats grass, so its head sits much lower to the ground. The black rhino eats shrubs, so its head is higher off the ground. We also saw at close range zebra, wildebeest, impala, black eagle, and waterbuck.

At a soda break, Jennifer and others rubbed a plant in their hands

White rhino crossing the road during a safari in Matobo
National Park, Zimbabwe.

with some water that foamed up just like soap. Later during the game
drive we stopped and walked several hundred feet toward a grazing
white rhino. We stood behind a large bush within 20 feet (6 meters) of
the rhino, close enough to see small birds on the rhino's back. We
stood with the wind coming toward us so the rhino, which has poor
eyesight and a keen sense of smell, did not detect us at all and kept
nibbling grass. Toward the end of the drive, we saw a mother white
rhino and her baby, and also a giraffe eating branches on a tree. Once
outside the park, our guide pointed out the sign that said "Poachers
may be shot on sight!" Many poachers lose their lives every year from
the fully armed game scouts (park rangers). A rhino horn can fetch
about US $100,000 on the black market and is prized by poachers.
Rhinos are very easy to hunt because they are territorial and mark
their territory with fresh dung every two days. In a country with seventy percent unemployment, the benefits of poaching outweigh the
tremendous risks to some people.

   We covered approximately 4,000 miles (6,400 kilometers) on our
tour of sub-Saharan Africa. Spread out over a thirty-day period, some
days the driving lasted four to six hours and other days we drove for
twelve hours. Driving long distances in Africa is much slower than in
the United States. We drove on the major thoroughfare through each
country, but African highways resemble backcountry two-lane roads

in the United States, with no shoulder and usually no lane markings. One-lane bridges, police checkpoints on the highways and flat tires add further time. At nine out of ten checkpoints, the police would wave us on after lifting the barricade, but on occasion, our guide would turn off the engine and show the officer his passport.

As we drove, we watched the African countryside go by. We only saw wild animals in national parks or reserves. Usually we drove past savannahs and agricultural fields broken up by small groups of buildings—usually two or three for sleeping and a separate one for cooking—surrounding a small courtyard. In Zimbabwe, these buildings were circular; in the other countries, they were rectangular.

Due to the uncertain rains in Africa, the people grow a variety of crops on the same plot of land—corn, pumpkin, cassava, and bananas—to insure at least one crop produces food. Most locals travel via dirt footpaths a few feet off the main road. Most vehicle traffic (which was not much) consisted of large trucks, buses, and mini-vans transporting people from village to village. Usually all the vehicles carrying people are packed full; occasionally one or two passengers hang out the window with their arms on the roof of a mini-van!

Our fourth day, we went to Hwange National Park. The park itself was inaccessible due to all the flooding in the area, including our normal campsite, so we stayed at a very nice game lodge for the evening. The lodge used to cater to photographers, but due to the drop in tourism over the past couple of years, it now caters to international game hunters. We went on another game drive, in the area where the hunting occurs. On this game drive we saw more zebra and many varieties of antelope in a large grassy stretch of land.

Suddenly as we turned left onto another road a male elephant stood in the road in the distance. We crept toward him and stopped about 100 yards (90 meters) away. We sat in silence watching him when someone in our group dropped a lens cap and startled him. Elephants have extremely good hearing and Jennifer, watching the elephant through binoculars, saw him lift his head at the noise. The elephant darted into the bush and we drove up to the area. Once he saw us, he mock charged us and then ran away. Within two seconds he had disappeared into the thick bush. Amazing!

We drove back to the lodge area at night. Our driver used a handheld spotlight to find animals. We saw many glowing eyes in the open grassy area, and identified more zebra, an owl, a springhare and a few jackals. At the end of our drive, within 100 feet (30 meters) of our lodge, we spotted a young male lion roaming around in the 2-foot-(60-centimeter-) high grass with the full moon rising just behind him! This was the Africa we came to experience—sleeping in the bush with all sorts of wild animals nearby.

The next day, we arrived in Victoria Falls in northwest Zimbabwe near the Zambian border. We spent two nights at the Drifters Inn (Drifters operates many of its own inns around its tour areas) and had time to explore the falls, one of the seven wonders of the natural world. (The others are: Mt. Everest, the Northern Lights, Great Barrier Reef, Grand Canyon, Paricutin Volcano, and the Harbor at Rio de Janiero.) The highlight of our visit was an elephant ride safari with the Elephant Company. The Elephant Company takes orphaned elephants and trains them for the safari rides. We each had an elephant and sat directly behind an elephant guide. A main guide walked in front of the elephants, carrying a rifle for his and our safety, and a videographer filmed us with a camcorder. (We bought the video for posterity.)

We only saw an antelope and one baboon in the ninety minutes we rode the elephants. We later watched the elephants being trained and fed them as well! We were the only two customers that afternoon, a reflection of the eighty percent tourism drop. The main guide said the three-year-old business is barely holding on. As some of the only tourists in the city, our group was like gold for the different adventure operators. Some people went white water rafting on the Zambezi River, one of the best rivers to white water raft on in the world.

The next day we entered Zambia, a country slightly larger than Texas with a population of almost 10 million. When we crossed the Zambia border, we noticed a huge increase in economic activity. Numerous construction projects on the Zambia side of the falls are closing the gap with the more established tourist facilities on the Zimbabwe side. Later, as we neared our campsite for the evening, we passed a parking lot of over one hundred semi-trucks. We found out later the trucks were stopped at the border and most wait two or three days for permission to cross the Zimbabwe-Zambia border!

We stopped first at Victoria Falls and saw it from that vantage point. Just like in Brazil, the spray drenched us as we approached the falls. Since we visited during the wet season, the water cascading over the falls covered the walkways in continuous sheets. At other times of the year, the spray is much less intense. We then drove east to begin our two-day canoeing adventure on another, much wider and slower part of the Zambezi River.

The first day we canoed 28 miles (45 kilometers), with Zambia on our left and Zimbabwe on our right. When we first started to canoe, we were the slowest as the group was about 1,000 feet (300 meters) in front of us. We later changed into separate canoes which worked out for the best for everyone. The flooded river (about 10 feet (3 meters) above its normal flow) moved very fast, helping us to go further than usual. Of course, the fact that Drifters' usual campsite was completely under water was another reason to continue further than usual! We were not heartbroken, as we stayed the first night in a wonderful tent chalet with a fancy open-air bathroom through the back of the tent. Since we were one of two married couples on this trip we had first priority with the tent chalets. The bathroom floor had large flat slabs of stone with small pebbles in between. A reed screen enclosed the bathroom area, so it was like we were showering outside. It looked like we stepped into one of those dream-house design magazines! We enjoyed a beautiful sunset over the river from the large deck of the mini-resort.

The second day we canoed for just ninety minutes (9.3 miles (15 kilometers)) to our next day's campsite. We saw numerous hippos and a couple of crocodiles in the river as we canoed. Statistically, hippos are the wild animal that causes the most human deaths in Africa. Hippos graze on land during the night and wallow in the water during the day, where they feel the safest. Early in the morning, hippos returning from a night of grazing run over village women collecting water from rivers. In the water, a hippo can charge a canoe if it feels threatened, but usually canoe and hippo pass each other peacefully.

When we reached our campsite we watched seven hippos in the water across the river from our campsite. Hippos spend most of the day fully submerged under water. When they need to breathe, wiggling ears pop out of the water followed by eyes and a quick snort of the snout and then the hippo is fully submerged again. Every once in a while a hippo would raise its massive head completely out of the water and open its mouth before disappearing under the water again. In the morning we saw two of the hippos copulating!

We enjoyed relaxing at our campsite. We showered in a reed curtain enclosure at the base of a huge tree. A small water tank with a nozzle allowed a continuous shower. Amenities including a water buffalo's skull, some wood shelving units and a small mirror decorated the enclosure. As we sat around the campfire that evening we saw the space shuttle Discovery docked with the International Space Station fly overhead. It looked like a very bright star moving much faster than the other satellites in the sky. Very cool!

After we went to bed, it started to pour down rain. Unfortunately we pitched our tent in a low spot and soon 2 inches (5 centimeters) of water flooded our tent! We evacuated into the large kitchen shelter for an hour, then moved the tent and dried it out. This was the first night of ten evenings in a tent, eight nights of which it rained, sometimes with ferocious winds! Little did we know we chose to visit Africa at the end of a delayed wet season! We usually packed away our tents wet and rolled up damp sleeping bags during the ten days to follow. We experienced warm sunshine during the daytime hours, so we were only damp half of the trip!

After our canoeing adventure, we started the beach portion of our tour. We traveled further east through Zambia into the small country of Malawi. Malawi is slightly smaller than Pennsylvania and has a population of 10.7 million. Malawi is known as "the warm heart of Africa." All throughout this country as we drove past the small and large villages, children and adults would wave and shout as our truck passed them. We loved waving at so many smiling faces! School boys in Malawi were also eager to hold our hands. As we walked near schools or towns, six- and seven-year-old boys would run up and walk with us, holding our hands until they parted to go to their homes.

About an hour inside Malawi, we had a flat tire (conveniently around lunch time) near a small village. About sixty villagers, half of them children, came out to watch us. Our guide/driver was underneath the truck jacking it up. All of a sudden he dashed out from under the truck and at full speed started to chase the thirty kids watching him. The kids scattered in all directions, but soon realized this fast white man was just playing with them and everyone laughed and laughed! After finishing with the tire, our guide simply turned around toward the kids and about twenty of them took off running.

We entered Malawi two days early because a national park we wanted to visit in Zambia was completely washed out. We spent three nights at Senga Bay on the shores of Lake Malawi, the eighth largest fresh water lake in the world. During the day as we walked out of our campground, young men in their twenties waiting at our campground gate joined us, wanting to sell us things or take us on a tour of their village. We toured the local fishing village with a couple of them. We walked through the market, saw the school, and saw the sardines drying out from the previous evening's catch. We tried the local "beer," which was anything but! (It is actually one hundred percent alcohol made from the remains of the corn kernels after they are ground into flour.) We watched the men who fish at night relaxing in makeshift day tents and repairing their nets. We walked along the beach with our guides and came to a small inlet where we climbed in a carved out log to cross about 30 feet (9 meters) of shallow water. Another local young man straddled the back of the log and paddled us across. The log was incredibly wobbly and, with only 4 feet (1.2 meters) to go before the other shore, a small wave came and knocked Erik out of the boat, then Jennifer fell out! Fortunately, we fell in only 2 feet (60 centimeters) of water, but were both soaked, including the backpack and the camera in Erik's pocket. The camera recovered and apparently we were the talk of the town that night!

We continued our tour of the village (although we were very wet) where we saw women cooking the typical lunch of the village. Jennifer sampled the porridge-like food made with corn flour and water that is rolled into a small ball in the hand and used to pick up steamed greens or stewed fish. (Erik was not in the spirit to try new food after getting completely wet.) About 2,000 people in 500 families live in this village. They sometimes share a cooking area, but even if not shared, the cooking area is separate from the sleeping room. Each home also has a separate toilet and a separate area for bathing. The village has no running water or electricity, so the women carry the household water on their heads from several taps in the village. They burn wood or charcoal made from wood to cook. Most of the villagers eat lunch outside or on the front step of their house.

One evening the local community invited our group to dinner. We ate at a long table in a room lit by oil lamps. Our meal consisted of local fish, rice, pumpkin, steamed dark greens, salsa and a coleslaw-type dish. After dinner we watched young women perform traditional dancing to the beat of a drum. Our group sat in chairs for the performance while many villagers stood behind us. Little boys offered to sell us necklaces with small wooden pendants. Jennifer must have said, "No, thank you" about twenty times and "no" another thirty times before one boy gave up!

We drove further north to Chilumba, another beachside campsite on the northern end of Lake Malawi. Three other overland tours camped with us. We toured the other overland vehicles and talk to the passengers on those trips. After looking over the other trucks, we thought Drifters had the best one. We camped right on the beach. That night the thunder was very intense over our heads. Most of our group

Jennifer speaking with schoolchildren, Chilumba, Malawi.

(not having lived in the Midwestern United States) had never heard thunder that loud before! Needless to say, we packed away wet tents the next day.

We then headed north into Tanzania and encountered our first major road construction. Because only one main north-south road exists through the center of Malawi, the detour around the construction site consisted of a 60-mile- (100-kilometer-) long dirt road bulldozed next to the main road! Due to the severe rain, trucks and cars stuck in the mud blocked the detour road, so we drove on the detour road for a while, then back to the main road, to detour the detour road and the stuck vehicles!

Tanzania is about twice the size of California and has a population of 37.2 million. Greek traders visited Tanzania as early as 400 BC. Arab traders soon followed bringing Islam and the religion was entrenched by the eleventh century AD. The Portuguese discovered Tanzania in 1498 and took over governance in 1525. Arabs displaced the Portuguese and increased the slave trade in the early eighteenth century. Tanzania was a German colony between 1891 and World War I. Today, approximately thirty-five percent of the population is Muslim and Tanzania has a different feel from the other African countries we visited—South Africa, Zimbabwe, Zambia and Malawi.

Once in Tanzania, we drove for another eight hours to our campsite enjoying the mountains with eucalyptus and pine trees, the flatlands, and then more mountains. The next morning we drove to Dar es Salaam, the largest city in Tanzania. We left our truck in Dar es Salaam and boarded a ninety-minute ferry to the spice island of Zanzibar in the Indian Ocean.

Zanzibar joined Tanzania in 1963. Before that, Zanzibar was an independent island country. We spent three days at a bungalow resort on the north end of the island, near the village of Nungwi. We ate our meals in open-air restaurants on the beach. The ocean tide retreats quite far, so the beach at low tide is about 200 feet (60 meters) wider than high tide. Consequently, many fishing boats sit "stranded" in the sand during low tide. The tide comes into the beach area at a height of 6 feet (1.8 meters), so at high tide we both swam in the Indian Ocean and battled the strong ocean current that pushed us northward.

Erik snorkeled at a coral reef along the Mnemba Atoll, a two-hour boat ride from the village. The large coral reef teemed with sea life, including a variety of colorful fish and sea urchins. We also toured this mostly Islamic village and watched a group of four men building a wooden fishing boat by hand. It takes two months to complete a boat. The boat costs US $1,500 and will last about ten years. The men use all hand tools and bend the wood planks by heating the wood over a low burning fire, a very interesting technique to watch.

After relaxing on the north end of Zanzibar Island, we headed back to the main city on the island, Zanzibar Town. On the way we stopped at a spice farm for a ninety-minute tour. We tasted pepper, nutmeg, cinnamon, cloves and ginger. One of the guides climbed a coconut tree and chopped down enough coconuts so we each had our own coconut to drink and eat the meat. The coconut water was refreshing without much taste and the soft, bland coconut meat did not resemble the shredded coconut familiar to us in the United States. Some members of our group tried to climb the coconut tree, but could not climb even 3 feet (90 centimeters).

Later in the old section of Zanzibar Town, known as Stone Town, we toured two former holding rooms for slaves ready to be auctioned at the slave market. These small, cramped rooms (one for men and the other for women) held around seventy slaves bound for the Middle East and other parts of Africa. The slaves were held here for one or two days without food or water so buyers would know which were the strongest and offer a higher price. It was quite a sobering experience.

That night we ate dinner at a busy, open-air food market on the waterfront. About sixty different vendors lined the sidewalk cooking and selling their treats. Many stalls had a myriad of seafood which you picked out and had cooked to order. We sampled a pizza that was dough stuffed with meat, eggs, cheese, and chopped vegetables. It was delicious and great fun to watch the chef make! We also tried chicken kebobs with an excellent hot sauce and a drink made from fresh crushed sugar cane mixed with lime. We were very full by the end of the evening!

The next afternoon we ferried back to Dar es Salaam and headed for Arusha and our trip to the Serengeti, the highlight of our tour. Last Sunday we left our truck at the campsite in Arusha and set out in three 4x4 Toyota Land Cruisers for three days of bush camping and game drives. It took us most of the day to drive out to the center of the Serengeti National Park.

On the way to the Serengeti, we drove past many nomadic herders known as the Masai. These herders, dressed in distinctive red blankets and wearing beaded earrings in their extended earlobes, live for cattle. They believe all cattle in the world belong to them and all land belongs to cattle. They migrate throughout eastern Africa following the best grazing and cross international borders without passports. They construct temporary village shelters as they move from place to place. They have a warrior tradition and sometimes kill locals who complain when the Masai graze their land. The Masai also periodically "liberate" cattle from local farmers.

When we reached the edge of the Serengeti Plain, we opened the roof hatches of the Land Cruisers to stand up and gaze at all the wildlife and the vast plain. The scenery reminded Erik of western Kansas—flat grasslands with thunderstorms in the distance. We saw four female lions walking in 2-foot (60-centimeter) grass along the side of the road, a cheetah roaming the plains, several leopards lounging on tree branches, and many spotted hyena.

The most amazing thing about the Serengeti Plain is the miles and miles of various herds of animals. We passed herds of gazelles, zebras, ostriches, impalas and wildebeests. In game drives in other parts of the plain we saw hartebeest, a dik dik (the smallest antelope in Africa), mongooses, giraffes, waterbucks, wart hogs, jackals, baboons, and hippos. We also saw numerous varieties of birds we cannot even begin to name. We also witnessed a small part of the wildebeests' continuous migration clockwise around the Serengeti. We drove through the area where the wildebeests had just finished breeding and were starting to move to the west in search of other food sources. We saw hundreds of them cross the road in front of our Land Cruiser!

Heading out of the Serengeti and into the Ngorogoro Conservation Area, we camped on the rim of this ancient volcanic crater. The next day we enjoyed a five-hour game drive into this "living Eden." Wild animals fill the crater floor. We saw herds of gazelles, zebras and wildebeests; dozens of male elephants; several black rhinos and hyenas; and several buffalo crossing a shallow lake filled with flamingos.

Suddenly we came upon four male lions sleeping in the middle of the road! Four other lions slept in the nearby grass. We stopped the vehicles to observe them and one of the male lions woke up and lazily walked over to a shaded area next to one of our Land Cruisers. The lion then proceeded to lay down right next to the vehicle! They probably had spent the night hunting and eating, since they had many open sores on their torsos, probably caused by wildebeests defending themselves. We were amazed to see these large cats sacked out in the sunshine and a herd of wildebeests grazing not more than 200 feet (60 meters) away!

From the crater we drove back to Arusha, and then onto Nairobi, Kenya to end our overland tour. Nairobi is a typical African capital city, meaning a few high rises, a scattering of hotels and few tourist sights. We spent the majority of our two days here in the fanciest Internet cafe yet writing this e-mail and replying to several weeks of messages. We found less e-mail facilities in Africa than South America, so we are enjoying the flat-screen monitors and a relatively fast connection. Tonight at "Buffalo Bills," a restaurant next to our hotel, we will eat the mixed game platter (ostrich, zebra, wildebeest, impala and buffalo)!

Early tomorrow morning we fly to Cairo, Egypt for a three-week tour of Egypt and Jordan. Then on April 29 we fly to Israel for fifteen days before going onto Greece and Turkey.

Love, Jennifer & Erik

8

Athens, Greece
Friday, May 4, 2001

Dear friends and family,

Greetings from Athens, Greece! In the past month we traveled throughout Egypt and Jordan and arrived in Athens for a month-long stay in Greece. We decided to skip Israel due to the escalating violence there; so now we have an extra two weeks in Greece!

We flew from Nairobi, Kenya to Cairo, Egypt on April 6. By the way, our dinner of mixed game meat in Nairobi was delicious. We found the zebra a bit tough, but the wildebeest simply melted in our mouths. We even tried some crocodile! On our flight to Cairo, we met another American newlywed couple traveling the world for one year. We ate dinner with them on our first two nights in Cairo before meeting our tour group. For one dinner we enjoyed a typical Egyptian meal including lentil soup and grilled chicken on a small balcony overlooking Cairo. It was wonderful!

Egypt is a Muslim country of 70.7 million people and is just a little more than three times the size of New Mexico. The Middle East is unlike any other part of the world we have visited thus far and, although we were still in Africa, we felt we had left that continent. Egypt was the first country we visited where we could not read the signs or the numbers on the license plates. We noticed the men dress as Westerners, but most women wear scarves over their heads and many also wear long coat-like dresses over their clothes. Egyptian women do not wear shorts or short-sleeved shirts. We arrived on Friday at noon, the time and day for the weekly prayer in the Muslim religion. Our initial experience of deserted streets and closed shops was unique for a city of 17 million people! Also, Egypt and other Islamic countries practice a strong tradition of *baksheesh* or tipping. Suddenly we were tipping people for practically every service performed which took a couple of days to get used to! Another unique feature of the Middle East is the smoking of *nargilehs*. We saw people, usually men, sitting in cafes smoking a pipe attached to a base that looked like a pump with bubbling, colored water. People smoke a fruit flavored tobacco product through this large device while they relax.

Late Friday afternoon, we joined the Egyptians strolling along the Nile and spent an hour atop the Cairo Tower orienting ourselves to the city. Cairo is an interesting blend of modern and mud-brick buildings. Mosques with two narrow minarets (the towers on a mosque from which the call to prayer is made) dot the skyline. Cars, buses and mini-vans clog the streets and numerous roundabouts. Men stroll down the sidewalks with elbows linked. Women dress with covered heads and long black outer garments. From the top of the Cairo Tower we watched a synchronized diving meet in a municipal pool.

On Saturday, we spent a full day sightseeing in Cairo. We first visited the Coptic (Christian) area of Cairo where Joseph, Mary and baby Jesus found refuge after their flight from Herod. The fifth century AD St. Sargius Church, the oldest church in Cairo, sits atop the refuge cave of the holy family. We also visited the nearby Ben Ezra Synagogue, the oldest synagogue in Egypt, and the Coptic museum where we saw textiles, metalwork, and frescoes from the early (third through fifth centuries AD) Christian era of Egypt.

Then we went to the bazaar area of town where we visited Bayt El Suhaymi, a merchant's house built during the Ottoman period (sixteenth and seventeenth centuries AD). This huge mansion, a fine example of Islamic secular architecture, was completely renovated in the late 1990s. We explored several very large rooms with tall ceilings, pillows for furniture, and windows screened with intricately patterned *mashrabiyya* made of wood. We loved the merchant's small bedroom with glass stars in the domed ceiling and large bathroom. We thoroughly enjoyed the beauty and tranquility of the spaces and the myriad of small narrow staircases. From the mansion we walked through the bazaar in the crowded narrow streets of old Cairo. Small coffee shops were everywhere, small storefronts sold all types of goods, and the smell of spices filled the air. It was a feast for all the senses! We stopped at the El Ghuri Madrasa Mosque where, for a small fee, we went inside this beautiful wood-paneled mosque and climbed up into the minaret that overlooked old Cairo.

On Sunday morning we met our new tour group for a three-week tour of Egypt and Jordan. We traveled with Exodus based out of London. Our new group came from Ireland, Australia, New Zealand,

and England. Again, we were the only two Americans. Our tour leader was a Christian Egyptian from Cairo. We started with a tour of the Egyptian Museum where we saw hundreds of antiquities, most of them thousands of years old. We also saw the famous treasures of King (Tut) Tutankhamun and the Mummy Room where we saw the bodies of pharaohs Seti I and Ramses II. Tourists packed the museum; in some places we stood shoulder to shoulder with people. Our guide claimed we visited on a "slow" day!

We then toured the Cairo Citadel, a former fortress and large landmark visible from most parts of Cairo that dates from 1171 AD. We visited two mosques inside the fortress. We first saw Mohammed Ali Mosque, built between 1830 and 1848, and Ottoman in style. This large, white building has several domes rising in steps to support the central dome. Two narrow minarets grace one side of the mosque. We next visited El Nasr Mohammed mosque, built in the early fourteenth century AD. In this Mameluke-style mosque, recycled Roman, Byzantine and Pharaonic columns support a brick arcade surrounding a central courtyard. Geometric designs of inlaid marble decorate the main prayer niche under the arcade. We also revisited the bazaar area. This time most of the small shops in the bazaar were closed and the street empty — a stark contrast from the day before!

Back at the hotel we heard a loud celebration in front of the main hotel entry. A wedding reception was about to begin. We watched a bride and groom and their friends and family dance and sing outside of the hotel before entering it for the reception. Soon afterward the hotel elevator stopped with us in it. We pressed the elevator alarm, but the wedding reception drowned it out. Through the half-inch (1.3 centimeter) opening in the door, we caught the attention of a woman going downstairs. The maintenance man soon came and we left the elevator after fifteen minutes.

Our second day we toured Memphis, the ancient capital of Egypt, and the pyramids to the west of Cairo. Pharaonic Egypt extended from 3100 to 332 BC. Three main kingdoms, the Old, Middle and New, were responsible for building the pyramids, temples and Valley of the Kings. At Memphis, we saw many large statues of Ramses II and a sphinx much smaller than the famous Sphinx at Giza. Ramses II was one of the longest reigning pharaohs. A military man, he ruled from 1279 to 1213 BC. We marveled at a huge statue of him lying on its back because the legs broke off centuries ago. The statue was so large we climbed to a second-floor catwalk to view the front. We drove to

Saqqara to see a tomb of a high priest of Egypt constructed in 2400 BC and the Stepped Pyramid of Zoser constructed in 2700 BC. Beautiful relief carvings depicting scenes from daily life decorated the walls of the priest's tomb. We walked around the stepped pyramid complex viewing many tombs, passageways, and pits. Jennifer mounted a camel just for a photograph, and suddenly the camel stood up and started walking away with her on it!

We then visited the Red Pyramid and the Bent Pyramid at Dahshur, both built by Old Kingdom pharaohs between 2650 and 2500 BC and only recently opened to the public because they sit in the middle of a military area. At the Red Pyramid (built from reddish limestone), we climbed to an entry a quarter of the way up and then descended in a small shaft at a forty-five-degree angle down to view two large empty chambers at the very bottom center of the pyramid. We suffered sore legs for the next several days from that climb. We visited the exterior of the Bent Pyramid, named for its change in angle half way up the pyramid. The original angle of the pyramid was too steep and cracks started to form, so the architect decided to change the angle after building half of the pyramid!

After lunch we arrived at the famous pyramids of Giza. We walked near the base of the Great Pyramid of Cheops, the only surviving member of the seven wonders of the ancient world, and viewed all three pyramids from an observation area. We also saw the famous

Jennifer on camel near Stepped Pyramid, Saqqara, Egypt.

Sphinx nearby. Western conveniences are not far from these ancient sights, as we saw a Pizza Hut across the street from the Sphinx!

Before returning to our hotel, we stopped at a papyrus institute where artists make elaborate paintings on papyrus paper, a paper made in ancient Egypt from the common reed-like Nile plant. The artists demonstrated how they press the water out of the papyrus and weave the leaves together into paper. Back at the hotel we watched the sun set directly behind the great pyramids—one of the coolest sunsets we have ever seen. We even saw sunspots due to the large amount of sand in the air.

That night we boarded an overnight train south to Aswan, Egypt. This area is "Upper" Egypt, even though it is in southern Egypt, since upper refers to the higher part of the Nile. Upper Egypt is home to the Nubian people, displaced by the Aswan High Dam and Lake Nasser (the second largest man-made lake in the world) constructed in the late 1960s. Nubians are tall and dark skinned, unlike the majority of Egyptians who have light brown skin. Nubians bridge the lighter skin of the Middle East people with the darker skin of sub-Saharan Africans. We visited the newly opened Nubian Museum next to our hotel. We saw many displays about the Nubian history and people, and an incredible photo exhibit of the hundreds of ancient tombs and structures now lost at the bottom of Lake Nasser.

The next morning we flew forty-five minutes to Abu Simbel, two temples with colossal figures (over 65 feet (20 meters) tall) carved out of the side of sandstone hills in honor of Ramses II and his wife, Queen Nefertari. These temples were discovered buried in the sand in 1813. The Aswan High Dam would have submerged this monument; however, a worldwide effort organized in the late 1960s and funded by UNESCO saved Abu Simbel from being covered by Lake Nasser. Engineers cut the temples away from their cliff face and placed them on a new, artificial hill above Lake Nasser. This was especially tricky because the large temple demonstrates the understanding ancient Egyptians had of the seasons and the movement of the sun. In the far inner chamber of the temple (approximately 90 feet (27 meters) from the entrance) sit four statues, including one of Ramses II. Twice a year, for the past 2,800 years, the morning sun shines on the statue of Ramses II and other statues next to it on the birthday and coronation day of Ramses II, February 21 and October 21, respectfully. The engineers successfully preserved this phenomenon, although since the move, the day has shifted forward to February 22 and October 22.

Later that day, we toured Philae Island. The first Aswan Dam partially submerged the temples of Philae Island in 1902. The new dam threatened the temples even more, so the Egyptian government decided to move everything off the island and reconstruct it somewhere else. A coffer dam enclosed Philae Island and the entire Philae Temple complex (comprised of the Temple of Isis, the Temple of Hathor and the Kiosk of Trajan) was moved stone by stone to a new, higher island nearby. The new site reopened in 1980. The Romans, who governed Egypt from 30 BC to 368 AD, built this complex in an effort to legitimize their rule of Egypt. Much of the complex remains unfinished because each caesar constructed his part of the complex and any part unfinished when a caesar died was left uncompleted by the next ruler.

From Aswan we sailed for three days and nights down the Nile River in a felucca, the traditional sailboats of Egypt. We had two feluccas; one held eight passengers and the other held nine. Each felucca had two crew members. Those of us in the smaller felucca went to the larger one to eat three times a day. Our smaller boat had a wooden deck with only enough room for eight of us to lie on comfortably, four on each side facing each other. A large, white sail provided power and a long wooden rudder steered us. Our bags were stored under the deck and were accessed only once a day. A tarp covered us during the day for shade, but was rolled to one side at night so we could sleep under the stars. If we needed to use the bathroom, we pulled up to the shore, crossed a long foot-wide (300-centimeter-wide) plank from boat to shore, and found a private place on shore to relieve ourselves.

We spent a relaxing three days gazing at the Nile scenery, reading, sketching, or talking with our fellow passengers and Nubian crew members. We shared the Nile with only a few other feluccas, and what seemed like hundreds of large cruise ships. These ships carried at least a hundred people each and usually cruised by us one right after the other. One night, as we finished dinner, one ship cruised a little too close and too fast, creating a huge wave that crashed into our felucca, soaking some of our mattresses.

Before lunch on the second day we stopped to visit the Kom Ombo Temple. Kom Ombo is a double temple dedicated to the gods Sobek and Horus dating back to the third century BC. Wonderful hieroglyphs and images, some beautifully painted in red, blue and yellow decorate the walls and columns of the temple. Periodically a large section of carvings were missing, having been removed for display in

Erik relaxing on our felucca, Nile River, Egypt.

museums in other parts of the world. We wandered between the
columns and among the walls viewing an ancient Egyptian calendar
of temple rituals and carvings of medical and surgical instruments
used by the Egyptians. Because Sobek takes the form of a crocodile, we
even saw some mummified crocodiles!

As we floated along the Nile, we passed green fields tended by men
in long, white gowns behind buffalos or donkeys. Small villages sat up
on the banks away from potential flooding. Large sand dunes formed
a backdrop to the strip of green along either side of the Nile. The
evening before we ended our felucca adventure we visited a local village and toured one family's two-story, mud-brick house. We entered
into a combination sitting/dining room with two sofas and a table with
chairs. That room opened into a courtyard where the family cooked
and kept their chickens. The family kept more chickens upstairs in a
second floor coop. An enclosed small bathroom for the family with a
squat toilet in one area and bathing room next door stood on one side
of the courtyard. The combined bedroom of the parents and younger
children was off the courtyard in the opposite direction, next to the
cooking area. The family served us hot hibiscus tea in the sitting room
before we headed back to the felucca.

Easter Sunday we left our feluccas and toured the Temple of Horus
at Edfu. This temple, constructed from 237 to 212 BC, was discovered
in the nineteenth century AD, buried under sand and part of the city

of Edfu. This temple is one of the best preserved in Egypt with huge pillars inside the roofed temple. The god Horus takes the form of a falcon so two large statues of falcons flank the temple entry.

From Edfu, we took a convoy an hour drive north to Luxor, famous for the Valley of the Kings, Karnak Temple and Luxor Temple. We showered for the first time in three days then toured the massive Karnak Temple. Future pharaohs lived and trained at Karnak. We entered the temple through a corridor of about twenty ram statues on each side. We marveled at the Hypostyle Hall of the Temple of Amun. This densely-packed hall holds over one hundred gigantic columns (about 65 feet (20 meters) tall), each elaborately carved with hieroglyphs telling of ancient Egypt. The temple complex also contains two well-preserved obelisks. Other obelisks from the temple are now in cities all over the world. A large pond in the temple complex measured the level of the Nile, so the people would know when to start planting. In ancient Egypt, agriculture depended on the annual flooding of the Nile that soaked the riverbanks and fertilized the soil with silt as it receded. An underground channel connects the pond to the Nile, about one-half mile (1 kilometer) away.

At sunset we visited Luxor Temple, in the center of Luxor. This temple also was covered by sand and had part of the city built on top of it. In fact, a mosque built hundreds of years ago sits on part of the temple. The original front door of the mosque sits 40 feet (12 meters) off the ground above the excavated temple. The evening illumination on the large-seated statues guarding the entrance and interior columns added a new dimension to temple tours.

The next day we toured the Valley of the Kings about 9 miles (15 kilometers) west of Luxor. Just before touring here we visited Hatshepsut's Mortuary Temple at the base of a large sandstone cliff. Hatshepsut was one of the few female rulers of ancient Egypt, governing from 1503 to 1480 BC. Large formal ramps link three terraces built at the cliff base. Throngs of tourists crowded the ramps and terraces. We saw many colored reliefs on the temple exterior, including fish found in the Red Sea hundreds of miles away.

The Valley of the Kings sits on the other side of the cliff from Hatshepsut's temple. When the pharaohs stopped building pyramids near present-day Cairo, they were buried in separate tombs in the Valley of the Kings. The valley has sixty-two tombs. King (Tut) Tutankhamun's tomb, found in the 1920s, was the last one discovered. In 1995, however, a major discovery in tomb "KV5" of more passageways led to the discovery of even more tombs. Due to painting deteri-oration from the moisture in human breath, groups are limited to tour-ing only three tombs. We visited tombs of Ramses VII, Ramses IV, and Merneptah, successor to Ramses II. Each tomb represented a different style of tomb building. The tomb of Merneptah was the most impres-sive, with a very long entry passage leading to the sarcophagus. Elaborately painted images and hieroglyphs honoring the various Egyptian gods and describing the life of the deceased pharaoh adorn the walls in each tomb. In some cases the ceilings were painted dark blue with yellow stars to resemble night. In the evening we returned to Karnak Temple for an impressive sound and light show in English. During the show, we slowly walked through the complex as parts of the temple lit up in sequence to the narration.

We left Luxor in a tourist convoy. Egypt's economy depends heav-ily on tourism. In 1997, terrorists killed sixty Swiss, German and Japanese tourists at the Hatshepsut Temple near Luxor. Egypt no longer allows tour groups to travel individually. Instead, convoys of tour buses and minivans travel between the various tourist areas. The convoys consist of a police vehicle in the front, the tour buses in the middle, and another police vehicle at the end. Convoys were a new way to travel and we questioned our safety, as we were an easy target while in the convoy. In addition to the convoy, tourist police armed with AK-47s and metal detectors guard all hotels where foreign tourists stay.

Our trip from Luxor followed the Nile for an hour, and then we turned east into the desert. We arrived at Hurghada, a resort town on the Red Sea, in the early afternoon. We spent the rest of the day walk-ing around the small town, checking e-mail at the Internet cafe and watching one of our tour members have henna painted on the back of her hand. Henna is a dark brown substance used to paint intricate designs on the body, usually the hands and feet. Many Middle Eastern brides and their bridal parties have henna painted on their hands for the wedding.

The next day we joined an all-day snorkeling excursion. We snorkeled along the coral reef at three different spots, and ate a deli-cious fish lunch on board the boat. Each spot we snorkeled at was bet-ter than the last. The various colored coral was amazing. We also enjoyed seeing many varieties of colorful fish, numerous light purple jellyfish, an octopus and a sleeping stingray. We look forward to snor-keling at the Great Barrier Reef in April 2002!

The next morning we left Hurghada at 3:15 AM to join another convoy. We drove with them until Suez, where the rest of the convoy drove to Cairo and we continued east to the Sinai Peninsula. We drove through the tunnel under the Suez Canal and stopped to see a huge cargo ship passing through the canal. A ship takes fifteen hours to pass through the 103 miles (167 kilometers) of the canal. Ships passing through the canal represent seven percent of the world's cargo and their fees provide another major source of revenue for Egypt. The Sinai Peninsula is one large desert. The northern part of the peninsula is mostly sand, which changed into sandstone and finally granite mountains as we headed south. We stopped at a Greek Orthodox convent near Mount Sinai, a small, peaceful retreat on the edge of the Feiran Oasis. The oasis amazed us because we were driving through desert with granite rocks on the sides and suddenly palm trees and plants surrounded us in the middle of the desert! Very cool!

We arrived at St. Catherine's monastery after fourteen hours of travel. St. Catherine's is built at the base of Mount Sinai, the mountain where Moses received the Ten Commandments. We stayed at a lovely auberge, ate dinner and went to bed early because we started hiking up Mount Sinai at 2 AM the next morning to watch the sunrise. We hiked for two and a half hours to reach the top, using flashlights to see the path. People riding camels periodically passed us on the trail and enterprising Egyptians sold candy bars and snacks from small huts strategically located about every quarter mile (400 meters) along the trail. The last third of the trail was stone stairs, just like climbing up the side of the falls in Yosemite. We were tired when we reached the top, but the beautiful sunrise was worth it! We overheard another group reading from the Bible about Moses' numerous trips up the mountain and that added to the magic of the morning. A few small church groups from America and Korea were on the mountain top also holding impromptu services.

We returned to the bottom of the mountain by 7:15 AM, ate breakfast, and then visited the monastery. Greek Orthodox monks have occupied St. Catherine's for 1,500 years. Fortress-like walls surround the monastery that contains the well where Moses met his wife and the transplanted burning bush where Moses heard the voice of God. To prevent Crusaders from ransacking the monastery, a mosque sits next to the basilica inside the walls. We saw beautiful icons and mosaics from the fourth through sixth centuries AD in the basilica.

That afternoon we drove to the coastal town of Nuweiba on the

Gulf of Aqaba and boarded a catamaran ferry to Jordan. Erik remembered riding on a glass-bottom boat when his family lived in Amman from 1973-1975 (they moved there from Quito, Ecuador). This time, a choppy ride forced Erik to look straight ahead and watch an old black and white movie in Arabic to quell his motion sickness. We reached Aqaba without incident and met our guide and driver for the Jordan portion of our tour.

The kingdom of Jordan is slightly smaller than Indiana and has 5.3 million people. Jordan is a more affluent and less populated country than Egypt. The homes are larger and generally built from concrete blocks rather than mud bricks. Most people drive cars and the roads are paved. Jordan has strong ties to Palestine and many Palestinian refugees live here. Jordan's former king, King Hussein, governed for forty-five years and had strong ties to the United States. He was a very well-liked leader throughout the world and was a moderate pro-American leader in the Islamic Middle East. The current king, his son, has ruled for less than two years and, as far as we could tell, he and his wife are also very well-liked. A photo of the current king adorns every hotel lobby right next to a photo of his father, beloved King Hussein.

The next day we headed into the Wadi Rum desert for two nights of camping. We first stopped at the village home of the Bedouin family that ran our campsite. The Bedouins are the nomadic desert people that once guided trade caravans through the desert. The father had four wives and twenty-three children, with another child on the way. The house consisted of six rooms: four large rooms that functioned alternatively as the living room, dining room and bedrooms; a bathroom; and kitchen. The main four rooms had no permanent furniture. One room held a lone television with a child sitting on the floor watching it. The front two rooms had sitting cushions with low tables. Cushions used for seating and sleeping were rolled up against a wall in the fourth room until needed. (Jennifer was able to write this description because she went in their home to use the bathroom.)

Wadi means valley in Arabic. We enjoyed two days in this long narrow valley where Lawrence of Arabia also spent time. Various teenage sons of the Bedouin family drove older 4x4 Toyota Land Cruiser pick-up trucks. Five or six of us sat in the back of each pick-up on metal benches with a long cushion; a bumpy ride, but a wonderful way to view the scenery. Tall, red sandstone walls with eroded holes resembling toffee icing lined the Wadi Rum valley. In places the sandstone has sheared off and the rock is perfectly straight. The sand changed

from a light tan to a dusty red color and small shrubs dotted the landscape. We enjoyed a half-day drive through the desert, including a
stop at a small canyon that has fresh water for most of the year. We ate
a typical Bedouin lunch of rice and boiled lamb served on large plat-
ters placed on the ground. The New Zealanders got a kick out of the
lamb we were eating because on one piece was a stamp "New Zealand
lamb." Jennifer also enjoyed an expected camel ride that Erik grace-
fully declined. Jennifer chose a very tall camel and almost fell off when
the camel stood up for the ride and knelt down for her to dismount!

From the Wadi Rum we traveled to the ancient Nabataean capital
city of Petra. The Nabataeans, a nomadic people, became wealthy in
400 BC leading trading caravans through the Jordan desert. They
inhabited Petra from approximately 400 BC until the second century
AD, when the Romans built a trading road through Jordan and elimi-
nated the need for caravan guides. The Nabataeans built Petra in a
canyon to insure an adequate water supply. To protect this supply, the
Nabataeans constructed a dam at the top of the canyon and carved
two water channels into the rock to channel the water. We entered the
city through a three-quarter mile (1.2 kilometer) natural, twisting,
descending canyon which opened up onto a beautiful two-story
facade carved into the rose-colored sandstone, the icon of Petra. This
facade, like the majority of buildings in Petra, is a tomb. The
Nabataeans carved their interiors from front to back and top to bottom. They did not paint their tombs because the sandstone, comprised
of multiple layers of colored stone, naturally decorates the interior
walls and ceilings with colorful swirls. We spent two full days exploring the facades and interiors of the city. The sandstone is very soft so
intricate carvings are preserved only where the facade is protected
from wind and rain. We hiked to a beautiful facade in the southwest-
ern hills behind the city once used as a monastery during the early
Christian period and also to a high altar where we had wonderful
views of Petra. We also saw a beautiful mosaic floor inside the remains
of a Christian church from the Byzantine period (sixth century AD).

From Petra we drove to Amman, stopping to visit the remains of
Kerak Castle, the largest Crusader castle in this region. Jennifer thoroughly explored the five floors that remain of the original seven-story
castle. After lunch we stopped on Mount Nebo, allegedly the place
where Moses died upon seeing the Promised Land. We visited a beautifully restored church from the fourth century AD and foundation
ruins from a vast monastery built in the seventh century AD. The

church contains a well-preserved Byzantine mosaic floor, as well as exhibits of mosaic floors from churches in other parts of Jordan.

Once we reached Amman, we desperately needed haircuts. Erik last had his cut in Paraty, Brazil, and Jennifer in Cape Town, South Africa. We ventured down the shopping street in front of our hotel and found several barber shops, but no women's salons. Erik chose one of the shops and, while we were there, asked if they would cut Jennifer's hair. The next thing you know, Jennifer is also in a chair with a smock getting a trim. Well, we think Jennifer's "stylist" did not have experience cutting women's hair because the cut was very short and boyish-looking. We later learned women in Jordan cannot have men outside their family see their hair, so women's hair salons have black painted windows and (we presume) female stylists.

Jennifer and Erik in front of main
facade at Petra, Jordan.

The next day we finished our tour with a visit to the remains of the Roman city of Jerash. This city, built near the Roman trading highway, had a population of nearly 15,000 during the Roman times. We saw one of the best preserved and highly decorated Roman theaters in the Middle East and the remains of the beautiful temple dedicated to Artemis. The stairs leading to the temple are so steep you do not see the temple until you almost reach the top of them. Jerash retains the skeletal foundation of a typical Roman city, including the primary thoroughfare lined with columns and shops, entry gates to the city, a beautiful city fountain, and a typical secondary main street lined with columns. Jerash has an impressive oval plaza archaeologists believe was built to correct the improper angle of the main street. Unlike most Roman cities, the main street was not built on a true north/south axis, so they constructed the oval plaza so the main road would meet up with the south gate. After walking all over Jerash, it was off for a dip in the Dead Sea. Our buoyancy in the water amazed us due to the high salt content. Once you lift your feet up in the water, they bounce right up and it is nearly impossible to put them down again!

Most of our group left last Friday morning for home. We stayed an extra two days in Amman to meet up with an architecture friend of Erik's and enjoy the warm hospitality of Jordanians first hand. After a brief tour of Amman (a very modern city with not many sights), we drove west to an older city, Salt. We joined Erik's friend for a wonderful architectural walking tour of this town. Many children playing in the neighborhood enthusiastically greeted us. When we returned to the car, a handwritten note from a Palestinian child on the front windshield welcomed us to Jordan.

We left the warm hospitality of the Jordanians for the equally warm hospitality of the Greeks. Greece is a country of 10.6 million people and is slightly smaller than Alabama. Landing in Greece was very familiar, since we both had visited Europe several times before. We arrived in Athens last Sunday and another architecture friend of Erik's immediately took us under his wing. This was a real blessing, since this past Tuesday was the national holiday, May Day, and everything was closed.

Instead of wandering around central Athens looking at all of the closed shops and restaurants, Erik's friend whisked us off for a drive along the coast and a visit to the Temple of Poseidon at Sounio. As we drove through the countryside, we saw families picnicking for the holiday and gathering wildflowers that they would form into a wreath, honoring an ancient Greek tradition. We arrived at the summer home of a relative of Erik's friend on the eastern seacoast and were greeted by about fifteen relatives and family friends. We feasted on traditional Greek dishes, including grilled lamb, *choriatiki* salad (chunks of tomatoes, onions, green peppers and cucumbers with feta cheese and olive oil), and *tzatziki* (a mixture of creamy yogurt, cucumber, garlic and mint), just to name a few. After partaking in the food and enjoying the homemade wine, we moved the tables from the room and joined in the Greek dancing. What fun! Yesterday, Erik's friend's parents invited us to lunch at their house in Athens and we were treated to another delicious feast. This time we sampled homemade cured olives and stuffed grape leaves among the numerous appetizers and main dishes.

In between the feasting, we have walked all over Athens visiting the sights and taking in the ambience. We visited several museums and have a firmer grasp of Greek history and art than when we landed. We also wandered around the Agora, the marketplace and social center of ancient Athens. We celebrated Erik's 30th birthday with a visit to the Acropolis, where we found all of the other tourists visiting Greece! Crowds wandered around the various temples. In Greece, unlike in Egypt, you cannot walk through the temples; the various buildings are cordoned off. In Egypt, we wandered throughout the vast temple complexes viewing the columns and interiors up close.

As much as we have enjoyed Athens, we head to Corinth this afternoon for a two-week driving tour of the Peloponnese peninsula before we head off to the Greek Islands. From there we will spend about ten days in Turkey before heading for Scandinavia and Iceland for the bulk of the summer. This is our short European respite before venturing into Southeast Asia and India this fall.

Love, Jennifer & Erik

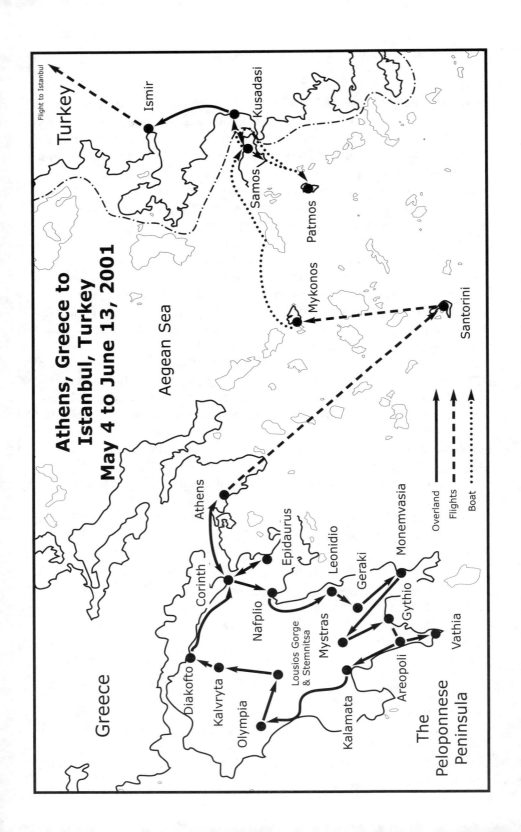

Athens, Greece to Istanbul, Turkey
May 4 to June 13, 2001

Greece

Turkey

Aegean Sea

Flight to Istanbul

Ismir

Kusadasi

Samos

Patmos

Mykonos

Santorini

Athens

Corinth

Epidaurus

Nafplio

Leonidio

Lousios Gorge & Stemnitsa

Geraki

Mystras

Monemvasia

Gythio

Olympia

Kalvryta

Diakofto

Kalamata

Areopoli

Vathia

The Peloponnese Peninsula

Overland

Flights

Boat

9

Fira, Santorini Island, Greece
Sunday, May 27, 2001

Dear friends and family,

We are thoroughly immersed in Greek culture, and like the Greeks, have even taken to a leisurely travel pace. (This is a breakthrough for Jennifer for which Erik is very grateful!) In our experience, the Greeks take life at a very leisurely pace—dinners are not hurried, the Greeks stop for coffee in the middle of running errands, and in general move at a much slower pace, except for driving, but more on that later! We too wake up when we feel like it, leisurely set off for that day's adventure, and finish with time to relax or relax during the day. That being said, we still covered much ground since we last wrote.

After sending out our last e-mail, we hopped on a bus for the ninety-minute ride to Corinth. Modern Corinth is basically a modern small town. We saw a Hollywood movie and, late the next morning, rented a compact car (our first car rental since Key West, Florida) to visit the sights in the Peloponnese peninsula, an important region in terms of Greek history.

In ancient Greece, Mycenaean kings fought in the Trojan War, the Olympics started in Olympia and Sparta fought Athens for control of classical Greece. Romans seized control of Greece by sacking Corinth in 146 BC. When the Roman Empire collapsed in 323 AD, the Peloponnese joined the Byzantine Empire. The Byzantines governed the Peloponnese for nearly one thousand years, until 1204 AD when the Crusader sacking of Constantinople ceded the Peloponnese to the Franks. From 1259 to 1460 AD, Venice, Turkey and the Byzantine Greeks struggled for control of the Peloponnese. Turkey defeated the Byzantines in 1460 and Venice and Turkey fought over the ports of the Peloponnese for the next three hundred fifty years. Stemnitsa is the birth place of Greek independence and the first modern Greek capital was at Nafplio.

Since Jennifer had driven in Europe on several occasions, Jennifer drove on our first outing. We drove first along the northeast coast of the Peloponnese to ancient Epidaurus, a sanctuary to the god of medicine and an ancient healing center active from the sixth through second centuries BC. Very little remains of the former sanctuary other than foundations, although we saw some seats and the starting line of a stadium used for athletic competitions during festivals. The best thing about Epidaurus is the restored third century BC theater, the only theater with a circular stage to have survived antiquity. The acoustics are amazing. From the top of the theater (fifty-one rows high) we heard a person drop a coin on the center of the stage! After visiting Epidaurus, Erik gave European driving a try and soon became our main driver.

The next day we visited ancient Corinth and Acrocorinth. Most of the ruins in ancient Corinth date from the Roman era. The Romans razed the Greek town in 146 BC and rebuilt it in 44 BC. Corinth was the largest Roman township in Greece, with a population of approximately 750,000. The museum at ancient Corinth had beautiful mosaic floors from the Roman era on display. We walked around the ruins and saw the platform where St. Paul preached to the Corinthians for eighteen months in 51 to 52 AD. We explored a very beautiful fountain complex built over the spring that provided water for the town. We also saw the five upright columns that remain from the fifth century BC Doric Temple of Apollo.

After lunch, we explored Acrocorinth, the fortress overlooking ancient Corinth. Not deterred by a little rain, we hiked through the three gates to the fortress itself. The fortress blends Roman, Byzantine, Frankish, Venetian and Turkish structures. (The lower gate is Turkish, the middle gate Frankish, and the upper gate Byzantine.) We admired the multitude of wild flowers while hiking to see a small Venetian church, the remains of a mosque, and the remains of the Temple to Aphrodite (located on the higher of Acrocorinth's two summits) where the Romans "paid homage" to the goddess of love with the temple's one thousand sacred courtesans. From Acrocorinth, we could see for miles and miles in all directions.

From Corinth we drove south along the interior to Nafplio. We stopped in ancient Mycenae, the center of the most powerful kingdom in Greece from 1600 to 1200 BC. The most interesting aspect of the site is the various grave shafts and beehive-shaped tombs (used from 1400 to 1200 BC). In one grave circle containing six grave shafts, archaeologists found nineteen bodies and thirty-one pounds (14 kilograms) of gold objects. We saw many of those objects at the National Archaeological Museum in Athens. Most of the site consists of the foundations of nobles' houses and artisan workshops on the hillside below the remains of the royal palace. Mycenae is a popular tourist spot. At one point we counted twenty coach buses in the parking lot, and from what we could see, half carried noisy high school groups on a field trip.

From Mycenae we drove to a picturesque town on the Argolic Gulf, Nafplio. The majority of Nafplio's buildings date from the second Venetian occupation of the Peloponnese (1686 to 1715 AD), so the town consists of narrow streets lined with two- and three-story buildings that climb the hillside. We stayed in a small pension overlooking the

Typical cafes, Nafplio, Greece.

town and the harbor. We ate breakfast on a terrace with the same view, but also looking at the steps to the Palamidi Fortress. We climbed those reported nine hundred ninety-nine steps from the town to the Venetian fortress. The fortress, built between 1711 and 1714, fell to the Turks in 1715 after only a one-week siege. Palamidi Fortress consists of seven self-sufficient forts with gun slits aimed at each other as well as outside. We thoroughly explored four of the seven forts before heading down to town for lunch at one of the numerous taverns with outdoor seating. We ate under a wooden trellis draped with blooming bougainvillea.

From Nafplio we leisurely drove down the east coast of the Peloponnese. Driving in Greece is an experience. Although the Greeks are very laid back, you would never know it driving—all they want to do is pass or overtake you! The few other vehicles we passed were tractors, mopeds and a small pick-up loaded with about seventy burlap bags of charcoal. While driving on one-lane streets through small towns, we relied on small, convex mirrors strategically placed to see around the corners of buildings for oncoming cars. Patience is required because inevitably you must wait for a driver stopped in the middle of the street to finish his conversation with someone on the street, and double parking is quite common! Fortunately our rental car was small—perfect for the countless number of three-point turns, and perfect for finding parking.

While Erik dealt with Greek drivers, Jennifer was our "navigator extraordinaire." We had few difficulties while on main roads, but reading signs was a new experience. Invariably the first sign explaining the direction at the next intersection was written in Greek. The second sign, in English, was almost at the intersection and too late to know which way to turn. Reading the road signs gave new meaning to the phrase, "I don't know—it's all Greek to me!"

The road from Nafplio hugs the coastline until it turns inland about 60 miles (100 kilometers) south. The inland road follows a river through a small town called Leonidio, and then climbs over the rugged Parnon Mountains. The scenery was breathtaking, as we drove through hairpin turns climbing over and descending down the mountains. We stopped for lunch at a small town, Geraki, just outside of more ruins. This time we climbed to the ruins of a medieval fortress built by the Franks in 1245. The fortress was ceded to the Byzantines in 1262, who promptly built and added to several churches. Agios Georgios, located inside the fortress, is a thirteenth century hybrid

Franco-Byzantine church with a beautifully carved marble screen and some frescoes. We saw even more beautiful frescoes depicting various scenes from Christ's life in a small church below the fortress walls. From Geraki, we took numerous small roads through several villages to the island of Monemvasia.

Monemvasia was separated from mainland Greece by an earthquake in 375 AD, and reconnected by causeway in the sixth century when inhabitants of the surrounding area built a fortress for protection. By the fifteenth century, this rock island supported a population of 50,000. *Monemvasia* means "single entry," and the causeway is the only land entrance to the town. The town consists of an upper and lower town, the lower town is still populated and the upper one has mostly ruins. No cars are allowed in the town, so we parked our car outside the city walls and entered the intact city gate.

After walking through the L-shaped gate, we entered a magical, medieval town! The cobblestone roads, at most wide enough for a packhorse, usually consist of single-person wide steps winding between the stone buildings. The whole lower town is no more than one-fourth mile (400 meters) long and one-eighth mile (200 meters) wide. The buildings terrace up the hillside from the city walls along the seashore. Our hotel, a renovated fifteenth century building, sat on the main street (which runs lengthwise through the middle of the town, halfway up the hillside) at the far end away from the city gate. We explored the myriad of windy, twisting streets of the lower town and walked along the city walls. We also explored the upper city remains, the commercial center of the Byzantine Peloponnese. The most impressive sight was the still intact thirteenth century Church of Agia Sophia that sits precariously on a cliff.

From Monemvasia, we headed inland to the Byzantine spiritual center, Mystras, located next to Sparta. The remains of medieval Mystras wind up a 2,037-foot- (621-meter-) tall hill in three principal levels. We hiked up to the highest point first and explored the remains of a Frankish fortress built in 1249 AD and added onto by the later conquering Turks. The fortress has two sets of walls surrounding two separate living areas, and affords a three-hundred-sixty-degree view of the surrounding green countryside.

From the fortress we descended to the upper town to see the palaces of the Byzantine despots, who governed from Mystras from 1262 to 1460. We also visited several Byzantine churches. Byzantine churches have uniform architecture and interior decorations. They are

Typical Byzantine church, Mystras, Greece.

small and symmetrical on all sides without space for a large congregation. The stepped domes with windows light the fresco-covered
interiors. We craned our necks to admire the numerous fresco-painted
domes. Several convents and monastery compounds dot Mystras. Our
favorite church was a small, fourteenth century one built into a large
rock with beautifully preserved, bordered frescoes depicting various
scenes from Christ's life. We also visited the lower town and the original church of Mystras, Mitropolis. This church, built in the thirteenth
century is entered through two separate courtyards. We saw more
frescoes and a beautifully carved, wooden throne.

The next day we headed to the Mani region of the Peloponnese.
This region is the central peninsula of the three peninsulas that create
the southern coast of the Peloponnese. The Mani people proudly claim
no foreign occupier has governed them. The peninsula is best known
for the numerous seventeenth through nineteenth century tower
houses, some of them deserted, throughout the countryside. Due to
the barren nature of the land, Maniots built these square, three-story,
stone houses as protection during clan wars over land. We stayed in a
three-hundred-year-old tower house during our visit. Erik had to be
very careful of the low door frames.

From Mystras we drove through Gythio and visited the Mani
Museum. We continued west to the remains of a Turkish castle (built

in 1670 in anticipation of a Venetian invasion), a couple of miles (3 kilometers) off the main road along a narrow dirt road. A grove of olive trees grew inside the castle walls. After climbing around on the crumbling walls, we headed back to the main road. All of a sudden the car just died! The car came to a rolling stop and the engine would not turn over. Nothing. Not even the little clicking noises of the starter. We assumed we needed a jump-start. We saw a small village about one-half mile (1 kilometer) away, so we pushed the car down the muddy dirt road until we reached the town. The village of about fifty people was deserted. Armed with our Greek phrasebook, we walked through the village looking for help. Fortunately, a man from the church who spoke English came to our aid. We pushed the car up a hill so he could pop the clutch and start it while going downhill. But we still had no luck! So he opened the hood (or "bonnet" for our British, Australian and New Zealand friends) and noticed the cord that connects the neg-ative part of the battery had come off. The screw holding the bracket on was loose and the cord had popped off on the bumpy dirt road! The car then started up with no problem—that was music to our ears! So we thanked the man for helping us and drove to our tower hotel in the village of Areopoli.

Using Areopoli as a base, we took a one-day driving tour of the Mani peninsula. Our first stop was the Diros Caves. The natural entrance to the caves is on a beach, but we entered down steps and boarded shallow boats that seated twelve. We toured the caves on a twenty-five-minute boat ride admiring the multi-colored stalactites and stalagmites. The caves, actively explored since 1949, have been traced inland for 3 miles (5 kilometers). It was really cool!

From the caves we drove south along the west coast of the penin-sula, admiring the view and the tower houses. We were headed across the peninsula when we spotted a town with numerous tower houses. Well, we were on a road high above the town, so we set out to find the road that would take us there without backtracking. Ninety minutes and numerous three-point turns later (including several on gravel roads with steep drop-offs), we backtracked to reach the town. But the backtracking was worth it. We thoroughly explored the numerous closely-packed, deserted, three-storied tower houses of Vathia, said to be the most dramatic of the traditional Mani villages.

From Vathia we were off to the southeastern tip of the peninsula for lunch at a small tavern overlooking a perfect horseshoe bay. This small village had no more than a dozen buildings. We ate overlooking the bay and Jennifer sampled the fresh local fish. After lunch, we headed north along the east coast and waited for about a hundred goats to move off the main highway. (This was the day to wait for animals as we had already waited for a pig nursing her young and two cows to move off the road before we could proceed.) We passed numerous bicyclists also touring the Mani, and promptly drove into a fierce thunderstorm, which followed us back to our base of Areopoli.

Fortunately, the sun shone the next day for our long drive to Olympia. We visited with our hotel owner in Areopoli who, upon learning we were American, showed us his family photo album of his visit to New York in 1980. Once on the road, we made a short stop in Kalamata to run errands (laundry, check e-mail, and purchase plane tickets and film), and then explored more narrow Greek roads on our drive to ancient Messini. We ate lunch in the small town of Mavromati that sits above the ruins of ancient Messini. Ancient Messini was founded by the Thebes in 371 BC after the defeat of the Spartans. The wall surrounding the city stretches for 6 miles (9 kilometers). We drove to the circular Arcadian Gate, and then down to the site itself. We walked all over the ruins where we saw a well-preserved theater, market area, healing sanctuary with baths, main paved street, mosaic floors from the Roman time, and an impressive stadium.

The next day we explored ancient Olympia—home of the Olympics! Ancient Olympia is a complex of temples and associated buildings dedicated to Zeus. As part of the festivities, the ancient Greeks held Olympic Games every four years, starting officially in 776 BC. During the games, the various Greek city-states stopped any wars with each other and instead competed in athletic events. By 676 BC, the games were open to all male Greeks. (Romans were later permitted after the Romans occupied Greece.) The athletic festival took place at the first full moon in August and lasted for five days. The athletic events included wrestling, chariot and horse racing, the pentathlon (wrestling, discus, javelin throwing, long jump, and running), and a form of boxing. Every two years (for the modern Summer and Winter Olympic Games) the flame for the Olympic torch is lit in ancient Olympia from the rays of the sun.

We entered ancient Olympia, with the remains of the second century BC *palaestra* to our right and the magistrate's residence to our left. Winning athletes were honored at the magistrate's residence. Boxers, wrestlers and long-jumpers practiced at the *palaestra*. Adjacent to the *palaestra* were the priests' house and the workshop where the famous ancient Greek sculptor Pheidias sculpted a 39-foot- (12-meter-) high ivory and gold statue of Zeus, one of the seven wonders of the ancient world. The statue originally stood in the Temple of Zeus at Olympia, but was moved to Constantinople during the fifth century AD and destroyed by fire in 475 AD. Beyond these buildings stood the *leonidaion,* an elaborate hostel for the dignitaries with a clover-shaped water garden. All of these buildings lined the west edge of the sacred precinct of Zeus, which housed the temple. The Temple of Zeus, a fifth century BC Doric temple, dominates the area. Although the columns no longer stand, we could tell the temple was immense. Pieces of the columns measured about 5 feet (1.6 meters) in diameter and 3 feet (1 meter) high. It looked as if twelve of these pieces made one column.

After admiring the ruins of the great temple, we walked through a third century BC archway into the stadium on the east side of the sacred precinct. The start and finish lines for the 400-foot (120-meter) sprint track, and part of the judges' seats are still visible. Some other tourists ran a mock race, which added to the atmosphere. We left the stadium and walked west past the foundations of the various city-state treasury houses on the north side of the sacred precinct. The city-states stored offerings to Zeus in their treasury houses. Next to the treasuries was a *nymphaeum* (fountain house) erected between 156 and 160 AD.

Row of columns lining a walkway in the ruins
of ancient Olympia, Greece.

This large, two-story semicircular structure once housed numerous statues in its niches.

We also visited the nearby site museum. The museum has models of how ancient Olympia used to look, a wonderful display of ancient Greek armor and several ancient Greek statues displayed in their own niches. Large sliding windows in the larger galleries opened to the outdoors so we heard birds and could smell the gardens as we toured the museum.

From Olympia, we headed east into the mountainous central area of the Peloponnese. We drove through numerous small villages tucked along the mountainside. We stayed at the only hotel in one of these small towns, Stemnitsa. Stemnitsa, a medieval metalworking town, is known for the nearby monastery where the revolutionary leaders of the Greek War of Independence (1821 to 1829 AD) held their first convention. We used the town as a base to explore the Lousios Gorge. We drove part way down the deep gorge, parked the car and went on a day hike.

We stopped first at the Monastery of St. John the Baptist, twenty minutes downhill from the car. We found an empty monastery because all the monks were at a nearby church celebrating the feast of a local saint. (That explained the many Greeks rushing past us on the path.) Women must wear skirts to enter the monastery, so Jennifer borrowed a not-so-attractive skirt provided for women visitors hanging outside on a wooden peg and wore that over her pants. The monastery is built into the rock of the gorge walls and cantilevers out in some places. From the monastery we visited the eleventh century church built into the rock with room for only eleven monks.

From the monastery we crossed the gorge and hiked up the other side to see the ruins of a monastery built in 960 AD, and the new seventeenth century monastery one-half mile (1 kilometer) down the road. The church of the new monastery has beautiful frescoes dating back to 1693. From there we continued along the gorge and crossed over the river again where we met an American woman writer staying at our hotel. Having already walked about 6 miles (10 kilometers) at this point, we dragged ourselves up the side of the gorge toward a small town for lunch. Halfway up we stopped at a small church and met an English couple (also staying at our hotel) that gave us a ride part way up the hill. We continued hiking for no more than five minutes when the American writer pulled up in her car and drove us into the town where we wanted to have lunch. What a godsend!

After recuperating over lunch, we taxied back to our car and headed downhill again, this time in the other direction to visit ancient Gortys, a healing sanctuary. These ruins consist mostly of a bathhouse with an entry hall, changing rooms, and an area with seats for individual baths. When we returned to the hotel, we learned a national strike in Greece closed all tourist sites, including Olympia, for the day. We were glad our schedule had worked out the way it did! We enjoyed a wonderful dinner with the American writer and learned that she lives in the United States for six months out of the year and Leonidio (the small town we drove through on our way to Monemvasia) the other six months. Sounds like a wonderful life to us!

We left Stemnitsa early the next morning and drove north through the mountains to the coast town of Diakofto to board the afternoon train up the Vouraikos Gorge. The train, built between 1885 and 1895, uses a rack-and-pinion (cog) system to climb over 2,300 feet (700 meters) in 14 miles (22.5 kilometers). The views were spectacular! The train first passes through citrus groves, and then climbs through the gorge, criss-crossing white water rapids in the river. It was one of the most beautiful train rides either of us has taken. We even saw one of the original Boeing 727 planes Aristotle Onassis bought to launch Olympic Airways in the 1960s. The plane sits on the side of the highway and is now a music/dance club. The train ride ended at the ski resort town of Kalvryta, where the Nazis massacred 1,436 men and boys on December 13, 1943, as punishment for resistance activity. A large white cross overlooks the town in their memory. We ate dinner back in Diakofto with a young Australian couple we met on the round-trip train ride, and drove them to Corinth the next morning.

From Corinth, we hopped on a bus to Athens and then took a taxi to one of two Mail Boxes Etc. in Athens to mail our souvenirs, books and undeveloped film from Africa and the Middle East back to California. After lunch, we took a taxi to the "new" Athens International Airport. The airport opened a couple weeks before we arrived in Athens. The airport is great—sleek and modern. Unfortunately the highway out to the airport from the center of Athens is not finished yet, nor is the hotel next to the airport. We were scheduled to take a 6:20 PM flight out to Santorini Island on Olympic Airways. Two cancelled flights, a very expensive four-hour stay at a hotel, and sixteen hours later, we finally left Athens for Santorini on Aegean Airlines. Olympic Airways had canceled the evening flight and our 5:30 AM flight the next morning (the one we woke up at 2 AM to catch) due to strong crosswinds in Santorini. Aegean Airlines flew to Santorini at the same times as our canceled Olympic flights, so we decided to fly with them.

Santorini Island is part of the Cyclades Islands in the Aegean Sea. Santorini is probably the most popular island among tourists and is said to be one of the most beautiful islands in the Aegean. Around 1650 BC, the once intact island exploded in one of the largest volcanic eruptions ever known. When the volcano blew, seawater poured into the area that was once the middle of the island and created a caldera. The caldera, the largest in the world, measures 7 miles by 14 miles (11 kilometers by 22.5 kilometers). The volcanic island in the center of the caldera is still active—with its last eruption in 1956. Surrounding the caldera are the crescent-moon-shaped islands of Santorini and Thirasia, a smaller island that on a map looks like it would complete the footprint of the ancient larger island.

During our fiasco at the Athens airport, we met two very nice Americans also going to Santorini. We shared a taxi to the small town of Ia in the north part of Santorini where our new friends were also staying. Ia is a charming village overlooking the caldera, and less than half the size of the principal town on Santorini, Fira. Ia has one long narrow pedestrian street made up of cobblestones and lined with restaurants, hotel entrances, art galleries, jewelry shops, and the occasional grocery store. The typical architecture of Ia and Santorini are bright white boxy buildings that terrace down the steep side of the caldera toward the blue water, hundreds of feet below the town. The roof of one building also acts as the terrace or balcony of the building above it, and so on and so forth down the cliff. In Ia, we stayed in a room one hundred seven steps beneath reception and the main pedestrian walking street. Cobblestone staircases wind their way around buildings, and the occasional donkey carries a load of goods down the walking streets. It all makes for a very beautiful cityscape!

During the past ten to twenty years, Santorini has experienced a huge tourist boom. Many of the hotels, shops and restaurants are recently remodeled from former residential buildings. The ceiling of many rooms and shops is a large, single, curving vault. In Ia we stayed in a cave-like room carved directly into the black volcanic rock with a large, curved, vaulted ceiling. The whole room was painted white. Two wooden barn-type doors opened to the 30-foot- (9-meter-) deep by 10 foot- (3 meter-) wide room. A small bathroom with no windows was off to one side. We had a deck that overlooked the caldera and the waters of the Aegean Sea. We both enjoyed the architecture and Erik especially enjoyed looking at the ultramodern swimming pools at a few of the nicer hotels.

Ia is the place in Santorini where everyone comes to watch the sunset, including many cruise-ship passengers that are bused in. When we were there, however, hazy clouds obscured the last twenty minutes of the sunset. We considered ourselves fortunate, as the crowds of tourists really swell from June through August and apparently you can hardly walk down the street.

We spent quite a bit of time with the two American women that became our friends at the Athens airport. We enjoyed their company immensely during several dinners and two day-trips we took in and around Santorini. This past Tuesday, the four of us took a fifty-passenger, schooner-like boat out to the rocky volcanic island of Nea Kameni. We cruised for thirty minutes to this famous landmark next to Santorini. We hiked to the top, where we could see small craters resulting from various eruptions (the latest eruption being in 1956, the year a massive 7.8 earthquake also destroyed most of the houses in Fira and Ia), and sulfur fumes coming out of vents in the earth. Our guide scraped away a couple of inches (5 centimeters) of topsoil to reveal the moist, hot and gaseous soil below. From there we sailed to another nearby volcanic island of Palia Kameni. We jumped out of the

Buildings cascade down the hillside in Ia, Santorini Island, Greece.

boat into the chilly saltwater and swam to the shallow muddy shore and the "hot" spring (which wasn't exactly hot). We then swam back to our boat and sailed for thirty minutes to Thirasia Island for lunch, then back fifteen minutes by boat to the main port of Ia on Santorini.

Another day we toured all of Santorini Island with our American friends. We rented a compact car for the day and, since Erik had all the Greek driving experience under his belt, he drove. We stopped first at the incredible ruins of ancient Akrotiri on the southern part of the island. Ancient Akrotiri was a village destroyed by the massive volcanic eruption in 1650 BC. Excavations began in 1967 AD and today only three to five percent of the site is excavated. The excavations revealed two- and three-story buildings with intact cornerstones, wood-framed doors and windows, and much pottery, also displayed at the site. Archaeologists have found no human remains at the site, which supports the theory that the ancient people were forewarned of the impending eruption and had time to evacuate. Many beautiful frescoes were also discovered here and are displayed in Athens. (Unfortunately that section of the National Archaeological Museum is closed due to earthquake damage.) Yesterday we saw incredible photographic reproductions of these frescos located at the conference center here in Fira.

After ancient Akrotiri, we visited the red and black beaches of Santorini—so named for the color of the sand. We also visited the highest point on Santorini, Mt. Profitis Ilias at 1,860 feet (567 meters), where we had a stunning view of the island. We wanted to visit the monastery there, but it was closed. The monastery shares the summit with a modern military base and what seems like hundreds of telecommunication antennas, many of which were on the monastery roof. Later we hiked most of the way up to ancient Thira, settled by the Dorians in the ninth century BC. Even though it was not even 3 PM, the site had just closed, but we still got a very good workout hiking up to the windy summit!

Thursday, we said farewell to our American friends and stayed three nights in Fira, Santorini. Fira, more commercialized than Ia, is the port cruise-ship passengers visit for the day. One evening we saw a 200-foot (60-meter) line (queue) of cruise-ship passengers waiting for the cable car down to the dock. Fira also hosts the clubs and discos not found in Ia. This evening, if all goes well with Olympic Airways and the weather, we fly to Mykonos Island for four nights. We then visit the islands of Patmos and Samos before going to Turkey. On June 13, we fly to Copenhagen, Denmark to begin our six-week visit to Scandinavia. Erik studied architecture in Copenhagen from August 1993 through June 1994, so he is looking forward to returning there. Until Copenhagen!

Love, Jennifer & Erik

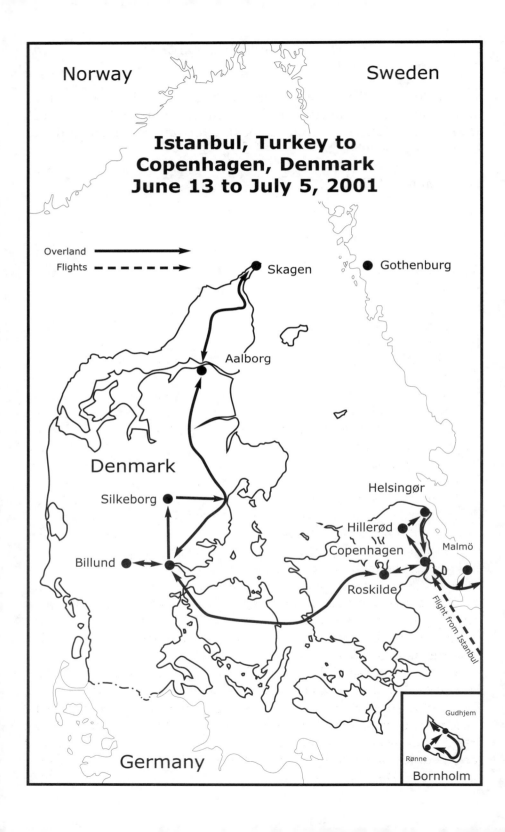

10

Copenhagen, Denmark
Thursday, July 5, 2001

Dear friends and family,

   Whew! We intended to send this e-mail when we first arrived in Copenhagen, but one thing led to another and after three weeks in Denmark we are just now getting this out. It seems like ages ago since we were in Greece, but that's where we left you last.

   We caught our twenty-minute flight from Santorini Island to Mykonos without incident. We stayed at a small hotel on the port where the small fishing boats are tied up. When we arrived the gusty winds caused all the little boats to bob up and down ferociously. We spent most of our three days on Mykonos exploring the myriad of narrow, twisting streets in the main town on the island. White houses, with bougainvillea draped over colorful balconies of blue, green and red, line streets wide enough for only two people to walk abreast. Tourists from cruise ships crowded the narrow streets and wandered through the numerous shops. We visited a maritime museum filled with the models of shipping boats from all ages, and two separate houses displaying middle-class life on Mykonos in the eighteenth and nineteenth centuries. We also saw the famous large windmills on the edge of town, and nearly bumped into Matt Damon who was finishing up a film shoot nearby. We also enjoyed the famous nightlife, visiting a piano bar one night that reminded Jennifer of one of her favorite haunts in San Francisco.

   One day we visited the island of Delos, the most important archaeological site in the Cyclades Islands. In the third through first centuries BC, Delos supported a large temple complex dedicated to Apollo (allegedly born on the island) and a town of 30,000. We first toured the residential section, walking uphill past the foundations of the poorest and middle-class sections to the section of homes for the wealthy merchants and ship owners. These two- and three-story homes, dating from the first and second centuries BC, had rooms facing an inner courtyard paved with amazingly beautiful and detailed mosaics. We saw several floors with intricate designs of flowers, faces and animals. A third century BC theater and cistern were in the center of the wealthy section. The cistern was indispensable because Delos is incredibly arid. After exploring a three-storied house and viewing several mosaic floors, we hiked back down the hill to explore the immense sanctuary to Apollo. A paved road lined with the remains of market stalls led to the remains of temple, after temple, after temple! We were most impressed by the five lions carved in the seventh century BC that guard the road to the sacred lake where Apollo was born. These are the only lions that remain from the original line of sixteen.

We intended to spend four days on Mykonos, but our ferry to Samos was cancelled, so we left a day early and had our first taste of Greek ferry travel. We took an overnight car/truck ferry the size of a small cruise ship that arrived late into Samos, so we missed the only ferry from that port to Patmos Island that day. Fortunately, another ferry for Patmos left from another port on the island. Two delayed ferries, one bus ride, and twenty hours after we left Mykonos, we finally arrived in Patmos. Patmos, about one-half the size of Santorini Island, is comprised of two large parts connected by a narrow middle. We stayed at the port town, Skala, located in the narrow middle and soaked in the ambiance.

Patmos is a tranquil island, not flashy like Mykonos. Visitors return year after year to enjoy the peaceful nature of the island. Most tourists are Dutch and Swedish families with small children. While Patmos attracts return visitors, it also attracts visitors who make the island their home for six months out of the year. Two such couples have opened ethnic restaurants, so we enjoyed a break from Greek food. (We started this break on the other islands, but indulged heavily on Patmos.) We enjoyed a wonderful Indonesian restaurant run by a Dutch couple who directed and filmed television documentaries before opening their restaurant. We also enjoyed beautiful sunsets and wonderful Italian food at a restaurant on the western part of the island run by an Austrian couple.

One day we rented a car, with Erik again behind the wheel. We drove all over the island investigating the numerous beaches and narrow roads. Our favorite beach was on a cove in the southwest corner of the island. We hiked thirty minutes along the rolling hills to reach it. In renting a car, we were the exception to the vehicular traffic on

Patmos. Nine out of ten tourists and residents use mopeds as their sole form of transportation. Watching the mopeds go by is something else! What amazed us was how many people, animals and goods can be packed on a single moped. We commonly saw an adult with a dog in between her legs, two adults and a small child, or an adult, a small child and groceries hanging off the handlebars. These days, as Americans, we do not normally see young children casually riding with an adult, both without helmets. In Greece, safety consciousness is different. It reminds Erik of what early- and mid-twentieth century America, must have been like, when people were able to do as they wished without a myriad of laws mandating safer environments.

Patmos is a place for religious pilgrimages. Around 95 AD, Christ's disciple, John the Evangelist, spent two years on Patmos after being banished from Ephesus in nearby Turkey. While in a cave on Patmos, John heard the voice of God and, over the course of four days, transcribed the book of Revelations. The cave sits in the hillside halfway between the port town we stayed at and the original island settlement high on a hill. Early one morning, we hiked thirty minutes along an old Byzantine path to the cave. We entered the cave through a small monastery. The cave is about the size of a small Byzantine church. We saw the fissures in the rock supposedly created when the voice of God interrupted John's praying.

From the cave we climbed another thirty minutes to the former main town of Hora and its monastery. This walled town has narrow, stone-paved streets that lead to the monastery high atop the town. The monastery, constructed starting in 1088 AD, is still in use, so we saw only a small portion of it. The monastery has ten chapels because Greek Orthodox practice permits only one service at an altar a day. We entered the main courtyard and visited a chapel. Fourteenth century frescoes and a two-story, intricately carved gilded wood altar screen decorated the interior. The detail in the altar screen carvings was breathtaking. We also saw the long wooden trough where the monks once kneaded their bread, and the large beehive-shaped oven they cooked it in. We visited the museum with fabulous religious art works, including icons, boxes for holy relics, beautiful gold and silver sacred utensils, books, and gold-embroidered vestments.

After five relaxing days on Patmos, we were booked on the small hydrofoil ferry back to Samos. However, howling winds cancelled the ferry, so we relaxed one more day, and returned to Samos via several additional islands on the next day's ferry. Once in Samos, we purchased tickets for the morning ferry to Turkey. What a difference it was to enter Turkey! Early in the morning we boarded the on-time ferry, stood in two efficient customs lines for our visa and entry stamps to Turkey, caught a bus to Izmir, effortlessly bought two plane tickets to Istanbul, boarded the on-time flight, and a representative of our hotel met us at the Istanbul airport. Before we knew it, we were exploring the streets of Istanbul, Turkey.

Turkey is a secular Islamic country that occupies two continents — a very small part in Europe, and the vast majority in Asia. Turkey is slightly larger than Texas with a population of 67.3 million people. A strategically important country, Turkey is a member of NATO and seeks to become a member of the European Union. Unfortunately, their economy needs to improve. A few months ago, their currency dropped from 650,000 Turkish liras to the U.S. dollar to over 1,000,000 liras to 1 U.S. dollar in a period of a couple days! When we landed, 1,000,000 Turkish liras equaled 85 U.S. cents. At first, we found it challenging to adjust to all the zeros at the end of everything you bought and differentiate between the 500,000 and 5,000,000 notes, but we managed. We spent a week in Turkey, just about all of that time in Istanbul proper. All and all, we really liked Turkey and want to come back and explore more. We found the Turkish people very nice and humble. A U.S. Air Force member based in Turkey said Turks would either give you their last meal or have nothing to do with you. We saw much more of the former.

Istanbul (formally Constantinople) straddles both continents and is comprised of three parts. One part borders the Bosphorus straits on the Asian side of Turkey. (The 20-mile- (32-kilometer-) long Bosphorus straits connect the Black Sea to the north with the Mediterranean Sea to the south.) The newer part of Istanbul sits along the European side of the Bosphorus straits. The third part, Old Istanbul, sits along the southern finger of the European side, separated from the newer part by the Golden Horn. Istanbul sits at the crossroads of Europe and Asia and has been an important seat of government for hundreds of years. Roman Emperor Constantine used the city as the capital of the new Eastern Roman Empire in 330 AD, ushering in the Byzantine Empire that lasted (with a brief interruption by the Crusaders from 1204 to 1261) until the Ottomans conquered Istanbul in 1453 AD. Upon arriving in Istanbul, we visited Galata Tower, a tower built in 1348 AD located in the newer section of European Istanbul. We used the panoramic view to acquaint ourselves with the layout of the city and admire the unique skyline dominated by monumental domed mosques perched atop the numerous hills of Old Istanbul.

We spent most of our six full days in Istanbul exploring Old Istanbul. We stopped first at Topkapi Palace, home of the Ottoman sultans for four hundred years. After the Ottomans conquered Byzantine Constantinople in 1453, they constructed Topkapi Palace, the seat of government as well as the sultan's residence. Topkapi is an extensive complex with four courtyards, the imperial kitchens (with ten chimneys), a treasury, numerous libraries, small octagonal-shaped buildings for relaxation, a large residential area, and three rooms that comprise the "divan."

The "divan," named for the sofa that lined three walls of the innermost room, is where the equivalent of the sultan's cabinet met daily to discuss governing the Ottoman Empire. Today the innermost room is restored to its sixteenth century decor with hand-painted Iznik tiles. These beautiful white tiles decorated with geometric and floral designs of blue, turquoise, red and green were hand-painted in the town of Iznik during the fifteenth through the seventeenth centuries. The two outer rooms exhibit Rocco decorations of a later era.

For most of the first hundred years, only the sultan resided at the palace as the harem, the concubines for the sultan, resided in the Old

Erik and Iznik tiles at Topkapi Palace, Istanbul, Turkey.

Palace. In 1541, the Old Palace burned down and the harem moved to Topkapi. The power of the government then shifted to the mother of the sultan, who ran the harem and decided which women to introduce to the sultan. The harem area we toured generally dates after 1665, when a fire destroyed the harem and divan. The interior of the harem is designed to keep men other than the sultan away from the women of the harem. Cooked food for the harem was placed on shelves along an outside hall. The harem had a separate garden and living quarters for the women; only the sultan's quarters connect with the harem's. The interior of the living quarters is decorated with numerous Iznik tiles. The ceilings are usually domed, with windows around the edge to allow light into the room. This feature is also typical of mosques. The apartments for the equivalent of the crown prince had beautiful stained-glass windows and wood shutters inlaid with tortoiseshell and mother of pearl.

There were several Turkish style baths in the palace as well as an indoor and outdoor swimming pool for the sultan and harem to enjoy. Most rooms lacked furniture, since the sultans and family mainly used cushions and low tables for furnishings. While enjoying the gardens and various pavilions at the back of the palace, we noticed two fire-boats going to meet a large Princess cruise ship. It was the *Golden Princess*, one of the largest ships we have seen. We spotted the same ship in Kusadasi the day before, when we arrived in Turkey, and here it was steaming into port. What a sight!

We next visited the Turkish and Islamic Art Museum. We saw a chronological exhibit of the world-famous Turkish rugs. Turkish rugs are still a valued souvenir. From the moment you set foot in Istanbul, rug shop employees pressure tourists to view their rugs. These men hang out in front of popular tourist attractions like the Blue Mosque and Aya Sofia, approach passersby and start a conversation asking where you are from, or something along those lines. Since our hotel was near this neighborhood, every day we were approached at least four times. About a minute into the conversation, they invite us to take a look at their store, usually a five to ten minute walk away. When we declined, they repeatedly asked us to come with them for a look—even when we told them we had no home!

We also enjoyed the mosaic museum displaying sections of a large mosaic floor from the Byzantine Great Palace. The floor dates to the sixth century AD and originally measured approximately 180 feet by 213 feet (55 meters by 65 meters). The museum displays approximately one-seventh of the original floor. Numerous domestic scenes, hunting figures and animal figures separated by plain white tiles adorn the floor. A 3-foot- (1-meter-) wide floral pattern edged with a ribbon borders the entire floor. The subtle detailing and coloring of the mosaic pictures was simply incredible and mind-blowing!

We relaxed sipping apple tea at a Turkish cafe, listening to Turkish music, and overlooking the remains of the hippodrome. The hippodrome, estimated to have held 100,000 people, is where the Romans held various sporting events, including chariot races. Roman emperor Septimius Sevenes constructed Istanbul's hippodrome in 200 AD and Constantine enlarged it when he moved his capital to Istanbul. Only half of the original hippodrome remains (now a park). At one end (originally the middle of the hippodrome) are the upper third of a sixteenth century BC Egyptian obelisk (all that survived shipment from Egypt), a fifth century BC bronze column from the Temple of Apollo at Delphi, Greece, and a third column whose origins are unknown. The Romans used to race chariots around these columns.

One of our favorite places was the sixth century AD Roman cistern. Restored in 1987, this cistern stored up to 21,000 gallons (80,000 cubic meters) of water brought to Istanbul from a nearby forest via a fourth century AD Roman aqueduct. Three-hundred thirty-six recycled Greek and Roman columns support the 460 foot by 230 foot (140 meter by 70 meter) area. The builders added to or cut the columns as needed to achieve a uniform height. We walked over the standing water on boardwalks among the rows of dimly lit columns. Very cool!

We also visited two Byzantine churches. The famous Aya Sofia is an amazing piece of Byzantine architecture. Built around 532 AD, its 100-foot (30-meter) dome hangs over the sanctuary (an area the size of the underground cistern) without apparent support. The dome has fallen in several earthquakes, and numerous exterior buttresses support the building. Presumably gold-tiled mosaics decorated the entire interior but were destroyed by the Crusaders in 1204 AD and further removed by the Ottomans when they turned the church into a mosque in 1453 AD. A few Byzantine-style mosaics survive in the upper gallery and the side entryway. Kariye Camii contains the best-preserved Byzantine mosaics. Again, the Crusaders destroyed the original frescoes and mosaics and the Ottomans paneled the sanctuary with marble to cover the mosaics there. Mosaics in the arched ceilings of the two narthexes of the church, dating from 1316 to 1321 AD, survived covering by the Ottomans. These mosaics depict parallel detailed scenes from the life of Christ and his mother Mary. Gold-tiled background separates these breathtaking and realistic scenes.

We also visited several mosques including the majestic Blue Mosque built between 1609 and 1616 by Sultan Ahmet I opposite Aya Sofia, near Topkapi Palace. Most sultans built a mosque, complete with surrounding complex. For example, between 1550 and 1557, Suleyman built a mosque surrounded by a library, cemetery with tombs for Suleyman and his wife, public kitchen, primary school, bath, and wrestling ground. The public baths arise from the need for Muslims to be clean when entering a mosque. Iznik tiles decorate each mosque and several windows below the domed ceiling brightly lit the mosques. The domes and minarets of the numerous imperial mosques make Istanbul's skyline very distinctive. We also visited the covered grand bazaar (said to be the world's largest covered bazaar) and spice bazaar, but they were tame compared to the bazaar in Cairo!

After so much sightseeing, we treated ourselves to a Turkish bath. Erik tested the waters at Cemberlitas Hamam, a sixteenth century AD bath. Our guidebook said Cemberlitas was a good place for an intro-duction, so Erik walked in and paid for a bath and massage. Erik was quickly escorted upstairs to a small individual changing room, one of many surrounding the lobby from above, and given what looked like a very long dishtowel and a pair of wooden clogs. Erik changed, wrapped the towel around his waist, walked carefully down the stairs in his wooden clogs and proceeded into the main chamber of the *hamam*. This chamber was for men only; an identical chamber for women was on the other side of the building. The marble chamber had a domed ceiling with little star skylights so the ceiling resembled the night sky. Elaborate columns, arches, and washbasins with fancy faucets lined the walls. An elevated 3-foot- (1-meter-) tall marble plat-form with an interior heat source sat in the center of the large room. Men in towels laid on this octagonal-shaped platform.

A man told Erik in hand gestures and Turkish to lie down and wait for his massage. Of the thirty men inside the room, half were cus-tomers and half worked there giving baths and massages. All wore identical towels. As Erik waited for his massage, he heard grunts and groans of men, and he was unsure if they were coming from the giver or the receiver of the massages. The large chamber was like a steam room, so after five minutes, Erik was sweating profusely.

Soon a small muscular man in his sixties with a few of his front teeth missing tapped Erik on his toe and motioned him to slide to the edge of the elevated platform. The man placed a scrubbing mitt over his hand and proceeded to scrub away an amazing amount of dead skin from all over Erik's body. The Turks swear by this way of getting clean; they cannot understand our western ideas of soaking in a tub. After the dead skin was removed, the man lathered Erik up with about 12 inches (30 centimeters) of soapy bubbles and roughly massaged Erik all over. The man then rolled Erik over on his stomach. Erik found it difficult to stay on the platform because the friction coefficient of bubbles, marble, and his body was just about zero! After a short massage, the man walked on Erik's back, massaging him that way. The man then sat Erik down near a washbasin and vigorously scrubbed Erik's scalp with his fingers and fingernails. After massaging Erik's arms, legs and shoulders for the fourth time, the man poured lots of hot water all over Erik with a small bowl. Erik then went into another small room where a man thoroughly dried Erik off and gave him yet another vigorous scalp massage. Erik felt like a new man. He now understands the Turkish definition of clean.

Having exhausted the major sights of the old city, we spent a day and a half exploring other parts of Istanbul. We cruised up the Bosphorus straits, stopping at a fortress the Ottomans built in four months in 1452 AD as part of their conquest of Istanbul. The fortress (about the size of an American football field) has six towers, five gates and walls 16 to 49 feet (5 to 15 meters) high. We also visited the residential palace built by the sultans in the mid-1800s and another summer palace completed in 1865. Both palaces are incredibly opulent and western in decor with beautiful hand-woven Turkish rugs. The residential palace had beautiful gilded ceilings, crystal chandeliers and intricately carved woodwork. It was a stark contrast to the decor at Topkapi Palace.

On the evening of June 13 we flew non-stop from Istanbul to Copenhagen, Denmark's capital. Denmark is a small Scandinavian country twice the size of Massachusetts that sits north of Germany and west of southern Sweden. It has a population of 5 million, about a third of which live in the Copenhagen area. Denmark is a very design-oriented country with simplicity, efficiency and elegance being the main motivating factors in their industrial and architectural designs. Danish is the official language though most Danes also speak fluent English, so traveling here is very easy. Denmark, a largely maritime and agricultural country, is a member of the European Union (EU) and NATO. Denmark voted to join the EU by a close margin and last year barely rejected adopting the EU's common currency, the Euro. So on January 1, 2002, the Danes, Swedes and Brits will keep their own currency while the other EU member states will scrap their francs, marks, lire, drachmas, and so on, and only have the Euro.

Denmark starts the part of our grand adventure where we visit many friends and family. Erik lived in Copenhagen from August 1993 through June 1994, spending his fourth year of architecture school at Denmark's International Study Program, so we visited the two host families he once lived with. In addition, Erik's second cousin (who is Swedish and married to a Dane) lives south of Copenhagen. Finally, one of our African travel friends lives in southern Jutland (the mainland of Denmark). Returning to Denmark, Erik noticed many changes since he lived here. For instance, the Danes redesigned their currency and modernized some of the local trains. Copenhagen airport also has an impressive new international terminal, a new bridge links Denmark and Sweden, and a new train links Copenhagen's central station to the Copenhagen airport.

Erik's relatives invited us to stay in a small summer cottage behind their house surrounded by beautiful gardens. We stayed just thirty minutes by train from downtown Copenhagen. In Copenhagen we explored museums, walking streets, churches, modern architecture, and favorite haunts of Erik's from his time here. On our first day in Copenhagen, Erik showed Jennifer where he went to school and we paid a quick visit to the architecture school headmaster.

We then climbed to the top of the Round Tower. This small observatory, built by King Christian IV in the seventeenth century AD, has a spiral brick walkway inside wide enough for four horses to pull the king's carriage. From the top of the Round Tower we saw the dozen or so mint-green (aged copper) spires on churches and government buildings that define the Copenhagen skyline. Another day we toured Copenhagen's canals, modeled after those in Holland, by boat. Erik had not done this before and we enjoyed sailing past the Little Mermaid statue and seeing some of the new Copenhagen architecture, including the new Royal Library (known as the "Black Diamond") completed a couple of years ago.

Another day we toured the Danish crown jewels at a former royal residence. Later, just after viewing the changing of the guard at Amalienborg Slot (the current residence of the Danish royal family), we had to move quickly out of the way of two black cars speeding into the palace. Erik recognized the lone passenger in the back of one car as the Danish crown prince Frederik. The Danes love to talk about the royal family, especially crown prince Frederik's love life, as he is in his thirties and not married. While in Denmark, we have learned much about the Danish monarchy, the oldest in the world. Erik found it especially interesting that of the three children of King Christian IX (reigned 1863 to 1906), one became King of Denmark, one became Queen of England (marrying King Edward VII), and the third became Czarina of Russia (marrying Czar Alexander III).

We also wandered through the area of Copenhagen known as the "free state" of Christiania. In 1971, a large group of hippies took over an abandoned naval base and declared it their free state, not subject to Danish laws or taxes. Christiania became and still is a place of open drug use. Even today, so called "soft drugs" such as marijuana and hash are tolerated and sold openly along "Pusher's Street." The government shut off the public utilities to the abandoned base to dislodge the hippies, but the Danish public supported the hippies and the government eventually agreed to let Christiania be a social experiment; however, the police still occasionally raid parts of this neighborhood. Today Christiania functions a bit more mainstream. Christiana is well known in Copenhagen for its well designed and manufactured bicycles and the numerous arts and crafts produced there.

We spent our first weekend with one of Erik's host mothers. On Saturday we visited the Louisiana Museum of Modern Art (not associated with the U.S. state of Louisiana) and saw the latest works from Anselm Kiefer and Sigmar Polke. Jennifer really liked the textile art of Sigmar Polke. Sunday was castle day! We went to Hillerød to visit Frederiksborg Slot, a Danish Renaissance castle largely built by King Christian IV between 1600 and 1620 AD. Danish kings used this castle for over 200 years until a fire destroyed the interior in 1859. A wealthy Danish brewer renovated the interior and turned it into a museum. From Hillerød we drove northeast to Helsingør to visit Kronborg Slot, a fifteenth century AD castle that Shakespeare used in 1602 as the setting for "Hamlet." The castle sits strategically at the northeastern tip of the island that Copenhagen is part of and overlooks Sweden just a few kilometers away.

With Sweden a twenty-minute ferry ride away, we saw many Swedes bringing inexpensive beer from Denmark back to Sweden. Making a Danish beer run is so popular, Swedes can board a coach bus that is loaded with beer underneath and pulls an additional trailer for more beer. We saw hundreds of cases of canned Carlsburg beer being loaded onto the bus. We were not sure if this was a weekly, daily or hourly bus.

After six days of sightseeing in Copenhagen and the surrounding area, we spent a few days at Denmark's easternmost point, Bornholm Island. Bornholm is much closer to Sweden than the rest of Denmark, with Poland to the south, and Germany to the southwest. The Nazis occupied Bornholm and the rest of Denmark in World War II. During the Nazi occupation, the Danish parliament, local authorities and police operated until the resistance movement disrupted the Nazi activities one too many times. The Nazis then had complete control of the Danish government until their surrender in 1945. King Christian X rode on his horse through the streets of Copenhagen every day of Nazi occupation with large crowds of locals cheering and following him. In May 1945, when most of the Nazi forces surrendered, the commander on Bornholm refused to surrender to the Soviet troops (he wanted to surrender to the British instead), so the Soviets bombed Rønne, the largest town in Bornholm, until the Nazis surrendered. The Soviets then occupied the island until the spring of 1946. Except for Bornholm, Denmark was not bombed during the war.

We stayed in Gudhjem, a very small fishing village on the island's northeast coast. We rented bikes to explore various parts of the island. We first visited a modern art museum 3 miles (5 kilometers) to the north, and then we rode to one of four twelfth century AD round churches on the island. We also visited a fortress, Hammerhus Slot, in ruins from the thirteenth century. We planned to ride the next day as well, but the rains came so we traded in our bikes for bus tickets. We visited another round church and a medieval cultural center. This fabulous center had people dressed in medieval clothing making food, playing with their children, and sewing. Erik even tried his hand at medieval archery. Later we visited the small village of Svaneke and ate delicious smoked salmon before completing a tour of the southern part of the island.

Back in Copenhagen, we visited Denmark's Frilandsmuseetan, an "open air museum" with over sixty reconstructed buildings from Denmark and southern Sweden. These are mostly farm buildings and were constructed with local materials during the sixteenth through nineteenth centuries AD. Furniture and farm equipment from various periods in the nineteenth and early twentieth centuries furnish each house. For example, one house was furnished from the early 1800s, another from 1850, another from 1920, and so forth. Afterward we had dinner with Erik's other host parents, who lived close to the museum.

On Saturday, June 23, the Danes celebrated their midsummer, known as Sankt Hans Aften. Midsummer festivities are celebrated all over Scandinavia. Erik's relatives treated us to a typical outdoor lunch in their garden. We had pickled and curried herring, thin dark bread, cheese, crackers, beer and schnapps. Traditionally, the Danes light bonfires all over the country, especially on the beaches. Erik's relatives have a sailboat so we took to the water to enjoy the festivities. The first bonfire erupted around 9:30 PM, although the sun still had more than an hour before it would set. We cruised for ninety minutes up and down the beach area south of Copenhagen. We saw thousands of people along the beach either watching their bonfire burn, or preparing to

Round church on Bornholm Island,
Denmark.

light one. About every 100 or 200 feet (30 or 60 meters) we saw another bonfire. At one time, we counted thirty-four bonfires from our vantage point, a half-mile (800 meters) from the beach. As darkness descended, fireworks started to go off all over the place. What a fun experience!

The day after midsummer, we took a train over the new bridge from Denmark to Sweden, and visited a huge housing and design exhibition in Malmö, Sweden. The new bridge, Oeresundsbron, opened in July 2000. Traffic flows on the upper deck and trains on the lower. Before this convenient bridge, you had to take a thirty-minute ferry to reach Sweden from Copenhagen. We found the housing exhibition absolutely incredible. Many different architects designed multi-family housing and condos near an industrial park and the beaches of Malmö. We wandered through approximately forty different units with very modern designs. Erik picked up many new ideas about residential and interior design. We also saw some houses of the future, decked out with flat computer monitors all over the house. In one we saw a flat monitor at the end of a bathtub running a live video of the beach and the new bridge beyond. (Erik wants one of those!)

The next day we visited Roskilde, the first capital of Denmark. We really enjoyed the Viking Ship Museum that houses five partially reconstructed Viking ships discovered in the Roskilde fjord in the early 1960s. The Danes sunk these ships around 1000 AD to act as a barrier to ward off an attack by Norwegian Vikings. It required nearly twenty years of preservation and reconstruction to display the original ships. The museum grounds contain replicas of Danish Viking ships you can ride in, as well as construction of other replicas using traditional Viking shipbuilding techniques. This is also the time of year for the Roskilde Festival, a large multi-day international rock concert. Bands from the United States and United Kingdom usually top the attractions. Even though the festival was still a few days away, we saw hundreds of teenagers and young adults arriving in Roskilde, most with their stock of essentials for the concert: beer, beer, and more beer—and the occasional sleeping bag.

The night before we left for Jutland, we went to Tivoli, an amusement park in downtown Copenhagen that is over 150 years old. Walt Disney visited Tivoli and it is said used its layout as inspiration for Disneyland. We enjoyed the park with lots of small lights, lovely gardens, numerous restaurants, and rides for the young and the not so young. We saw Manhattan Transfer in concert in Tivoli's glass pavilion, one of Jennifer's favorite groups. It was a fabulous indoor concert.

On June 27 we took a train west, to the mainland of Denmark known as Jutland. We spent two days in Billund visiting a friend from our Africa tour. Billund is home to Lego and Legoland. Jennifer had heard of Legoland growing up, and Erik had never made it there when he lived in Denmark. After lunch and looking at Africa pictures, we were off to Legoland.

We had an absolute blast! Legoland has two parts, the part with fun rides and the part with miniature cities and towns made of millions of Lego bricks. The miniature displays completely entranced us. We first saw a full model of an airport, inspired by Munich's airport, at 1:50 scale. Lego airplanes of incredible detail moved around and readied for takeoff. We even saw baggage moving out of one plane and onto a truck. At one point a three-year-old boy darted through the flowers onto the tarmac of the Lego airport in pure excitement. His father ran after him and picked him up before he damaged the display.

We also saw huge Lego models of Amsterdam; Los Angeles; Bergen, Norway; the Klampenborg train station in Copenhagen; a Japanese city and surrounging countryside; an oil platform in the North Sea; and a town in Scotland. Architect Erik was completely overwhelmed—the attention to detail was amazing. Two working Lego locks with real water lifted up Lego boats about a foot (30 centimeters) long. In the Los Angeles section, a movie set with lights, camera, and moving vehicles filmed a movie. We saw Lego copies of many castles in Denmark and Germany. If anyone is a model train buff, this would be your dream come true because over twenty different working Lego trains—Danish, Dutch, German, Japanese, Finnish, Swedish, and Norwegian—run through the exhibits.

Lego is probably one of Denmark's best-known exports. The company started as a small wooden toy company, and in the late 1940s, created the plastic building blocks that quickly became popular the world over. The word *Lego* is a take off of the Danish words "to play well." Later, after they created the plastic building blocks, the company found out that in Latin, *Lego* means "to put together, to combine." Lego, a well-respected corporation, has factories all over the world, but Lego's Billund factory remains the largest. Our friend's mother has worked in that factory for over twenty-five years, and before we left Billund we toured where she works. We found it fascinating to see Lego pieces combined in different sets, sealed in plastic and put into boxes to be shipped all over the world.

After leaving Billund, we spent a couple days in Silkeborg, a lovely small city on the shores of a long narrow lake. We rode on one of the world's oldest paddle steamers the length of the lake. We passed many houses lining the lake that each had their own little dock and boats. We stopped at Himmelbjerget, one of Denmark's highest points at 482 feet (147 m). After lunch, we climbed for fifteen minutes to the top—a bit easier than Dead Women's Pass in Peru! We also enjoyed displays in the Silkeborg Museum on ancient rural life in the area and the "Tollund Man," a well-preserved corpse from around 200 BC. This dark brown corpse was found in a nearby peat bog in the 1950s. The tannins in the bog preserved the corpse so well we could see the lines on his face and the leather cap tied around his head!

From Silkeborg we took a bus and two trains to Skagen, Denmark's northernmost town. Skagen is a popular tourist spot for Danes, Swedes, Norwegians and Germans alike. Cloud-free skies warm numerous beaches during the summer months. The land mass narrows the further north you go, and ends up at a point where the North Sea meets the Baltic Sea, creating unique waves as the two seas meet. Many people crowded around the northernmost point of Denmark for photos. Old Nazi concrete fortifications, the size of small houses and used to ward off a possible Allied invasion, dot the beach. At the turn of the century a hundred years ago, Skagen was a thriving artist colony. Skagen's summertime "light" attracted the artists because they

Typical Danish houses, Skagen, Denmark.

could paint outdoors until nearly midnight and the skies were usually clear. We visited an art museum displaying the works of painters P.S. Kroyer, and Anna and Michael Ancher—the principal artists in Skagen's art colony.

A few hours ago we returned from Aalborg where we celebrated the fourth of July at the Rebild Festival, the largest American Independence Day celebration outside of the United States. The festival first started in 1912 to encourage Danish-Americans to visit Denmark and look up their roots. Each year about 10,000 people come and celebrate the friendship between the United States and Denmark. The festival takes place in a natural amphitheater in the hills of Rebild, a small town 15.5 miles (25 kilometers) southwest of Aalborg.

It took several minutes to find a seat on the bushy hillside that surrounded the stage area. We perched precariously and occasionally started to slide down the hillside if we were not careful. The hour-long ceremony was quite moving, complete with everyone singing the Danish and American national anthems, as well as "America the Beautiful." That night back in Aalborg, we enjoyed a barbecue in the park, and live musical entertainment. We admired classic American cars displayed by local classic car organizations. Three thousand lawn candles looped around the trunks of trees and throughout the park lawns. It was a stunning visual landscape. We figure this public candle display could not take place in the States very easily due to liability concerns. At midnight, we enjoyed a short but fantastic fireworks display.

Tomorrow we drive to Sweden for two weeks. Then we visit Finland, Iceland and London before going to Southeast Asia on August 14. Until Singapore!

Love, Jennifer & Erik

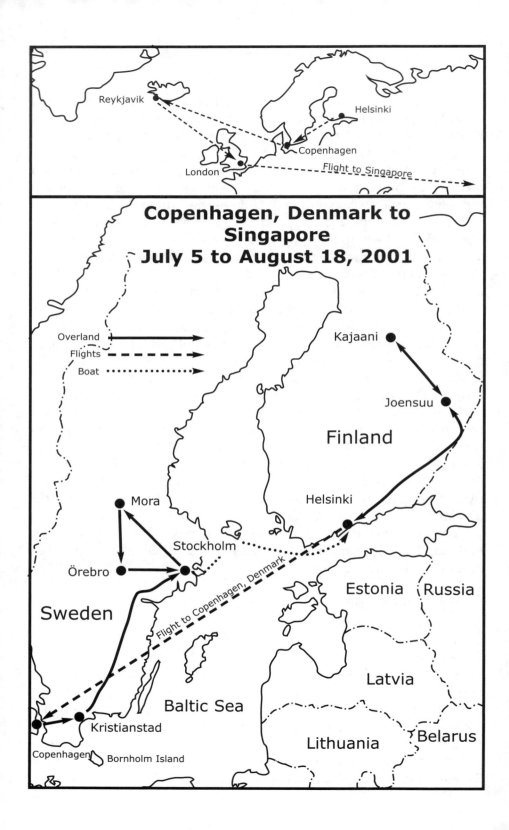

Copenhagen, Denmark to
Singapore
July 5 to August 18, 2001

Overland
Flights
Boat

Reykjavik

Helsinki

Copenhagen

London

Flight to Singapore

Kajaani

Joensuu

Finland

Mora

Stockholm

Helsinki

Örebro

Estonia   Russia

Sweden

Flight to Copenhagen, Denmark

Baltic Sea

Latvia

Kristianstad

Copenhagen   Bornholm Island

Lithuania   Belarus

11

Dear friends and family,

We left Denmark on July 6 for Sweden with Erik's cousin via the new bridge connecting the two countries. Sweden has a population of almost 9 million living in a country slightly larger than California. The Kingdom of Sweden, a peaceful country, was neutral during both world wars. Sweden exports Volvos and Saab cars and is the world's third largest exporter of music. Sweden is also home to the worldwide furniture store IKEA and the Nobel prizes.

While driving past the dairy farms and rolling hay fields, we noticed large, round, white bundles that resembled giant marshmallows in the fields. Turns out in Sweden, Finland, and Iceland, the farmers store their cut hay in round bundles wrapped in plastic. The hay is cut, allowed to dry slightly on the ground, and then raked into round bales. These bales are fork lifted onto a machine that spins the hay about twenty times, tightly sealing the hay in white plastic. These covered bales sit in the field until transported for storage near the farm buildings. In Iceland, farmers use mint-green plastic as well as white, so they can find the bales easier in the snow. Apparently, wrapping the hay preserves more nutrients since the hay does not have to be dried as much. It also diminishes the risk of fire, and requires less barn space on the farms. In Iceland, farmers recycle the plastic and make plastic fence posts.

We arrived in Sweden during a major heat wave that did not last very long. We enjoyed the nice weather during an outdoor garden party at Erik's cousin's summerhouse with relatives that lived nearby. We spent a couple of days enjoying the forested lake and preparing for the party. We visited with around twenty relatives on Erik's maternal grandfather's side. Both of Erik's maternal grandparents were born in Sweden and immigrated independently to America in the 1920s. They met and married while living in Michigan, then moved to California in the 1940s.

One of the relatives took us on a day tour of the Skåne province of Sweden. We visited a castle that also was a monastery, and a well-preserved manor house called Glimmingehus. During the sixteenth century, Denmark owned southern Sweden and a very wealthy Danish lord built this fortified house. The lord only resided in the house periodically, having similar houses all over Sweden. Upon the lord's death, his son declared the house too "old-fashioned" and built another one at the top of a nearby hill. Consequently, Glimmingehus was used for storage since the mid-sixteenth century and not renovated. As we toured the building, we saw various defenses including holes to shoot arrows at people coming into the house and upper balconies for archers. We toured a large kitchen and storage area in the basement, a general gathering room on the first floor, a banquet room on the second floor, and separate bedrooms for the lord and his wife. Because travel was difficult in those times, the lord's banquets lasted several days and his guests slept in the general gathering room.

After enjoying an outdoor dinner in the seventeenth-century town of Kristianstad, we rode a train to Stockholm, Sweden's capital city, to visit Erik's former host brother. Erik spent the summer of 1989 in Örebro, Sweden as an exchange student with American Field Service, an organization that promotes world peace through international student exchanges. Before we left Kristianstad, we found out a college friend of Erik's was also in Stockholm with her brother, so we had even more friends to see! We toured Stockholm's City Hall built in the early twentieth century. Each December, Sweden hosts a dinner for the Nobel Prize winners (except for the Nobel Peace Prize which is given in Norway) in a covered courtyard area that resembles an Italian piazza. After dinner a dance is held in an upstairs ballroom decorated with mosaics. We also climbed the bell tower for a fantastic view of the numerous islands that comprise Stockholm.

Our favorite sight was the Vasa Museum; a specially-designed museum opened in 1990 to house the *Vasa*, a Swedish warship completed in 1628 AD that sank in the Stockholm harbor twenty minutes into her maiden voyage. The completely intact ship was rediscovered in the late 1950s and raised and preserved over three decades. The body of the ship is huge, measuring 200 feet by 38 feet (61 meters by 11.7 meters) and 63 feet (19.3 meters) high. Built as a new design with two decks of cannons and beautiful carved wood on the front and back, the ship sank because it did not sit low enough in the water for her size. The preserved ship sits in the middle of the museum surrounded by ramps for close up views. The museum also has wonderful displays of the various artifacts found in the ship, as well as a replica of the lower gun deck you can walk through. We found this museum as interesting as the Viking Ship Museum in Denmark.

From Stockholm, we headed northwest into the province of Dalarna to spend time visiting relatives on Erik's maternal grandmother's side. Erik's grandmother came from a large family, so we visited many people. We soon learned the ins-and-outs of Swedish hospitality—specifically, you cannot visit someone without the host serving a meal (usually) or dessert and strong coffee. We certainly did not go hungry in Dalarna, and had plenty of sugar and caffeine. Lying in bed one morning, Erik felt his cheek twitching and thought, "Oh gosh, is my nervous system going crazy from all the sugar and caffeine I had yesterday?" It turned out that it was only a fly landing on Erik's face over and over! Since it was strawberry season, we enjoyed garden fresh berries on waffles and Swedish pancakes—very delicious!

We also enjoyed some of the Dalarna sights. We visited Mora, known for the Vasaloppet, a 56-mile (90-kilometer) cross-country ski race held each March. Started in 1922, it is said to be the "oldest, longest and greatest" cross-country ski race. Even the King of Sweden has competed! Mora, Minnesota also hosts a Vasaloppet race each February, but it is only a 36-mile (58-kilometer) race. Mora, Sweden is also the home of the Swedish portrait artist Anders Zorn. We visited his home, built in the late nineteenth century, and the adjacent museum. Mora sits on the north shore of the beautiful Lake Siljan and we enjoyed driving along the shore. Rolling hay fields dot the countryside broken up by stands of trees and farm buildings painted dark red with white trim. We also visited Sundborn, the home of Carl Larson who was a contemporary of Zorn's. Larson is known in Sweden and abroad for his Japanese-style watercolor paintings of his family in their home. Many say Carl Larson is Sweden's most beloved artist. Larson's artist wife, Karin, decorated their home in a new way. Her use of bright colors and geometric designs in the fabrics for the furniture launched a new style of interior design in turn-of-the-century Sweden.

From Dalarna we traveled south to Örebro to visit Erik's former host parents. Jennifer enjoyed seeing the farm where Erik stayed and meeting some of the people Erik met in 1989. We spent two relaxing

days in Örebro before returning to Stockholm to board an overnight
ferry to Helsinki, Finland. We booked a cabin with twin berths. The
ferry resembled a small cruise ship with several decks and amenities.
We left Stockholm at 5 PM and enjoyed an enormous and delicious
Swedish/Finnish smorgasbord while passing through the Stockholm
archipelago. Jennifer was amazed at the number of ways they served
herring. After dinner, Erik enjoyed the sauna and cinema; we passed
on the casino, karaoke bar and disco.

Finland is about two-thirds the size of Sweden, or slightly smaller
than Montana, with a population of approximately 5 million. Finland
borders Russia and was ruled by Russia from 1809 to 1917, so the language and the feel of the culture differ from Denmark and Sweden.
Finland is the only Nordic country adopting the Euro on January 1,
2002. Finland has more trees and fewer farms than Denmark or
Sweden. During our six-hour, 250-mile (400-kilometer) train ride from
Helsinki to Joensuu, we passed through mile after mile of birch and
pine forest. In Joensuu, we stayed with the parents and family of a former Finnish exchange student Erik met in Modesto, California in 1989.
Their home sits along one of the numerous small lakes in Finland and
Erik enjoyed the wood-burning sauna every night. The Finns take
their saunas very seriously, as they invented it. Erik and his friend
enjoyed heating up in the sauna then cooling off in the misty lake.

While in Finland we had our first experience fishing off a trawler.
Erik's friend, who enjoys fishing, arranged for a boat trip on two of the
nearby lakes. We were amazed the captain kept twelve fishing lines
from getting tangled. After placing a small wooden ski off each side of
the boat, the captain attached four fishing lines to each ski and had
four poles off the back of the boat. Although the fish were not biting
that night, we enjoyed sailing for five hours on the water and leisurely
passing the forested coast.

We also visited an exhibition of Finnish housing in Kajaani and
spent a rainy afternoon touring models of single-family homes, apartments, and even a retirement center. Erik especially enjoyed seeing
new ideas for home saunas. We both enjoyed the new Nordic designs
for homes and admired the high quality of materials used.

After a short overnight in Helsinki, we flew to Iceland for ten days.
We both loved Iceland and highly recommend it as a place to visit.
Iceland is roughly the size of England with a population of only
280,000. The Norwegian Vikings settled Iceland between 800 and 900
AD. Until the early twentieth century, the majority of Icelanders lived

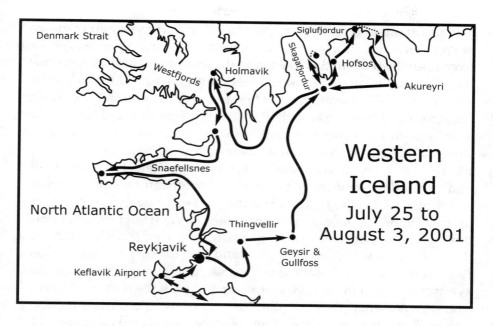

Denmark Strait

Westfjords

Holmavik

Siglufjordur

Skagafjordur

Hofsos

Akureyri

Snaefellsnes

North Atlantic Ocean

Thingvellir

Reykjavik

Keflavik Airport

Geysir & Gullfoss

Western Iceland
July 25 to August 3, 2001

on small farms throughout the country. In the last part of the twentieth century, Icelanders have migrated to the cities and 110,000 people now live in the capital, Reykjavik, with another 60,000 in the surrounding area. Reykjavik continues to grow with one family migrating to it every day.

Iceland, the land of fire and ice, is a land of rugged beauty. It reminded us of the American west and parts of the Peruvian desert. Iceland is young geologically, only 15 to 18 million years old, and is located on the separation of the North America and Europe Plates. The pull of the plates forms new land in the middle of the country and causes Iceland to grow approximately 1 inch (2.5 centimeters) each year. This split produces much volcanic and geothermal activity. We saw numerous old lava fields (many covered in lichen and moss), dormant and extinct volcanoes, three glaciers, and geothermal activity in almost every part of Iceland we visited. We also saw beautiful fjord-carved coasts with green hills and mountains. Iceland is basically treeless. The trees that once forested Iceland were cut down during the thousand years of settlement. The introduction of sheep to Iceland prohibited reforestation, as sheep eat everything and do not allow the tree seedlings to grow. Iceland uses driftwood that washes ashore from Siberia and has young, small, man-made forests, as well as young trees in towns next to people's houses.

Our first day in Reykjavik we enjoyed the art museum, home and works of the Icelandic sculptor, Asmundur Sveinsson. An aside about Icelandic names: Families in Iceland do not share the same last name. Rather, the last name of an individual shows the first name of that person's father. So, for example, the first name of the sculptor Asmundur Sveinsson's father is Svein. If the sculptor had a daughter, her last name would be Asmundursdottir, and his son's last name would be Asmundursson. Women do not change their last name when they get married, so one family usually has four separate last names—the dad's, the mom's, one for all the sons and another for all the daughters.

We also joined the Icelanders in a geothermal-heated public swimming pool. Along the side of the pool were several hot tubs ("hot pots") of varying temperatures, each approximately 15°F (8.3°C) hotter than the next. Erik was surprised he could not tolerate the hottest one. Reykjavik has several of these pools and, from our experience, so does every small town in Iceland! Harnessed for only the past one hundred years, geothermal power now heats eighty-five percent of Icelandic homes, heats the municipal swimming pools and hot pots, provides hot water for home showers and is even piped under some streets and sidewalks in Reykjavik to keep them cleared of snow in the winter. Swimming or using a hot pot requires a certain amount of preparation. Icelanders do not use much (if any) chlorine in their pools, so bathers must take a pre-bathing nude shower with soap, washing all parts of the body. After that, you put on your swimsuit and are ready for the pool!

On our second day in Iceland, we joined a German and a Swiss family for a nine-day tour with Isafold Travel on their "North by Northwest" tour. We traveled east from Reykjavik to visit Thingvellir, site of the world's first parliament. In 930 AD, the various chieftains of Iceland realized that they needed a uniform type of government for the country and set up the world's longest running parliament. Every summer for approximately two weeks, the thirty-six regional chieftains from all parts of Iceland met at Thingvellir to set up new laws and rule on various legal and criminal matters. This council lasted for more than 800 years, until the last meeting in 1798, when a national court and parliament at Reykjavik replaced it. Today Iceland has a sixty-three-member parliament that meets during the winter months.

From Thingvellir we visited Geysir, a hole in the ground that spouts hot water and gave the name to geysers all over the world. We stood close to another geyser to see it bubble just before spouting water about 70 feet (23 meters) in the air! From Geysir we visited the Gullfoss waterfall, where we viewed the spectacular two-tiered waterfall. We are lucky the falls still exist. In the 1920s, the government wanted to create a power plant over the falls, but one woman, Sigridor Tomasdottir, walked 60 miles (100 kilometers) to Reykjavik to keep the government from spoiling the falls. From the falls we drove through the stark interior, between two glaciers, to another area with fumaroles and bubbling geothermal water. Icelanders let their sheep free-graze on the interior lands during the summer. A fence stretching across the interior separates the sheep from the north from those of the south, making it easier to find lost sheep in the fall and protecting the animals from infectious disease.

We continued our drive through the largest desert in Europe and ended up on the north coast of Iceland, between two of the numerous peninsulas created by fjords. Endless hayfields fill the fertile valleys of these peninsulas. The first two nights we stayed in the Skagafjordur peninsula known for the breeding of the Icelandic horses. When the Vikings settled Iceland in the ninth century, they brought their finest Germanic horses with them. To insure these animals would be free from disease, Icelanders soon banned the importation of horses. Thus, for the last 1,100 years, Icelandic horses have maintained their original genetic traits. The horses are short, measuring approximately thirteen to fourteen hands, and retain five different gaits. We saw a demonstration that included the *tölt* (a running walk where the rider does not move in the saddle), and the pace (a gait even faster than the gallop). It was wonderful to watch these beautiful animals run!

After the Icelandic horse demonstration, we drove along the fjord coast to visit an outdoor "hot pot." This natural geothermal spring is associated with one of the numerous Icelandic *sagas*. *Sagas* are the oral stories of the original settlers told and retold until they were written down between the twelfth and fifteenth centuries AD. *Sagas* are very important to Icelanders, as they tell their history.

In this *saga*, "Grettir the Strong" lives as a fugitive on Drangey Island. He is a fugitive for killing one person too many. He makes a life for himself on that island, but one night his fire burns out. So he swims to the mainland approximately 1 mile (1.6 kilometers) away, warms up in the hot pot, gets a burning ember to take back, and swims back to his island home with the ember in his mouth. Later that afternoon we visited this island by boat and climbed up a steep trail to the 600-foot (200-meter) top where Grettir lived. Today the top of the rocky island is covered with thick grass and the locals collect the eggs and hunt the various birds that breed in the rocky cliffs. We saw fulmars, grullemots and puffins. The cliffs are stained white from bird droppings.

That night we ate an unusual dinner—one that consisted of food Icelanders ate 200 years ago. We had marinated shark, smoked sheep's heads, a type of "fish jerky," turnip mash and lamb. The sheep's head was served in the skull cut in half from the jaw to the back of the head. To help us eat this unusual food, our guide provided us with ample amounts of Icelandic beer and schnapps. After dinner our guide pulled out his guitar and we sang Icelandic and American folk songs. We were surprised at how many American folk songs everyone knew the words to. When we returned to the guest house, Erik and another group member got on their knees and pleaded with the owner to reopen the hot pot for a late night dip!

The next day we drove east to the other side of the fjord to visit the wonderful Icelandic Emigration Museum in Hofsos. For the first 1,000 years of settlement, life in Iceland changed very little. Most people farmed using Icelandic horses and raised sheep and dairy cows. Grain does not grow in Iceland, so Icelanders did not raise beef cattle. People lived in turf houses due to the lack of timber. Some people fished, but few depended on fishing as their sole means of support. By 1874, nearly 84,000 people lived in Iceland, but the available farmland no longer supported the population. Between 1874 and 1900, nearly 16,000 Icelanders emigrated, most to Manitoba, Canada and a lesser amount to the United States. This twenty percent population loss spurned new innovations, allowing the remainder of the population to prosper in Iceland. Coincidently, herring appeared off the north coast and created a new fishing industry from 1900 to 1968 (when the herring suddenly disappeared). Today much less land is cultivated, as Iceland has fewer sheep and horses (thus less need for hay) and depends more on cod fishing.

We continued north along the coast to the tip of the peninsula and the town of Siglufjordur, one of the most important ports during the herring years. In some years this town accounted for over twenty percent of the nation's export of herring. We visited a museum and enjoyed a hilarious staged demonstration of cleaning and salting herring during the 1950s. Herring was processed only during the summer, so workers came from all over Iceland for three months. The mostly young female workers were paid by the barrel and worked almost continuously, as the sun barely sets during summer.

Notwithstanding the port, Siglufjordur is a narrow fjord surrounded by peaked mountains. Jennifer joined the other families to
hike between these mountains to a deserted fjord on the other side.
Erik opted not to climb 600 feet (180 meters) through the snow, but
rather sailed with the voluntary coast guard that picked up the hikers
on the other side. Jennifer enjoyed hiking up the mountainside covered in various wildflowers and even "skiing" in her hiking boots
down the other side. The scenery was beautiful. Melting snow caused
several streams through the turf that eventually drained into the lake
behind the fjord.

On our trip back west toward the Westfjords, we stopped by a turf
house. This particular house had nine separate turf houses connected
to each other by a covered tunnel. Rectangles of stacked sod formed

Erik and fellow travelers relaxing in
an outdoor Icelandic hot pot.

the walls and a sod roof (supported by a wooden frame) covered the building. Two guest rooms constructed in 1841 and 1878 stood opposite each other at the front of the house. The kitchen (dating to 1750) and the dairy (where the milk was separated and the butter made) faced each other next to the guest rooms. The kitchen was the only room that was heated. Typically, different parts of sheep hung in the kitchen above the fire to be smoked. Next to the kitchen and dairy were the room for assembling the food and the pantry for storing smoked and cured food. Another guest room (used as a classroom for boys during the winter) and an emergency access door for the back of the house were the next rooms. The farmer, his family and all of their help slept in a large room at the back of the house. The help slept in bunks in a large middle section and the family slept in two alcoves on the ends. People used their body heat to keep warm in this unheated room. The precious wood was used for cooking fuel only. A well-built turf house could last 100 years. The kitchen could last longer because the residue from the fire coated the walls and gave it added strength.

We spent the next several days driving through the beautiful countryside of Iceland and the Westfjords. We stopped to hike, watch seals and dolphins, and enjoy more hot pots while simultaneously looking for whales in the Arctic Ocean. In the seventeenth century, the isolated Westfjords had many accusations of witchcraft and some subsequent executions. We visited an interesting and informative exhibition on Icelandic sorcery and witchcraft and noted the Icelandic accusations of witchcraft coincided with those in Salem, Massachusetts.

As we headed south from the Westfjords, we stopped and planted aspen seedlings as part of Isafold Travel's participation in a reforestation project. We planted the trees in a fenced-in area to protect them from the sheep. We spent the final three nights of our tour in former boarding schools. During the mid-twentieth century, many rural middle- and high-school-aged students attended boarding schools for their secondary education. Because many Icelanders have migrated to Reykjavik, several boarding schools have closed and been converted into hotels and guesthouses to support the ever-increasing number of foreign tourists.

The final day of our tour we first visited the birthplace of Leif Eriksson (son of Erik the Red), the "real" discoverer of North America. In 1000 AD, Leif Eriksson and his party sailed to various parts of Newfoundland and some say even as far as New York City harbor! Earlier, Erik the Red was exiled from Iceland (having killed one neighbor too many) and discovered Greenland. He named it Greenland, not because it was green, but to attract settlers. Iceland, on the other hand, is much more "green" than Greenland will ever be. It makes far more sense for the names to be reversed!

We then drove around the Snaefellsnes peninsula, the peninsula to the north of Reykjavik. Every geological feature in Iceland can be found on this peninsula. At the far tip of Snaefellsnes, we explored a black pebble beach with the remains of a wrecked British ship from the 1940s. It was quite beautiful to see the rusted metal strewn over the black beach. This area is also well known for the beautiful glacier-topped Mount Snaefellsjokull, the setting for the beginning of Jules Verne's "Journey to the Center of the Earth."

We traveled another three hours back to Reykjavik and stopped at our guide's home to meet his wife and for a good-bye champagne toast. Later when our guide drove the other members of the tour to their hotels, his wife generously drove us to the Blue Lagoon for our final Icelandic hot pot experience before our red-eye flight to London. The thermal spa is located near the Keflavik International Airport and the U.S. Air Force base at Keflavik. (The United States has had an Air Force base here since Iceland joined NATO in the early 1950s.)

Blue Lagoon was simply magical. This swimming/hotel complex built five years ago captures the geothermal waters of a local geyser. The unique pool is a massive man-made lagoon surrounded by a 4-foot- (1.2-meter-) tall wall of black lava rocks, with an active geyser at the far end. The closer you swim to the geyser, the hotter it gets. The water contains an unusually high concentration of silicon (among many other minerals), so we were careful not to get it in our eyes. The combination of steam coming off the water, the low sun and modern architecture created a unique and beautiful last image of Iceland.

After enjoying the full colors of the "midnight sun," we boarded our plane at 3 AM, and arrived in London three hours later. Later that morning, Jennifer's sister and her husband arrived in London from Chicago, so we met them at Heathrow airport. We spent nine wonderful days together in London. What a treat to have family members join us on our trip! Jennifer had been to London four times previously, and Erik went to graduate school in London from 1995 until 1996, at the Architectural Association, so it was old hat for us. Jennifer's sister and her husband were first-time London visitors, so we all toured the popular spots in town. We also visited three friends from our South American travels that live in London, as well as Erik's host mother from Denmark, visiting London at the same time as us. We also ate dinner with Erik's former architecture classmates from the University of Kansas who also went to school with him in London and now run their own architecture firm there.

We enjoyed seeing several things for the first time. Because it was summer, we toured the State Rooms at Buckingham Palace. We saw the magnificent rooms used during ceremonies and balls, as well as the palace gardens not previously open to the public. We also enjoyed the reconstructed Globe Theater. Built from the dream of Sam Wanamaker, an American actor and director, it is the only building in London with a thatched roof. It was fantastic to see a theater from Elizabethan times and understand how Shakespeare's plays were performed for the audience. Another new sight for us was the Hermitage Rooms. The Hermitage in St. Petersburg, Russia has so many treasures it cannot display them all, so it opened a five-room gallery at Somerset House in London to display a different exhibit every year. We saw an exhibition on the treasures of Catherine the Great, and in November, a new exhibit will start.

We also enjoyed old favorites. Foremost, we enjoyed the Tower of London despite the heavy rains. The Tower of London, started by the Romans, was fortified by King William I in 1080 AD after he conquered England. The British royalty lived here for several centuries and continually expanded it. We enjoyed the four rooms that reconstruct the interior of the medieval palace as it looked at the end of the 1200s. The Tower of London became the infamous prison and execution spot for various unlucky royals during the reign of Henry VIII. The Crown Jewels are also housed here, and Jennifer and her sister enjoyed gazing at their brilliance. We also enjoyed touring the Cabinet War Rooms, the underground rooms in the heart of London constructed during World War II to house Prime Minister Churchill and his staff. The rooms look just as they did when Churchill used them and met with his War Cabinet. Jennifer and her sister also spent an afternoon viewing Princess Diana's dresses in Kensington Palace and enjoying afternoon tea at one of London's famous tea houses. (Meanwhile, their husbands explored the Imperial War Museum and a couple of pubs.)

Before we knew it, we were off once again; this time to our present location, Singapore! After a twelve-hour flight on Qantas Airlines, we arrived at this small island nation just over 3.5 times the size of Washington D.C. Singapore became an independent country in 1965.

A former British colony, Singapore was occupied by the Japanese in World War II, and now is the business hub for Southeast Asia. Singapore is a city-nation and seems like one big air-conditioned shopping mall. The amount of consumerism in Singapore is mind-blowing. You can find most American shops and hotels here, with a multi-story shopping mall on nearly every corner. In 1965, the new government decided to do away with lawlessness and poverty, so they moved everyone in the country into high-rise apartments and cleaned up the streets to attract international investors. Their idea has worked successfully; almost everyone speaks English, and Singapore enjoys a high standard of living (ninety percent of the people own their own housing) and high per capita income. Singapore's population is approximately 4 million, with 1 million additional foreign workers. Between 200,000 and 300,000 workers (approximately the population of Iceland) commute forty-five minutes from Malaysia to Singapore every day. Singapore takes pride in its clean streets and low crime rate. Crime does not pay in Singapore, as drug traffickers are put to death and many criminals are sentenced to caning and long prison terms.

We are staying in the "Little India" section of town; so our first morning in Singapore, we had an Indian curry dish for breakfast. In Singapore, we enjoyed a city tour and their famous "Night Safari." Since everyone has moved into the city in recent years, a night safari was opened in 1994. It has been wildly successful; approximately 2,000 people visit the park every night. After a buffet dinner at the park, we took a forty-minute tram ride and saw many wild animals in a controlled environment. The park resembles a zoo, but the enclosures are hard to see at night. We saw lions, tigers, bears, giraffes, deer, porcupines, and Asian rhinos, among many other animals. After the tram ride, we went on a forty-minute walk through the park. Lights that simulate moonlight illuminated the park. The park is very well done, and we were impressed at how natural the habitat appeared.

Tomorrow we take an overnight train to Kuala Lumpur, the capital of Malaysia. We will spend around ten days in Malaysia before beginning our seven-week India trip. We will write again in India!

Love, Jennifer & Erik

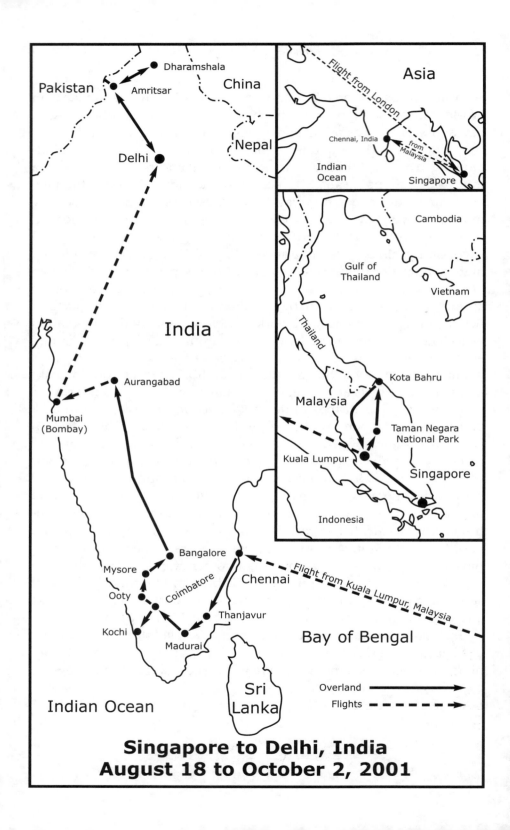

Singapore to Delhi, India
August 18 to October 2, 2001

12

Bundi, India
Saturday, October 6, 2001

Dear friends and family,

First, we are both safe and well and we thank all of you who have e-mailed us with concern. We apologize for the delay in letting you know of our safety. We initially intended to send this e-mail on September 13, but the attacks on America delayed that. Then we intended to send it on October 1, but we had one of our bags stolen off a train and spent the rest of the day purchasing new clothes and personal items. Thankfully we had our money and passports strapped to our bodies, so the loss of the bag was essentially a minor inconvenience. In light of September 11, we realized how lucky we are that we only lost some clothes—all replaceable stuff.

On Tuesday evening, September 11, 2001, we sat in our hotel room in Mysore, India in utter shock and disbelief watching the televised replays of the death and destruction in New York, Washington D.C., and Pennsylvania. Most hotels in India carry CNN International, FOX News (Erik's favorite), and BBC World, so we were very informed about the events back home. In addition to western news sources, we also read the Indian perspective of these tragic events in Indian newspapers. Here in India, people are very sympathetic to what happened in America. When people ask where we are from, we say "the United States" and they immediately mention or hand gesture about the attacks on September 11.

But back to where we last left you. From Singapore, we took a night train to Kuala Lumpur, the capital of Malaysia. Malaysia is comprised of two separate parts—Peninsular Malaysia between Thailand to the north and Singapore to the south, and East Malaysia, which is two states on the island of Borneo. The entire area of Malaysia is slightly larger than New Mexico. We limited our travels to Peninsular Malaysia. Malaysia has 22.2 million people, with approximately fifty-eight percent of Malay descent, twenty-seven percent Chinese, eight percent Indian, and the remainder indigenous and others. A constitutional monarchy governs Malaysia, although the king is strictly a figurehead. When Malaysia was created as an independent state in 1957, nine hereditary kings governed various sultanates within Malaysia. To preserve their status, Malaysia created a rotating monarchy system whereby the nine sultans hold the title of national monarch for a five-year term. At present, Malaysia is on its eleventh monarch since independence, and he is the son of Malaysia's second monarch. He is scheduled to rule until 2004, when the heir to Malaysia's third monarch will take the throne.

The Malays are Muslim, and Malaysia prides itself as being a moderate and modern Islamic state. The Muslim women in Malaysia dress in brighter colors than the women in Egypt, Jordan or Turkey. In Kuala Lumpur, the Malay women wear bright, solid pastel-colored headscarves that match their clothing of a long skirt made from small floral-print material and a matching long-sleeved tunic top that reaches their knees. The bright headscarf is typically clasped under the chin with a decorative pin. Outside of Kuala Lumpur, we saw Malay women dressed the same way, but some also dressed in pants and t-shirts with a headscarf.

Moving rapidly into the modern western world, Malaysia is an interesting mix of modern skyscrapers with older, more rundown buildings and markets comprised of movable stalls and handcarts. Our first encounter with modern Malaysia was a driverless subway. We thought "Wow, what advanced transportation," except we could not purchase an all-day or multiple ride pass. Later we learned that each subway line is run by a different private company, so to transfer subway lines we needed to leave one station and walk across the street to the other subway line, even though the two stations had the same name. Not the easy transfer of other metropolitan subway systems!

After settling ourselves in Chinatown, we hopped on the subway to see the Petronas Twin Towers, the tallest buildings in the world, completed in 1996. United States-based Argentinean architect Cesar Pelli designed these very modern, stainless steel and glass-panel towers. Based on an Islamic geometric pattern representing unity, harmony, stability and rationality, the towers are not your typical boxy skyscrapers. Instead, the buildings look cylindrical, with each floor consisting of two interlocking squares rotated by forty-five degrees with arcs interlinking the squares, leaving the points protruding. Each tower rises 1,483 feet (452 meters) with a "sky bridge" connecting the two twin towers at 558 feet (170 meters), or level 41, which we visited for a bird's-eye view of Kuala Lumpur.

From Kuala Lumpur we left the concrete jungle for the real jungle— in our case a jungle that has existed for 130 million years! We drove four hours northeast from Kuala Lumpur into the interior of Malaysia, and then took a three-hour ride in a covered longboat to Taman Negara National Park. We met several Americans, a Kenyan and a South African on our boat. The boat ride was wonderful; we glided upriver in a motorized boat admiring the lush green scenery along the shores. We were deep in tranquility when all of a sudden the motor stopped and the boat started spinning around in the current! Soon the clank, clank, clank of a wrench hitting the motor replaced the sounds of the jungle. After an agonizing five minutes, we heard the happy sounds of the motor starting and we were once again cruising along the river. We arrived late in the afternoon at one of the floating restau- rants that dominate the village across from the main park entrance.

After settling into our small bungalow, we ate dinner and ventured across the river in a water taxi for a night safari in the jungle. Ninety percent of animals and insects in the jungle are active under the cover of darkness as a protection from enemies. We set off single file behind a guide with a strong flashlight ("torch" for the Brits, Aussies, Kiwis and others) hunting for insects. That first night we saw a snake in a tree, a flying lemur (a small mammal) in the treetops and many insects—spiders, lantern sticks, walking sticks, scorpions, ants, crick- ets, moths and lightning bugs. We had so much fun that first night, we went for a night jungle safari all three nights we were at the park.

The next day we set off to explore the jungle by day. We hiked over the same path we had explored the night before, but it certainly looked different by daylight. Tall, tropical trees with vines clinging to them, leafy, fern-like plants, and several types of plants with palm-like leaves approximately 5 feet (1.6 meters) in length lined the dirt trail. Although it did not rain during our visit, the air in this tropical rain- forest was quite humid. In addition to exploring the jungle on the ground, the park service has constructed an extensive canopy walk in the treetops so people can experience the jungle up there. So, off we went. The canopy walk sits 98 feet (30 meters) above the jungle floor and consists of nine different catwalks (totaling 1,476 feet (450 meters)) strung between the trees. The walkways vary in length with the longest being 262 feet (80 meters). The walkway sways but is quite

easy to walk on. We both enjoyed walking along the treetops and seeing the jungle from above. Erik liked the walk so much he did it again
the next day.

We then hiked on a trail in the jungle and for about two hours we
did not see anyone else. We returned to eat lunch and then back to the
bungalow for a cold shower. As Jennifer took off her left shoe, she
noticed a pool of fresh blood coming from under her sock. A leech had
attached itself through her sock and later fell off (after it was full).
Jennifer had no idea it was even there, and did not feel anything out
of the ordinary. Fortunately, our insect safari guide the evening before
informed us that leeches are harmless, so that quelled Erik's anxiety.
Our South African friend also had a leech on her ankle, which attached
through two of her socks!

We also visited a Batek village, the native people of the Malaysian
jungle. We took a longboat twenty minutes down river to a semi-per-
manent village one-quarter mile (400 meters) from the riverbank. The
Batek people are nomadic, so they only stay in the village for a few
weeks at a time in houses on stilts built of wood and covered with
palm leaves. The families occupy different huts every time they return
to the village. When the families are in the jungle, they build a lean-to-
type structure to protect themselves from the rain. The tribe we visited
had about forty people in the village, as the rest had moved into the
jungle. Apparently only about 1,000 members of this tribe remain
today. These native people have very dark skin and curly black hair
and reminded us more of sub-Saharan Africans than Malaysians. We
visited with the women as they finished cooking dinner and watched
several young men play hacky-sack with a ball made from weaved
palm leaves. At least a dozen small children also ran around the village. We saw a demonstration of a blowgun made from bamboo.
These people use poisoned arrows to hunt monkeys, small mammals
and birds. Erik tried his hand at the blowgun and found it lighter and
more accurate that the one he tried in Ecuador.

We left the national park on another three-hour boat ride down
river. Luckily for us, we left on the day of a raft race, so we passed
about fifty different four- and five-person groups standing up while
floating down the river on wooden rafts steered by wood poles. It
looked like something out of "Huckleberry Finn."

After the boat trip we caught a local train north to Kota Bahru in the
state of Kelatan on the north coast of Malaysia. We traveled for ten
hours through the scenic jungle, and soon realized we were on the

equivalent of the local school bus. Friday is the Muslim holy day, so the local middle school and high school students rode our Saturday afternoon train back to their boarding schools. Malaysians are incredibly friendly, and we shared a local fruit, a mangosteen, with some of the female students on the train. A mangosteen is a fruit about the size of an orange, the color of an eggplant, and the shape of a pomegranate. To open the fruit you squeeze the bottom, which splits to reveal seven white fruit segments the size and shape of small tangerine segments. The segments are very sweet and tasty.

We had extra time in Kota Bahru because our planned excursion to the nearby islands was cancelled due to full accommodations. So instead of enjoying sandy beaches and snorkeling, we visited sights in Kota Bahru. We stopped first at the World War II museum. During World War II, the Japanese invaded Kota Bahru at the exact same time as they bombed Pearl Harbor. The Japanese invasion started a two-month campaign resulting in the Japanese occupation of Malaysia and Singapore during World War II. The British did not expect the Japanese to invade the peninsula from the north and were quickly overrun by the Imperial Japanese forces. The Japanese used bicycles (some they brought and the rest confiscated during the invasion) to move their troops south.

We also enjoyed the crafts and culture of the Malaysian state of Kelatan. Kelatan is closely associated with Thailand and was traditionally the home of the artisans for the Thai kings. Consequently the handcrafts in Kelatan are exceptional. We saw examples of beautiful goldthread embroidery, goldthread woven fabrics and hand-painted batik fabrics. In batik painting, the artist first draws a picture on white cloth with melted wax and then hand-paints the design with various colors after the wax has hardened. Once completely painted, the cloth is treated and the wax removed, leaving bright-colored designs outlined in white. We also saw the myriad of puppets used in shadow plays. Intricately designed flat puppets lit from behind perform these very popular plays. The puppets are designed according to a certain standard so everyone knows immediately which character is on stage. The puppeteer moves the various puppets and narrates the plays accompanied by music. We also saw a top-spinning competition. Men spin heavy flat tops by winding a tightly coiled rope smeared with resin around the top then fling the top onto a dirt pile. The spinning top is scooped up on a wooden paddle and set on a wooden post to spin, sometimes for as long as two hours!

One evening in Kota Bahru we enjoyed dinner at the daily night market. Due in part to the heat during the day, Kota Bahru comes alive at night, especially in the night market held in the town square. Stands selling food, clothes, and other essential items fill the square. The food stalls are grouped together in the middle with the non-food stalls on two opposite edges of the square. On the other two sides of the square vendors selling drinks set up tables and chairs. Once you buy your food, you sit at a table and order drinks from that vendor. Invariably each set of table and chairs faces a television set for entertainment, usually showing American wrestling. The food stalls sell a variety of foods—fish, chicken skewers, and rice served in banana leaves. Our favorite was a banana and beaten egg mixture wrapped in a large piece of flat dough (shaped like a tortilla but folded into a square) and cooked on a griddle. Very delicious!

Having exhausted our short time in Malaysia, we returned to Kuala Lumpur for our three-and-a half-hour flight over the Bay of Bengal to Chennai (formally Madras) on the southeast coast of India. Kuala Lumpur's new international airport, completed just a few years ago, is an hour drive southwest of Kuala Lumpur. For Erik, it was one of Malaysia's architectural highlights. The ceiling consists of elegant curving vaults, a theme repeated throughout the airport. White, tubular, angled columns hold up this unique ceiling. Two departure terminals are detached from the main check-in area. To reach our gate we rode a very cool automatic train that resembled something out of Star Trek. We ate an American feast at Chili's restaurant inside the airport and met a large group of American college students from Minnesota on their way to India for a four-month independent study program.

India is the largest democracy in the world. India's population of 1.1 billion people (3.5 times the population of the United States) is packed into one-third the area of the continental United States. Rarely do we drive more than fifteen minutes without passing through a village of several hundred to a thousand people. Even after traveling in many third-world countries in South America and Africa, we experienced more culture shock entering India than any other country so far. Nothing can really prepare one for the density of people, the poor sanitation conditions, and the traffic. During our first couple days in India, by early afternoon we were so tired, we had to return to our hotel room. Fortunately, our culture shock dissipated after a few days. We could only imagine the amount of shock first time third-world travelers going to India would experience.

India is twelve and a half hours ahead of Pacific Time. (The odd half-hour time designation keeps India on a different time than Pakistan.) Since India is on the opposite side of the world as the west coast of the United States, this is the furthest away from home we will be. India only has about three million foreign tourists arriving each year, and most of them travel in the north. By starting our travel in southern India, we were the only Westerners on all of our bus rides, tours, and in hotels for the first ten days. Indians clamored to have their picture taken with us. At a botanical garden in Ooty, India, a group of about thirty young men saw us, and one of them wanted to have his picture taken with us. Next thing we know, we spent the next ten minutes posing for pictures with group after group, family after family. It took us thirty minutes to cross the front lawn of the gardens! We even had our picture taken with a group of ten soldiers. Walking around in temples we send out the same picture-taking vibes, as many Indian families posed with us. We can now appreciate fully what rock stars or movie stars experience, as so many people want to gather around and take our picture!

Driving through India is a unique experience. Cars, trucks and buses clamor for the same road space as motor rickshaws, cycle rickshaws, mopeds, bicycles, cows pulling wagons overloaded with hay, cows just roaming the streets, cows peacefully sitting in the middle of

Typical Indian street scene, Chennai, India.

busy intersections, and pedestrians. It took several days to not look out the front window at what is going on since vehicles constantly pass other vehicles on the roads. We heard Indian roads are dangerous, but we have not seen any accidents. As crazy as the traffic seems, it has its own logical flow that everyone seems to understand and keeps everyone surprisingly safe. (Indians call it a "controlled anarchy.") When we pass other buses and trucks, the drivers repeatedly honk horns as they pass. During the night, the drivers flash their lights. On the backs of trucks near the rear bumper, hand-painted signs read "please honk" or "use horn."

We also have to contend with the air pollution from every motorized vehicle that at times can be suffocating. When we reach our hotel, we usually shower to wash the traffic pollution off us. Black soot and dirt from the roads gets under our fingernails and covers our clothes and the books we are reading. Two days after we wash a pair of pants, they are completely dirty again, especially after a long bus ride with open windows or many auto rickshaw taxi rides.

The small and quick rickshaw taxi is the quickest and cheapest way of getting around urban areas. These yellow and black doorless taxis have one wheel in the front and two in the back where we sit. The driver's steering wheel looks like the handlebars of a motorcycle, and he starts the rickshaw by pulling up sharply on a stick that lies on the floor, almost like starting a lawnmower. Their maneuverability is incredible; as we thought for sure we would hit cars as the driver swerves around them. Even though they have fare meters, we usually ask for a set price to get to a location, or the driver quotes us a price. Being Westerners, we were quoted inflated prices. If we don't like the quoted price, we simply walk away and nine times out of ten, the driver will drive up to us and agree to our price. Getting into a small rickshaw with our five bags (we purchased two sleeping bags in South Africa and added another bag to our luggage) is quite a feat, although manageable; after all, Indians can pile ten large dead pigs or ten people onto a seat designed for three!

We usually ride public buses between cities and they are quite an experience. They are very cheap, typically US $1 to US $3 for an eight-hour, 180-mile (300-kilometer) ride. The only difference between a deluxe bus and a normal bus is with a deluxe bus you have your own seat, and on a normal bus the seats are like a school bus, where three or four people sit. Our first bus ride in India was a "deluxe" bus for an eight-hour journey. When we arrived at the bus depot, we boarded to hear the bus music speakers blaring Indian music videos on the television. It was so loud that we could not even hear each other talk, let alone think! We would have given anything to return to the more pleasant sounds of loud Spanish rock music! We asked the ticket man to turn the volume down, and he did—down just one unnoticeable decibel level. After eight hours of this, we could really appreciate peace and quiet! Fortunately, that was our only video bus ride.

Several times we have ridden on long (six-plus hour) bus rides on the state-run buses. These can be quite crowded and uncomfortable. When Indians travel in India, they do not carry much luggage, usually a briefcase or small duffel bag. We are the odd exception carrying two big bags and three smaller ones. On the buses, we stick as much baggage in the narrow overhead racks and put our big bags on the seat between us, as the state-run buses have no luggage storage. Since each seat is expected to hold at least three people, when the bus gets full, we put our bags in the aisle and squeeze in more people.

In India, we have found some public behaviors that are quite different than our American customs. For example, when there is a line of people waiting for bus tickets or a cup of coffee, many people blatantly cut in front of us. Some Indians have a different notion of personal space as well. When standing in line, the person behind is right on top of you, not maintaining any space. Erik found this queuing behavior quite frustrating at first. Some Indians also need to be the first off of public transportation. When we landed in Chennai, the Malaysian flight attendants tried unsuccessfully to stop Indian men (mostly professionals) from standing up and opening the overhead bins while the plane was still taxiing to the gate. We usually let everyone get off buses first, especially if we need to unload our five bags.

In southern India we used state-run day tours to see various cities and their surroundings sights. We were usually the only Westerners on these tours, so we met many Indians visiting a city from elsewhere in India or abroad. We ate typical Indian fare on our tours and invariably visited a silk *saree* shop or other air-conditioned tourist shop. The tours were an interesting mix of temples, notable landmarks, palaces, shops, churches, boathouses and even one deserted amusement park. We noticed not much time was given to museums (which was fine with us as they are not usually air-conditioned) and much time devoted to temples. Hindu temples reached their architectural peak in South India since the Muslims did not conquer that part, so our tours gave us a well-rounded overview of temple architectural history.

Our Hindu temple sightseeing adventure started with a day trip from Chennai to the towns of Kanchipuram and Mamallapuram. We visited several temples started in the late seventh century AD and early eighth century AD and continually added onto. Because Hindus worship individually, freestanding public temples were not built until the seventh century AD. A typical Hindu temple complex has a large courtyard with the main gate facing east. In later times (twelfth century and after), *gopurams* topped the gates. *Gopurams* are brick and plaster pyramidal structures densely packed with intricately carved gods of the Hindu religion. In most instances the *gopurams* have ten levels of figures. Usually these figures are unpainted stone bricks. From the sixteenth century and later, *gopurams* are painted in bright colors. A covered, raised, colonnaded area that originally housed pilgrims surrounds the courtyard. A pool for bathing sometimes sits in one corner and an area where pilgrims cooked food in another corner. A marriage hall, typically a covered hall on a raised platform with many intricately carved pillars, sits separate from the main shrine. The main building of the complex, which houses the shrine, is typically in the center. Sometimes we could enter this part, but not usually. These shrines are usually very dark with carved columns and figures decorating the various halls.

Most Hindu temples are a beehive of activity. The gate is a steady stream of bare-footed men, women and children bearing offerings of fruit and flowers. Everyone must leave their shoes outside the gate, so we learned to visit the temples in the morning before the stones of the courtyard heat up from the sun. (Early we toasted our "baby-soft" American feet on several occasions.) Sometimes the temple has a decorated elephant that, in return for a coin donation, will bless your head with the end of his trunk. The temple complex is a contrast of dark brown buildings and brightly dressed worshippers. Women dressed in *sarees* have strands of fresh jasmine flowers in their hair that perfume the air.

In Mamallapuram, we saw one of the oldest freestanding Hindu temples built in the late seventh century. This is a rare temple since it has shrines to both Siva and Vishnu. Hindus tend to worship primarily Siva or Vishnu, and their temples are dedicated to one or the other god, not both. In Mamallapuram, we briefly saw the largest bas-relief in the world. This carving, measuring 90 feet by 30 feet (27 meters by 9 meters) tells a story from the Hindu religion in life-size figures of humans and animals, including elephants. The relief was incredible, even though we only saw it from the bus. (Our tour guide thought it more important to spend more time on a not-so-fun boat ride and a very empty and worn-down amusement park!)

We traveled further south through Thanjavur (stopping to visit a temple built from 1000 AD through mid-twelfth century AD) to Madurai. After visiting the Minakshi Temple (dating mostly from the sixteenth to eighteenth centuries), we found our favorite sight to that point—the Thirumalai Nayaka Palace. This is the most beautiful decayed palace we have ever seen. The palace was built in 1636 in Indo-Mughal style. Only a fourth of the original palace complex still stands. We entered the palace courtyard opposite the audience chamber. A raised colonnade with 240 columns measuring 39 feet (12 meters) tall surrounds the courtyard. Some of the columns and carvings were repainted so we could easily imagine the original grandeur of the hall. In addition to the vast space, the stunning carvings in various domes inside the colonnade and in the audience chamber are simply breathtaking. Superbly carved elephants flank the stairs leading to the audience room where the throne sat.

Having seen enough temples, we ventured north to Coimbatore to visit the aunt, uncle, and grandmother of one of our fellow travelers from our Africa tour. In what we have discovered is typical Indian hospitality, the family picked us up at the train station, warmly welcomed us into their home and graciously arranged for us to visit the neighboring state of Kerala where the family originates. The family owns several coffee, tea and rubber tree plantations in the area. Many family members live in the United States. We stayed at their beautiful home with surrounding gardens. The family is Christian (as are most people of Kerala) due to St. Thomas coming to this part of India in 52 AD and converting five families. The grandmother told us her family can trace a direct line back to those original converts.

On reaching Kerala, we spent a wonderful day and a half exploring Kochi and its environs. The first afternoon we went on an interesting and relaxing boat ride along the backwaters of Kerala. Kerala is located on the southwest coast of India and is known as the Venice of India. For centuries, traders used the natural interior canals to transport spices and other goods to the coast for trading. We joined a French couple on a boat constructed from wood and coconut shell fibers for a three-hour tour. We sat on metal folding chairs while two men powered the boat, one at each end, using paddles where the river was wide and poles in the narrow canals.

The vegetation in the backwater reminded us of the Malaysian jungle with many coconut trees. We saw how coconuts are cut from the trees and dried. The fibers are then removed from the coconut and soaked in the canal water for nine months to soften them so they can be used to make rope, rugs, and boats. To make a boat, planks of wood are essentially "sewn" together with coconut-fiber rope and gaps in the wood stuffed with coconut fibers. Once the boat is complete, the boat is submerged for several days to allow the coconut fibers to expand, making the boat waterproof.

The backwater inhabitants live and farm along the banks of the canals. We saw many women washing clothes in the canals. In one area we saw rice fields which our guide told us are planted once every three years to keep the government from confiscating it, as the government can take farmland not cultivated for three years.

The next day we visited Kochi itself. Several islands make up Kochi, so we took a boat tour to one of the oldest inhabited islands. We first visited a Jewish synagogue built in the late 1600s with beautiful eighteenth century Cantonese hand-painted blue and white ceramic tiles on the floor. We also visited the palace built in 1557 by the Portuguese for the Indian Raja of Kochi in exchange for trading rights. The palace has beautiful frescoes depicting scenes from Hindu religious texts. These frescoes were painted with vegetable and mineral pigments and

Cruising along the backwater canals of Kerala state, India.

finished with a coat of oil and pine resin. We also visited the church where the Portuguese explorer Vasco da Gama was buried in 1524, and remained until his body was removed to Portugal in 1538. We really enjoyed watching fishermen use Chinese-style fishing nets to fish off the shore. These nets, measuring about 30 feet (9 meters) square, are attached at the corners to large arching, wooden frames that are lowered into the water by a lever and weight system.

Our last night in Kochi we attended a *Kathakali* demonstration and performance. *Kathakali* is the traditional theater originally performed in temple courtyards. Today actors perform short programs for tourists throughout the year, and full-length performances during the festival period in January/February. A full performance lasts several hours; our demonstration lasted ninety minutes. In *Kathakali*, actors perform various stories from Hindu epics to music, without speaking. The musical accompaniment is a drum and a singer. The actors convey their characters through their make-up and costumes, and about a dozen different emotions conveyed through a standard set of facial expressions. The actors demonstrated each of the emotions to us and we were amazed at the individual facial muscles the actor could move without moving any other muscles. We have never seen eyes and eyebrows move with such precision and velocity! The costumes and make-up for the actors are quite elaborate and we watched the actors apply it. In one instance an actor spent ninety minutes applying his facial make-up and another forty-five minutes to put on his costume! That costume included stringing large pieces of stiffened fabric together under the costume in three separate layers such that the costume at the actor's hips measured about 3 feet (1 meter) in diameter. The facial make-up was incredibly elaborate, with a green face (denoting a good character) carefully applied around highly stylized and emphasized eyes, eyebrows and mouth. It was a wonderful evening!

After returning to Coimbatore for one more evening with our Indian hosts, we set off for Ooty and some very welcomed cooler weather. Ooty sits at 7,350 feet (2,240 meters) in the Nilgiri Hills. It is a large town surrounded by beautiful tea plantations, and the end of the line for one of the most famous railways in India—the Blue Mountain Railway. To maximize our experience, we drove the twisty road to the halfway point on the railway, Conoor, and boarded the train there. Along the road we passed trucks and buses around the hairpin turns and honked at monkeys sitting in the road. The train was an experience unto itself. Because we boarded the train at Conoor, the one first-class car was completely packed, as were the three second-class cars. After paying the equivalent of ten cents each for the ninety-minute train ride, we loaded our numerous bags onto the first available compartment (designed to seat ten people in two bench seats facing each other), joining several young men. Five minutes before the train departed, we learned that we had sat down in a "Ladies Only" compartment, so Erik and all the other men had to leave. Jennifer stayed in the compartment with all of the bags and many women, and Erik joined several male college students in another compartment. Once the train started moving, various groups of young college men started singing and clapping loudly in a friendly competition among the cars.

We took a private minibus from Ooty to Mysore down another twisty road through a wildlife reserve where we saw deer, peacocks, monkeys, antelope, and a wild boar. Because it was Sunday, when we reached Mysore, 40,000 lights outlined the impressive City Palace. It was stunning! When we reached our hotel we found out that the lights are on for only one hour each Sunday, and we only had fifteen minutes left! We dumped our bags and dashed across the street to take photos. Just after we snapped the last picture on the roll, the lights on the palace went out for the evening. We were happy to have photographed such a spectacular sight!

The next day, September 10, we took a city tour of Mysore. The highlight of the tour was the visit to the City Palace. The City Palace, one of the largest palaces in India, was built between 1897 and 1912 after the former wooden palace burnt down. To insure that this would not happen again, the new palace was built in the same Indo-Saracenic style as the former palace, but this time in gray granite. Mysore is famous for an annual ten-day festival held in October called the Dasara. Formerly this festival culminated in a large procession leading the maharaja and his family riding on an elephant (the elephant now carries a statue of a goddess) down the front gardens of the palace and into a large colonnaded, covered hall at the front of the palace. The palace is wide enough for two sets of bleachers for the spectators and plenty of room for the elephant.

As spectacular as the outside is (especially lit up), it cannot compare to the interior of the palace. The marriage hall contains an octagonal area in the center set off by two-story painted columns supporting a vaulted stained-glass ceiling decorated with a peacock motif. Painted scenes of the Dasara adorn the three walls of the hall. On the second level of the palace, an indoor/outdoor colonnaded area extends to the bleachers for the Dasara festival. The white columns with gold stripes and accents support scalloped arches painted light blue with gold trim. The domes inside the arches are painted in various colors with gold accents. The ceiling over the bleachers is painted with a central panel of the Hindu trinity of Brahma, Vishnu and Siva surrounded by the twelve zodiac signs. The private audience hall of the king was equally impressive. Elaborately designed silver doors and rosewood doors intricately inlaid with ivory motifs of the Hindu god Krishna lined the room. Light blue columns with gold trim and scalloped arches supported a rectangular, vaulted, stained-glass ceiling in the middle of the room. There was so much to see in the palace, Jennifer visited it twice.

On September 11, we spent a day touring three area temples. We shared a car and driver with a wonderful Indian couple married just one month after us. We stopped first at Sravanabelagola and the spectacular sight of a 56-foot (17-meter) monolithic statue erected sometime between 980 and 983 AD. The light gray statue of a prince after he gained enlightenment is superbly carved and conveys an air of tranquility and serenity. We next drove to Halebid to visit a temple started in 1121 AD and never fully completed. The inner temple is mostly complete and reminded us of a Frank Lloyd Wright building with low roofs and wide overhangs. The temple exterior is decorated with six rows of detailed carvings, including lines of elephants, lions, horsemen, and scenes from the Hindu epics. The last temple we visited in Belur was started in 1116 AD. Like Halebid, only the inner temple still remains. The intricate stone carving along the roofline is simply breathtaking. We saw water drops on the end of hair, the individual beads of a pearl necklace, and a life-size grasshopper in the finely carved rock. We really enjoyed wandering around the temple admiring the carvings.

We drove back to Mysore about the same time as the attacks in New York and Washington D.C. were happening. We returned to our hotel around 9 PM. Erik showered then turned on the BBC to see smoke billowing out of the Pentagon and the text below the picture read the World Trade Center Twin Towers had collapsed! Erik quickly told Jennifer the news while she was still in the shower. We sat on the bed in utter shock and disbelief watching the breaking news.

From Mysore we traveled on to Aurangabad to see the caves that preceded Hindu temples. We visited caves in two places—Ajanta and

Ellora. The older Ajanta caves, spanning from 200 BC to 650 AD, are Buddhist monasteries and worship halls carved out of a sheer cliff shaped like a horseshoe. The monks abandoned the caves in the seventh century AD, and the jungle overgrew them. The caves remained hidden until discovered by a hunting party in 1819. Consequently, many cave interiors are well-preserved. Most of the twenty-seven caves are monasteries, with only a handful being worship halls. Monasteries are flat-roofed excavations with a large columned central area, meditation cells on the sidewalls and large statues to worship along the back. Painted scenes from Buddha's life and stories of his followers decorate the walls with geometric and floral designs painted on the ceilings. The worship halls are narrow two-storied, vaulted halls edged with carved columns. The monasteries and worship hall columns are only decoration, as the caves are carved from solid rock.

The caves at Ellora span 600 to 1100 AD and comprise Buddhist, Hindu and Jain (a religion stemming from a reform movement to the Hindu religion) caves. These caves, located on a trade route, were used by both monks and pilgrims. The interiors of these caves generally lack paintings and other decorations, as the Muslims destroyed them when they conquered northern India. The most impressive of the thirty-four caves is the three-story Hindu temple carved out of the rock in the mid- to late-eighth century. This temple has a central shrine surrounded by a courtyard and a colonnade hall carved from the rock. The structure was carved from top to bottom out from an estimated 111,175 cubic yards (85,000 cubic meters) of solid rock. It is quite incredible! We also enjoyed the Jain temples with intricately carved columns and serene carvings of Jain teachers along the back wall.

From Aurangabad, we flew north to Delhi. One of the main sights in Delhi, the Red Fort, was closed due to militant threats after the September 11 attacks in America, so we visited other sights instead. We most enjoyed the modern Baha'i Temple designed to resemble an opening lotus flower bud. Constructed in the early 1980s, the building has forty-five "lotus petals" constructed from white marble panels. The shape of the panels reminded us of images of the Sydney Opera House (which we will see in March). Jennifer was impressed with how the design allowed sunlight to bathe the 1,300-person capacity open seating area. We also enjoyed Delhi's oldest monument—the Qutb Minar. The tapered minar, a tall 240-foot (73-meter), five-section tower, was erected in the 1190s AD to celebrate the victory of the Muslim kings over northwest India. The red sandstone tower dominates a complex that includes the remains of a mosque, a beautifully carved stone screen, several tombs, and a wonderful gate house built in 1311 that used "true" arches for the first time in India.

While in Delhi, we took a break from touring and assisted at the Landmark Forum, a three-day course offered by Landmark Education worldwide. The Landmark Forum is the first of a four-part "Curriculum for Living" that promises living life powerfully and living a life you love. Through conversations and sharing with the leader and other participants of all ages and walks of life, people look at what is, and what is not, working in their life and distinguish ways to transform the areas where they have a loss of power. Out of their participation, people experience more love in their relationships, more effectiveness at work, more effective communication and taking actions consistent with what's important to them. For example, the life we have today, including our trip around the world, is a direct result of our breakthroughs from participating in Landmark's programs. In our ten months of world travel, we noticed people all over the world have similar concerns, issues and perspectives. Assisting at the Landmark Forum further reinforced this view, as we observed people in a completely different culture producing the same breakthrough results for themselves as people who participated in Landmark Forums in the United States.

From Delhi, we took a train north then northwest to Amritsar, in the state of Punjab to visit an Indian couple we met on our fourth day in India. When we arrived, they drove us to the India/Pakistan border 15.5 miles (25 kilometers) west of Amritsar. Historically, India and Pakistan do not have friendly ties. Pakistan was once a state of India, but separated along religious lines when India became independent in 1947. Virtually no trade exists between the countries and only two trains per week enter Pakistan from Amritsar. Every evening at sundown, however, the border security hold a joint flag-lowering ceremony. The general public sits in bleachers with horrible views, but we had special front row seats, since our friend is in the Indian army. Just before the ceremony, we walked to a cement pylon that is the actual border, crossed to the other side and were "officially" inside Pakistan. We snapped some pictures and, after forty-five seconds, left Pakistan and crossed back into India. Erik was thrilled to visit since Pakistan is in the center of the news these days.

During the ceremony, we could only see the Indian guards with clarity. One by one, they kicked up their legs and feet, and quickly "stomped" down toward the border gates where they met their Pakistani counterpart, gave a quick salute and stood in formation for the flag lowering. Just before they stomped down to the border, the guards performed moves with incredibly fierce faces. By the sweat on their faces and their heavy breathing, you could tell they take this very seriously. When the flags were eventually lowered, each country played the bugle and then they both marched off with their flag. The public in each country's bleacher seating then shouted and cheered, like at an American college football game. The whole experience was a thrill to watch! As we drove away, our friend pointed out the electric barbed wire fencing that is 490 feet (150 meters) away from the border that stretches for hundreds of miles and a huge ditch that also runs for hundreds of miles to stop any invading Pakistani tanks.

After watching the sunset, we visited Amritsar's most famous sight—the Golden Temple. The Golden Temple, home of the Sikh religion, is built in the middle of a square pool of holy water. A wide marble sidewalk lined with a columned portico surrounds the pool. On one side of the pool, a restaurant and kitchen serves vegetarian meals twenty-four hours a day free of charge. A marble causeway links the Golden Temple to the sidewalk. The three-storied, small, boxy temple is covered in gold-leaf inside and out. We visited on a Friday night when many Sikhs come to the temple for their weekly prayers. The

Typical Indian traffic, Punjab, India.

complex bustled with worshipers listening to the evening prayers spoken over a loudspeaker and waiting to pray inside the Golden Temple.

Our friends invited us to dinner at their house. Dinners in Indian homes differ from those in America in one major aspect. In India, when we arrive at the home, we are greeted with drinks and appetizers and converse with the hosts until we decide to eat. Once the meal has been served and eaten, the dinner party is over and we are taken back to our hotel. We are used to American dinner parties where the host determines when dinner is served and the guests linger after dinner, conversing with the hosts.

Having exhausted the sights in Amritsar, we hired a car and driver and headed to Dharamshala, the city where the Dalai Lama lives in exile from Tibet. This town, nestled in the foothills of the Himalayan Mountains, sits about 5,800 feet (1,770 meters) above sea level. Since China invaded Tibet in the 1950s, many Tibetans have fled into India and Nepal. Almost 10,000 people of Tibetan descent live in this Indian mountain village with their spiritual leader, the Dalai Lama. We hardly knew we were still in India with all the monks clad in maroon robes walking around the village. Many free-spirited Westerners also come here for meditation retreats and New-Age activities.

After spending one more evening with our friends in Amritsar, we headed back to Delhi when our bag was stolen. Our bag was stolen around 5 AM, and our friend was so caring he stayed at the train station until 9 AM looking and talking with people about our bag. In India, we met some of the nicest people in the world!

We then traveled to Agra to see the famous Taj Mahal and are now in the state of Rajasthan, India's most popular state for western tourists. In order to get this e-mail out sooner rather than later, we will talk about these places in the next e-mail which we will send out from Nepal. We fly to Nepal on October 16, and will be in Nepal for two weeks before traveling to Thailand in early November. Until Nepal!

Love, Jennifer & Erik

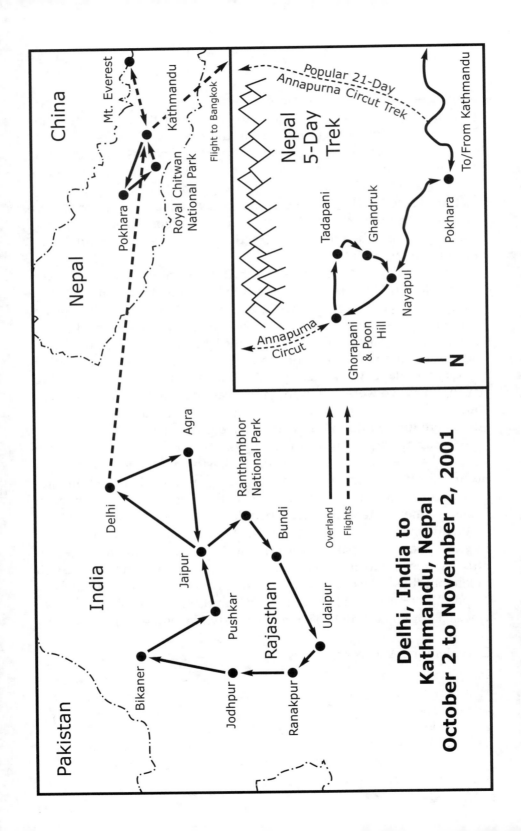

**Delhi, India to
Kathmandu, Nepal
October 2 to November 2, 2001**

Overland
Flights

China
Mt. Everest
Kathmandu
Pokhara
Royal Chitwan
National Park
Flight to Bangkok
Nepal

Popular 21-Day
Annapurna Circuit Trek
Nepal
5-Day
Trek
To/From Kathmandu
Tadapani
Ghandruk
Pokhara
Nayapul
Ghorapani
& Poon
Hill
Annapurna
Circut
N

Pakistan
India
Rajasthan
Delhi
Agra
Jaipur
Ranthambhor
National Park
Bundi
Pushkar
Udaipur
Bikaner
Jodhpur
Ranakpur

13

Kathmandu, Nepal
Thursday, November 1, 2001

Dear friends and family,

One year ago today we left California to start our travels, and November 19 will mark one year since we left the United States. We continue to be safe and had an amazing time in Nepal. More on Nepal in just a bit...

From New Delhi, we traveled to Agra, India. In a moment of weakness, we hired an air-conditioned car and driver for a two-week tour of Agra and the Indian state of Rajasthan, the state most western tourists visit. So we now have experienced another type of travel in India! Traveling by car and driver is comfortable; however, after having traveled in local buses and taking city tours, we missed interacting with the locals. We met fewer Indians in Rajasthan because we did not travel like we did in the south.

Agra is the home of the famous Taj Mahal. The Delhi emperor Shah Jahan built the Taj to honor the memory of his favorite wife, who died giving birth to her fourteenth child. It took twenty-two years to construct the monument and was completed in 1653 AD. We visited first thing in the morning and were the very first tourists (many followed soon after). We enjoyed the emptiness of the grounds and the early morning light on the white marble building. A brick wall surrounds the Taj, so we first glimpsed it upon emerging from the brick gateway. The monument stands majestically at the end of a large garden with long, rectangular, reflecting pools. The building and steps leading up to it are covered in white marble inlaid with onyx and other semi-precious stones in geometric and floral designs. Overall, it is simply a breathtaking monument and not to be missed if you are in India.

In addition to the Taj Mahal, we visited Agra Fort, a red sandstone fort enclosing several palaces of the Mughal emperors. The fort was started in 1570 AD and continually added onto during the 1600s. The

Carved facade, Agra Fort, Agra, India.

various palaces show the architectural shift from a predominantly Hindu style with stepped arches and carved animals, to more Islamic/Persian features with formal gardens and symmetrical pavilions. We most enjoyed an octagonal tower decorated with the same white marble as the Taj Mahal and inlaid with floral designs. An open balcony overlooks the river and the Taj Mahal in the distance.

From Agra we headed to Jaipur, stopping on the way at Fatepur Sikri, the capital of the Mughal emperors from 1570 to 1585. We visited lovely red sandstone palaces and other buildings, including an interesting private audience chamber. This two-story domed building had a circular platform one-story above the ground connected to the edge by four walkways. Outside a life-size Parcheesi board fills an open courtyard where the emperor would sit in the center and use slave girls dressed in four different colors as the "game pieces." Adjacent to this courtyard sits a large pool with a square platform in the center connected to the sides with four walkways. A beautifully carved gazebo sits at one edge of the pool.

Jaipur was our first introduction to Rajasthan, land of the Rajputs, the warrior class in the Hindu religion. Historically, numerous small principalities divided Rajasthan, each with a fort/palace. We started with Amer Palace, about 6 miles (11 kilometers) from Jaipur. Like most fort/palaces we visited, fort defenses surrounded several palaces. Various rulers built new palaces as more space and new palace designs were desired. The distinctive feature of the Amer Palace is the hall of mirrors, a private audience hall built during the 1630s. Glass mosaics in the shape of vases and small pieces of mirrors decorate the vaulted ceiling and produce a shimmering effect in candlelight and sunlight. As with most Indian architecture, the Amer Palace rooms blend indoor/outdoor features, with large archways leading from the room to gardens outside. In many instances bedrooms and dining rooms are three-sided, to permit air circulation.

The royal family of Jaipur moved their capital from Amer to Jaipur in 1727 and built the new city palace in the center of the new city. Jaipur was originally designed with extra-wide streets, so traffic flow through the old part of town is much easier than in many other Rajasthan (or Indian) cities. Being more modern, we found the Jaipur City Palace less interesting than others, but we liked the two-story guest house built in 1890 with cantilevered balconies and an open arcade in the upper story. This building now houses a textile and clothing museum that includes clothes of the former rulers.

Rajput rulers were very wealthy and indulged in excessive lifestyles. Indicative of these excesses were the two large silver urns in the Jaipur City Palace used by Maharaja Sawai Madho Singh to carry holy water from the Ganga River for his trip to England in 1897. The Maharaja, a devout Hindu, purified himself after any meeting with a non-Hindu. So, when he traveled to England for Queen Victoria's Diamond Jubilee, he commissioned the two silver urns (measuring about 6 feet (1.8 meters) tall and 5 feet (1.5 meters) in diameter) to carry the water.

The Rajasthani countryside differed from other parts of India. Indians grow agricultural crops in small fields. In the south we saw rice and sugar cane. As we traveled north we saw more corn, sunflowers and millet. We saw less farming in Rajasthan, as it is drier, but we saw more tractors than in the south. In the south, oxen plough the field and pull hay carts. The Indian women in the south dress in short-sleeved midriff tops with a *saree* wrapped around their waist and over one shoulder. The women in Rajasthan have a similar dress, but the *saree* is a bright, almost fluorescent, yellow, orange, green or fuchsia and embroidered with glittery edging. *Sarees* are versatile clothing as a woman can easily use the cloth draped over her shoulder to cover her head when walking outside or visiting a temple. In the northern parts of India, women wear a two-piece outfit called a *Punjab* suit. A *Punjab* suit consists of a pair of pants underneath a long, calf-length top that is either long- or short-sleeved. The men in Rajasthan usually wear turbans, and the way the turban is wrapped shows where that man is from. The only other time we saw the majority of men in turbans was in Amritsar, the center of the Sikh religion. Because Sikhs do not cut their hair, the men wrap their hair in a turban.

Udaipur, with the incredible Lake Palace, was our favorite Rajasthani city. The Udaipur fort/palace, started in the late sixteenth century AD, is Rajasthan's largest palace. The complex rises above the east bank of Lake Pichola and contains five separate palaces. We toured the two oldest palaces and admired the beautiful colored glass mosaics, mirrorwork, beautiful frescoes in the wedding bedchamber, and lovely blue-and-white eighteenth century Dutch and Chinese tiles. We also admired the intricately carved stone *jali* screens that allowed the women of the court to see outside, but not be seen from the outside.

After viewing the main palace, we set off by boat across Lake Pichola to visit the former summer palace of the Udaipur rulers, known as the Lake Palace. This beautiful, white palace sits in the middle of the lake, rising majestically from the water, as if it were a floating building. The palace, a five-star hotel since the 1960s, is beautifully restored. Floral motifs in blue and green, typical of Rajput interior design, decorate the large open sitting areas. We treated ourselves to a delicious buffet lunch in the dining room that overlooks the city palace on the shore of the lake.

After lunch we took the complementary boat ride back to the mainland and wandered the crooked narrow streets of the old town watching artists paint the miniature paintings famous in Rajasthan. These artists apply the same techniques used for hundreds of years. They make their paint from the powder of different stones mixed with water and apply the paint with fine brushes, including one made from a single hair of a squirrel!

From Udaipur we traveled north to visit Kumbhalgarh Fort. This fort, built around 1485 AD, is one of the finest examples of defensive fortifications in Rajasthan. Its 22-mile (36-kilometer) outer walls snake up and down the steep terrain and are wide enough for ten horsemen to ride abreast. This is the second longest wall in the world, after the Great Wall of China. At its height, the walls enclosed a palace, a garrison, a town of 30,000 residents, 365 temples, plenty of farmland to support the town, and a year's supply of water. As we drove away from the fort we saw at least one hundred schoolchildren in uniform heading uphill to the fort for lunch. We were amazed at the number of children living in the fort complex today.

From the fort we continued north toward Jodhpur, stopping in Rankapur to visit the famous Jain Temple there. This temple, built of white marble, dates from 1439 AD and has 1,444 uniquely carved columns. Each column is thoroughly covered with figures or designs. The temple floor constantly changes levels and a unique blend of covered, open-sided halls allows natural sunlight to light all sections of the temple. The four largest domes are intricately carved with progressively more complex images. We marveled at the interplay of the light on the beautifully carved marble columns, arches and ceilings.

Our favorite fort/palace was the one in Jodhpur. Fort Mehrangarh rises majestically from the plateau on the edge of town to dominate the surrounding countryside and densely packed, light blue buildings. We entered the walls of the fort and snaked our way through the various gates to the palace complex, rising three stories from the top of the plateau. We wandered through the various former palaces viewing displays of paintings, weapons, musical instruments, the various turbans of the area, seats for riding on the elephants, and covered litters. Again the palace interiors were decorated from various periods and include mirrorwork, gold-painted ceilings, and the incomplete pleasure hall. Originally every inch of wall space in this hall was to be elaborately painted, but the artist died partway through the project and no one could replicate his work. The parts of the room that are complete are stunning. The palace also boasts carved *jali* screens and a bedroom decorated in the mid-nineteenth century with large, round, glass ornaments suspended from the ceiling. The entry ticket to the palace quotes Jackie (Kennedy) Onassis as describing this fort/palace as the eighth wonder of the world, and we wholeheartedly agree!

Our favorite aspect of India was the food. We loved southern Indian breakfasts. We dunked *vada* (deep fried lentil "doughnut" rings) and *idli* (steamed, bland, spongy rice cakes) into two different sauces—*sambar* (a watery broth with cooked vegetables and spices) and a white chunky pureed sauce. We also dumped those sauces on *masala dosa*, a thin, crispy rice pancake wrapped around a spicy potato and onion filling. Delicious! For lunch or dinner we ate *thali*, a fixed dish of *dal* (lentils or chick peas), two vegetable dishes (one a curry and the other a drier, spicy preparation), hot pickled relish, rice and *naan* bread, all served on a metal tray. Erik especially loved the *naan* bread! In northern India, we enjoyed *dal makhani* (black lentils with small, red kidney beans cooked overnight in the oven), *malai kofta* (vegetable balls lightly fried and covered in a creamy sauce), and vegetable *kofta* (balls of minced vegetables in a sauce, usually tomato based and slightly spicy). We drank lots of mineral water to wash it all down (and cool our mouths), as well as the occasional *lassi* (a yogurt based drink, usually with fruit). Of all the countries in the world we have visited, India consistently had the best food, and we did not have food poisoning or bad stomachaches (known as "Delhi Belly") that many times afflict foreign tourists.

After spending seven weeks in India, we left on October 16 for Nepal, a country of 25 million people and slightly larger than Arkansas. Nepal's lowest elevation is 230 feet (70 meters) and its highest is Mt. Everest—the tallest mountain in the world at 29,035 feet (8,850 meters). Nepal is a landlocked country squeezed between India to the south and China to the north. The landscape is very diverse, with the towering Himalayas in the north and subtropical jungle in the south. When we visited the jungle area in the south, we could see the snow-capped peaks of the Himalayas in the north. A constitutional monarchy governs the kingdom of Nepal. In June of this year, Nepal's crown prince massacred the king, queen and many other family members before killing himself. The brother of the deceased king currently rules and his unpopular son was named crown prince just last week. The government has been a constitutional monarchy for only the last ten years, and the Nepalese fear the current king may return the monarchy to an absolute one. Tourism in Nepal is low because of the royal massacre and the events of September 11. Many tourists from all over the world have cancelled their trips to Nepal, but from our experience, Nepal is safe and the government fairly stable. We were surprised to learn tourism is low, even though we see hundreds of tourists on the street of Kathmandu.

Nepal reminds us of India, but has clear differences also. Like India, Nepal is largely Hindu, but Buddhist influences from Tibet are more apparent (eighty-six percent of the population is Hindu, almost eight percent Buddhist, and almost four percent Muslim). Nepal is the only official Hindu state in the world, as India does not have a state religion. The traffic is similar to India with narrow city streets, but fewer vehicles means it is less congested. Nepalese women dress in *sarees* like India but wear a long-sleeved shirt with their *sarees* and a shawl in the chilly early mornings and at night. The Nepali people have Indian features of the subcontinent and the Mongoloid features of the Chinese, so there is no distinctive Nepali look. Finally, like India, family-owned stores with a limited selection provide most goods and services. One store sells clothing, another material for *sarees*, another books, another jewelry, another soft drinks and water, another vegetables, another basic food staples, another motorcycle parts, and so on. These storefronts line the streets with little to no sidewalk and, if closed, are a line of metal, garage-like doors with an occasional sign indicating the type of store.

Our first day in Nepal we visited Bodhnath, the largest stupa in Nepal and one of the largest in the world. The stupa is a large, white hemisphere topped with a four-sided box decorated with two colorful eyes and a "nose" that looks like a curly backward question mark. A four-sided gold tiered structure with thirteen stepped levels sits atop the box and a large cylinder tops the tiered structure. Lines of alternating red, green, yellow, blue and white prayer flags fly from the top of the tiered structure to the plaza below the stupa. Tibetan refugees and artisan shops fill the plaza around Bodhnath. We visited several nearby monasteries populated with monks clad in burgundy robes and admired the prayer halls, elaborately decorated with beautiful fresco paintings.

After absorbing Buddhist culture, we next visited Pashupatinath, the most important Hindu temple in Nepal. We could not enter this Siva temple, but the temple graces a tributary of the holy Ganga River in India, so many cremations are held on its banks. In the Hindu religion, the dead are cremated within hours of their death. When we arrived, a shrouded body was removed from a white van and carried to a pile of logs neatly stacked about five levels high. The body was placed on top, covered with flammable branches and the logs lit with little ceremony. Temple workers tended the cremation fire while male relatives sat in a nearby covered pavilion to watch the two-hour process. From our vantage point across the river, we admired the unique architecture of Nepal temples. Unlike the single-storied temples of India, Nepali Hindu temples generally have a two- or three-tiered roof with large overhanging eaves supported by beautifully carved wood angled downward from the building to the eave edge.

After a short time in Kathmandu, we drove five hours to the west to Pokhara, the second-largest tourist spot in Nepal. On the mountain highway we experienced two traffic jams due to stalled buses and trucks and enjoyed spectacular views. Our guide pointed out a couple different landslides that took place during last year's monsoon season. The Nepal monsoon season ended in September, so for the most part, we did not have to contend with the rain and leeches that accompany it. Many trekkers start their trekking (i.e. hiking) adventures from Pokhara, the main access to the Annapurna mountain treks, the most popular in Nepal. Many people trek for twenty-one days around the permanently snow-capped mountains, climbing to a maximum height of over 17,400 feet (5,300 meters). We decided not to take such a long trek, and opted for a five-day, 28-mile (45-kilometer) loop from Nayapul to Ghorapani to Tadapani to Ghandruk and back to Nayapul. We reached a maximum height of 10,500 feet (3,200 meters). We had a wonderful time despite some sore knees and legs at the end of the five days. We hired a guide recommended by friends to show us around and a porter to carry our large backpack, so we only carried small day packs for our water, coats, snacks, and so forth. Most people trek independently, but for our first time, we decided to play it safe.

Trekking in Nepal is very different from our Inca Trail experience in Peru last Christmas. In Nepal, we stayed in "teahouses," basically small hotels/restaurants located about a thirty-minute walk apart. Many of the villages we passed through consist of nothing but teahouse after teahouse. On the Inca Trail, we camped in tents. In the teahouses, we had our own room with a double bed or two twin beds, and once we even had an attached bathroom with a western-style toilet! The price to sleep at a teahouse is usually US $1 or US $2, but they expect you to eat dinner and breakfast there (where they make most of their profits). The teahouses also expect you to bring your own sleeping bag, and they provide a bed with mattress and a pillow. Unlike the Inca Trail, we took wonderful hot showers every day after hiking! This made all the difference in the world on the days with cooler weather and rain. At one teahouse, the hot shower water was pumped directly from the boiling water in the main kitchen (this was a bit too hot). We marveled that these remote teahouses had nice hot showers, while the smaller hotels in Kathmandu have temperamental hot water.

When trekking, we woke up at 6 AM, watched the sunrise hit the incredible snow-capped Himalayan Mountains, ate breakfast and hiked from 8 AM until 3 or 4 PM, with an hour stop for lunch. We hiked uphill for several hours, and then an equal time downhill with some very enjoyable flat places. Most downhills had nice stone steps, but

Trekking among the terraced rice fields, Annapurna Range, Nepal.

sometimes we hiked down a narrow muddy path with occasional stones. Typically we covered 4.5 to 7.5 miles (7 to 12 kilometers) a day. When we reached our evening teahouse, we showered as soon as possible (to beat the many other trekkers getting in soon afterward) then relaxed or napped until dinner at 6 or 7 PM. The most popular dish at the teahouses is *dal bhat* (rice with lentils, curry potatoes and vegetables). Our guide and porter ate *dal bhat* for lunch and dinner every day. We ate *dal bhat* on occasion, but also sampled the wide variety of "Nepali-interpreted" western food on the teahouse menus.

We met many other trekkers from all over the world, mostly from the England, Europe and America. In the evenings we chatted with many of them, exchanging stories and e-mail addresses. Some we met were on a worldwide trip like us, so we traded travel advice on other countries. Others were completing three weeks away from the "civilized world" of asphalt and cars and would be curious about the news. Erik enjoyed catching them up on the latest on America's anthrax scare and the fighting in Israel and Palestine. (Erik is a news-junkie, so five days without new news made him anxious to return to Pokhara, especially since September 11.)

The trekking path is actually the "highway" for the mountain villages. While trekking we passed numerous locals and porters carrying a variety of goods, many times in woven baskets strapped directly on their foreheads. We assume they are used to this and have strong neck muscles. We also passed many animals. Donkeys and mules wearing bells carry the heavy loads to the teahouses and villages. Sometimes a group of donkeys would carry only bottled beer up to the teahouses!

During the first two days of our trek we saw hundreds (if not thousands) of goats herded down from the higher elevations toward the larger towns. This was Dasain festival time in Nepal, and most families buy a live goat and eat it a couple days later. Once every twenty minutes or so we stood on the side of the trail for a few minutes to let the goats pass. Three to five herders controlled about one hundred goats. The herders had long sticks to keep the goats on the trail. Wearing cheap flip-flops, they ran after their goats down stone steps slick with water and mud from post-monsoon rains. It was quite a sight to watch hundreds of goats (imagine a "sea" of goats) crossing a small bridge or descending a steep incline, and hear dozens of bells tied around various goats necks. Over one bridge, we watched two goats get knocked off the bridge by other goats and fall about 6 feet (1.8 meters) into the creek below! They eventually scrambled up the steep bank back to the herd. Each goat had a patch of colored spray paint on their back or a horn to indicate ownership. Once Erik thought it was St. Patrick's Day since several groups of goats coming at us had large patches of green paint on their backs!

As the goats headed downhill to the larger villages and cities, not-so-expensive chickens headed uphill so the poorer villagers could also eat some meat for the festival. We saw locals carry large chicken cages on their backs. Each cage was divided into twelve smaller segments (three across and four down). In the morning the locals descended the mountain with an empty cage and returned in the afternoon with each segment holding three or four live chickens. It was very funny to see the chickens sticking their heads out of the cages, possibly enjoying the scenery on their way uphill to be sold and eaten. In the large towns, dozens of live chickens were sometimes transported by hanging them upside down from the handlebars of bicycles. The first time we saw this, we couldn't believe our eyes!

On the third morning of our trek we climbed Poon Hill, a hill that trekkers hike up before sunrise and watch the sun hit the incredible Annapurna range of the Himalayas. This was our first close-up view of these mountains. We climbed about two-thirds of the way up, and watched one of the most incredible sunrises of our lives. Unfortunately, our camera stopped working just before the sunrise, so for that glorious sunrise and the remaining three days of trekking we took no pictures. (We figure this is a great excuse to have to trek again in Nepal in the future. Perhaps a longer trek next time...)

During the first and last day, we passed many beautiful terraced rice fields. We hiked during rice harvest time, so everyone was busy cutting and drying rice, as well as preparing the cut terraces for the next crop. Farmers in Nepal plant three crops in a year: rice or millet during the monsoon rains; wheat after harvesting the rice; and corn after harvesting the wheat. We watched men and oxen use a wooden plow to prepare the ground for the wheat using technology almost as old as agriculture itself. It made perfect sense because a tractor is just not practical on the narrow terraces that have a 6-foot (1.8-meter) drop between them. The rice fields and cut rice laid out to dry made for some amazing patterns in the mountain landscape, especially with the clear sky and tall Himalayas as the background. We adored trekking near the famous Himalayan Mountains. We would do it again in a heartbeat and highly recommend it for those who love to hike.

After resting in Pokhara for a day, we rode a cramped minibus to the Royal Chitwan National Park in south-central Nepal. What a contrast from the mountain landscape! The southern part of Nepal is near India and quite flat. After leaving our minibus, we walked across a wooden bridge and met about twenty jeeps to take people to their hotels in the area. Our hotel transport was the only non-jeep—a cart pulled by a horse! This was a new experience and we thought about what road travel must have been like before cars. We had a couple of relaxing days in the jungle. We went on an hour-long elephant safari where we saw four Asian rhinos resting in a small pond, and quite a few deer. The elephant even crossed a river, which was fun from the top of the elephant. We also visited an elephant-breeding center a few miles away. This time we rode in a cart driven by two oxen—even slower than the horse. The oxen were very temperamental, especially passing many of their cattle cousins peacefully grazing next to the road. After thirty long minutes on this ox cart, we crossed a river in a longboat and arrived at the elephant-breeding center. All of the adult elephants were chained down and several baby elephants roamed around freely. These cute four-month old babies were about 4 feet (1.2 meters) tall, weighed at least 500 pounds (225 kilograms) each, and had a tendency to sneak up on you if you were not paying attention.

One of the highlights of our trip in Nepal was the hour-long flight we took to see Mt. Everest on our one-year wedding anniversary. We flew with the small airline Buddha Air, which operates four sixteen-passenger turbo-prop planes. Along with another airline, each plane makes two hour-long trips each clear morning. Only two trips are possible because the winds pick up near the mountain by noon and preclude further flights. The flight was amazing. We each got a diagram of the profile of the mountains we passed, and each of us came up to the cockpit several times to see directly out of the front of the plane, as the co-pilot pointed out the mountains, especially Mt. Everest. We were still a good distance away, but close enough to get a good look at the tallest mountain in the world. It was a great first-year-anniversary gift to each other!

The day after our anniversary, we took a two-day tour of the Kathmandu Valley. The Kathmandu Valley includes three former Nepali capital cities that existed prior to the uniting of the kingdom of Nepal in 1768 AD. Our favorite city was Bhaktapur. The town has a well-preserved medieval center. For two hours we wandered from plaza to plaza, listening to music stores play Buddhist monk chant music, taking in the village life, and enjoying the temples, narrow streets, and medieval architecture. Three- or five-tiered temples with overhanging roofs dominated the plazas. The wooden front doors of the temples were carved with three figures one atop the other. Three-storied houses with a wood balcony overhanging the street on the third floor bordered the narrow streets. Burlap sacks filled with potatoes, bunches of corn in dried husks, and long strands of dried spinach leaves hung from the balconies.

As it was rice harvest time, rice drying on woven mats filled the plazas and any open sunny space. Women shoveled the rice into a large pile to separate the grains from foreign material and to help dry the grains. In Nepal, three to four people cut a field of rice by hand and leave the stalks to dry in the sun. A few days later the stalks are threshed in the field and the rice grains transported into the village or town in a large bag or basket for drying. The stalks are transported into the village later and stored in large haystacks near the houses. We were amazed at the amount of rice we saw drying all over Nepal!

From Bhaktapur we drove past more harvested rice fields to the east end of the valley and climbed to the ridge where we spent one night at Nagarkot. Nagarkot, a tourist area next to a strategic army post, has the best views of the Himalayas from the Kathmandu Valley. We enjoyed another spectacular sunrise over the Himalayas (this time we had a working camera). On our trip back to Kathmandu, we

Rice drying in a plaza, Bungmati, Nepal.

stopped at two more medieval villages—Patan and Bungmati. Our favorite was Bungmati, where we again wandered through narrow streets and large plazas filled with drying rice. Our final stop before returning to Kathmandu was Swayambhunath, a fourteenth-century Buddhist stupa sitting on a tall hill overlooking Kathmandu. Geologists believe Kathmandu Valley was once a lake and the hill the stupa sits on was an island in that lake. We enjoyed wandering around the monastery perched on the hilltop and watching the monkeys run all over the place.

Tomorrow we fly to Bangkok and start our travels through Thailand, Laos, Vietnam and Cambodia. We will visit these four countries through Christmas, and fly to New Zealand just before New Year's Eve. We will update you again from Vietnam. Until then!

Love, Jennifer & Erik

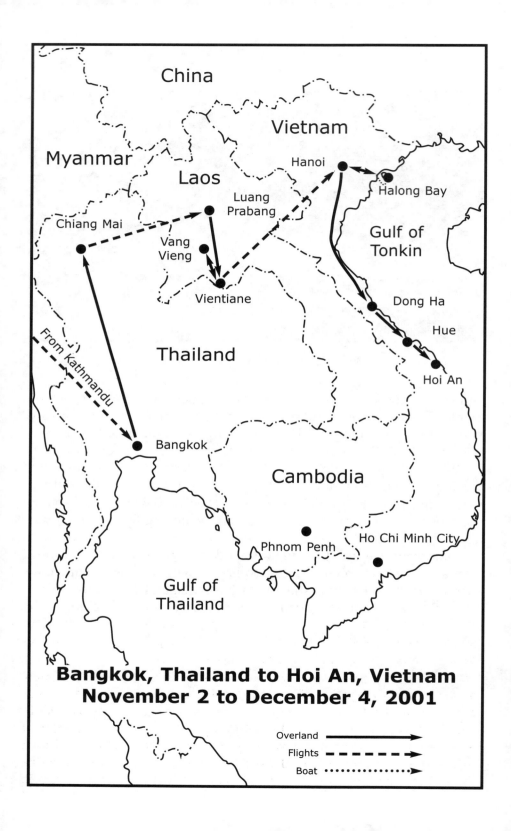

China

Vietnam

Myanmar

Laos

Hanoi

Halong Bay

Luang
Prabang

Chiang Mai

Gulf of
Tonkin

Vang
Vieng

Vientiane

Dong Ha

Hue

Thailand

Hoi An

Cambodia

Bangkok

Ho Chi Minh City

Phnom Penh

Gulf of
Thailand

**Bangkok, Thailand to Hoi An, Vietnam
November 2 to December 4, 2001**

Overland

Flights

Boat

14

Hoi An, Vietnam
Tuesday, December 4, 2001

Dear friends and family,

Early on the morning of November 2, we flew from Kathmandu, Nepal to Thailand, a country slightly smaller than France with a population of almost 62 million people. Our arrival into the capital, Bangkok, was a culture shock of sorts—it was so western! We breezed through customs at the airport, grabbed our bags and jumped into an air-conditioned cab (with a meter being used for once) playing a radio station with American music and an American DJ. As the taxi drove onto the new, express tollway into downtown Bangkok, we questioned whether we were still in Asia—we were, but this felt more like America than where we had been for the past two months, India and Nepal. Erik, excited to be back in familiar western surroundings, spent the rest of the day wandering through the nearby shopping malls, eating KFC and McDonald's, seeing a Hollywood movie, and shopping at the nearby 7-Eleven! We augmented Jennifer's wardrobe (replacing some of the clothes stolen in India and retiring others) with great shopping deals. After a quick fix of raw American-like culture, we visited some Thai sights.

Thailand is predominantly a Buddhist country (ninety-five percent of Thais are Buddhist), so we first visited Buddhist monasteries, or *wats*. *Wats* are low-walled compounds consisting of a main temple or *viharn*, an ordination hall, a library, rooms for the monks, and often a stupa containing relics of the Buddha. *Wats* are places of education, worship, meeting and healing, and a village is not considered a "complete" community without one. In the various *wats* we visited in Thailand, we saw educational meetings, practitioners and students of Thai massage, and young boys playing sports. Nearly all Thai men attend a *wat* for some part of their life. Many stay for three months after their mandatory service in the army. Wherever we traveled in

Thailand we saw Buddhist monks dressed in orange robes with shaved heads. Traditionally a young village boy could receive an education at a *wat*, so (until recently) many young monks were boys from poor families.

Our first stop was Wat Traimitr, home of the Golden Buddha. This *wat* houses a 10-foot- (3-meter-) high, 700-year-old Buddha sitting in a meditation pose made from five and a half tons of solid gold! This originally stucco-covered Buddha was moved as part of the expansion of the Bangkok port in 1957. During the move, the Buddha fell and the stucco cracked, revealing the solid gold image underneath. Apparently, during the sixteenth century AD, when the Burmese invaded Thailand, the Thais covered their valuable Buddha images with plaster to disguise them. From Wat Traimitr we visited Wat Pho, home of the Reclining Buddha. This large *wat* is famous for its 150-foot- (46-meter-) long, 50-foot- (15-meter-) high, gold-plated, reclining Buddha. Scaffolding hid the front of the Buddha when we visited, but it was still breathtaking, especially the soles of the feet inlaid with mother-of-pearl depicting the 108 auspicious signs of the Buddha. We wandered around the various parts of the *wat* and happened upon a monk ordination ceremony. The monks sat in the center of the temple and the family of the new monk gathered on one side. During our visit, the family individually approached the new monk and offered him gifts. Outside we passed an area set up for a luncheon reception after the temple ceremony.

We stopped last at Wat Phra Kaeo and the Grand Palace, the former royal residence. Wat Phra Kaeo is the former royal *wat* and has various styles of temple architecture. We saw traditional Thai temple architecture with tall wooden buildings supporting steep, tiered roofs. Colored glass tiles decorate the outside and invariably a snake/dragon adorns the handrail that lines the steps to the temple. Several Ceylonese-style, gold-plated stupas with a squat circular base rose to a point hundreds of feet in the air. We also saw temples designed with a Khmer (Cambodian) flavor and a model of Angkor Wat (which we will see in Cambodia). The Khmer-style temples look like beehives, uniformly cylindrical with a small dome at the top and long, narrow windows carved in the cylinders. We enjoyed seeing the various types of architecture all in one place. A colonnaded cloister with painted story panels depicting the Thai version of the Indian epic *Ramayana* surrounds the *wat* compound. The *wat* compound bustled with people lighting candles and visiting the sights.

The Grand Palace, the former home of Thai kings built in 1728 AD, was much less interesting, as the buildings are not highly decorated and the interiors were closed. We did like the exterior of the funeral hall used for the lying-in-state of the deceased king and queen. Thais adore their royal family, especially the king. We were surprised that before a movie in a theater, the whole audience stands for a two-minute multimedia tribute to the king.

Having sampled Bangkok (we will stay there again for several days when we leave Cambodia on December 17), we took an overnight train north to Chiang Mai, Thailand's second largest city. What a difference from Bangkok! Chiang Mai is an absolutely charming city in the hills of northern Thailand and a good choice to spend the six days we needed to get our visas for Laos and Vietnam. We situated ourselves just inside the old city walls and within walking distance of numerous *wats*. The temples of northern Thailand are tall, rectangular buildings with a steep two-story, high roof. Usually two slightly smaller entries, also steep roofed, sit in front of the main temple, so the effect is a three-tiered building gradually getting larger. Wood columns that disappear into the high ceiling support the interior of the temple. Painted murals adorn the inside and beautifully carved wood decorates the outside. The exterior wood is usually painted red with gold paint in the carved spaces. The banister of the temple steps is usually a multi-colored, glass-tiled snake/dragon. Gold ornamentation that resembles a gold snake rising into the air accents the peaks and edges of the temple roofs.

Erik bought several small canvases and painted in the hotel room while Jennifer toured Doi Inthanon National Park and took several Thai cooking courses. Doi Inthanon is Thailand's highest point at 8,517 feet (2,596 meters). The road to the top winds through terraced rice fields and hilltribe villages. The tour stopped at the beautiful Wachiratan Waterfalls on the way to the summit, and Mae Ya Falls on the way back. Jennifer also visited two hilltribe villages, one of the Hmong tribe and one of the Karen tribe. The Karen tribe lives lower on the hillside and builds their wooden homes on stilts. The Hmong are from higher altitudes and build narrower houses with steep roofs that come near to the ground for more warmth.

Jennifer's favorite part of Chiang Mai was the Thai cooking courses. Having not indulged her passion for cooking for nearly one year, Jennifer enrolled in three full-day courses. Thai cooking courses offer a hands-on cooking experience. Jennifer joined fellow Americans as

Front staircase to a *wat* temple, Chiang Mai, Thailand.

well as Canadians, Aussies, Norwegians, Israelis, Dutch, Germans and Brits trying their hand at Thai cooking. On two of the days, Jennifer visited the market with the class and helped pick out the fresh vegetables, herbs and other ingredients to make the *pad thai*, spring rolls, curry paste and various soups and curries. The Thais use three different types of basil in their cooking, several unique varieties of eggplants, three types of chilies, lemongrass and numerous other unique seasonings. Jennifer saw how coconut cream is made from squeezing fresh grated coconut. The best part of Thai cooking school is each student has a wok and prepares their own portion of the dish being cooked. On most days Jennifer made six different dishes so Erik had yummy leftovers to sample!

One unique feature of many Thai houses and buildings is they have a miniature house in front of the main house, perched 4 feet (1.2 meters) off the ground on a pedestal. These small shrines sit in front of houses, gas stations, shops, and other buildings far enough away that the shadow of the building does not fall across the shrine. These fully decorated houses are for the resident spirit of the building compound. Thais give offerings of food, incense, flowers and candles to the spirits to keep the spirits content and call on the spirits to help in emergencies.

On November 11 we flew from Chiang Mai to Luang Prabang, Laos. Laos is a landlocked country slightly larger than Utah with a population of 5.6 million. We did not know very much about Laos before going there. The country has been at war for the past three hundred years and now is at peace. Laotians are among the friendliest people we have met, and the children laugh and play more than any other children we have seen. The government follows a communist philosophy and the country has been open to foreign tourism for only the last ten years. More than half of the foreign tourists are Thais, and we landed at the Thai-assisted, newly upgraded airport. Luang Prabang is a peninsular city at the confluence of the Mekong and Khan Rivers, and nestled in a valley surrounded by mountains. Like the rest of Laos, Luang Prabang is laid-back and quiet. Few cars drive by and the motorcycles and bicycles pass by slowly. We arrived on a Sunday afternoon and walked the quiet streets watching children playing and people relaxing.

We only had a couple of days to enjoy this wonderful city since we needed to complete paperwork for our Vietnam visa in the capital, Vientiane. In Luang Prabang, we first explored the Royal Palace Museum, housed in a palace built in 1904. The king of Laos lived here until 1975, when he was removed by the communist revolution. The palace was interesting for the ordinariness of its rooms and the display of gifts to Laos from various governments during the twentieth century. We were most fascinated by the piece of moon rock given to Laos by the United States in 1972.

The real treasure of Luang Prabang, and the reason it is a world heritage site, are the more than thirty *wats* located in this small town. Notwithstanding the communist government, the Buddhist monastery tradition is strong in Laos. Laos historically has strong ties with Thailand, and practices the same form of Buddhism as Thailand. All over in Luang Prabang we saw orange-clad monks going about their daily activities. These monks have restored the various *wats* and these buildings are spectacular. One of the former royal *wats* has a beautifully carved wood facade painted with gold. The Luang Prabang *wats* resemble those in Thailand. Buildings are painted red and accented with gold-painted wood carvings. Stair banisters are decorated with multi-colored glass tiles. The steep roofs of Luang Prabang *wats* are layered within a single roof. Each *wat* is uniquely designed, and we enjoyed wandering around a dozen or so of the more famous ones.

Having had a hefty dose of *wats* (what we called "being watted out"), we spent our second day on the Mekong River. We joined three

Typical *wat* building, Luang
Prabang, Laos.

other travelers (two from England and one from America) on a covered longboat for a day tour. We headed upstream on the Mekong
River for an hour enjoying the lush green vegetation, beautiful mountains and farmers tending the land along the river bank. As the
Mekong recedes from its height during the rainy season, the farmers
use bamboo poles to mark the new fields of vegetables. The upper
banks were green with the growing rice crops planted earlier.

We stopped at Ban Xang Hui village to see how they make rice
whiskey. Historically this town was known for its pottery, but as
demand for pottery declined, they started using the pottery to make
rice whiskey. We then stopped at a pair of caves to see hundreds of
Buddha statues before setting off across the river for lunch in yet

another riverside village. Laos definitely has a laid-back pace of life and, after a leisurely lunch with our fellow travelers, we toured the nearby village and returned to Luang Prabang by boat. The village houses were built on stilts. The more affluent houses had reed walls surrounding the lower level and wood planked upper floors; less affluent ones had reed walls on the upper floor and no covering on the lower level. Interestingly, the village lacked domesticated animals; only a few chickens and turkeys ran around the dirt streets. Apparently Laos still has sufficient wild game and many Laotians obtain their meat that way. We assume the villager we saw running out of his house and into the woods with an AK-47 was going to shoot dinner and nothing else.

The next morning we reluctantly boarded a bus heading south to the capital, Vientiane. It was a scenic, although cramped bus ride. Laos is very mountainous, with wooded craggy peaks rising along the roadside. Between the poor condition of the road and its twisting nature, it took eleven hours to travel 260 miles (420 kilometers) to Vientiane. Like the rest of Laos, the capital city is very quiet. We stayed in the heart of the city and saw almost no traffic.

After dropping off our visa paperwork, we set off to explore the town. We took a short promenade along the river bank then headed back toward town stopping to visit the former royal *wat* and Wat Si Saket, another *wat* famous for the Buddha statues housed in niches — 6,840 statues are housed in the main temple and cloisters! Not having had enough *wats* yet, we headed further out of town to Wat Sek Pa Luang, a wooded *wat* known for its steam sauna. A variety of herbs, including kaffir lime, lemongrass, camphor bark and lemon scented the sauna. In the small wood sauna, Erik chatted with local college students. Erik talked with one student about English pronunciation and jokingly asked the student to pronounce the word "conspicuous." The student laughed and didn't even want to try that one!

Having exhausted most of the sights in Vientiane and with our Vietnam visas in hand, we headed back north and spent our last two days in Laos visiting Vang Vieng, a small riverside town sporting fabulous scenery and interesting caves. We opted not to participate in the more adventurous day tours (which included kayaking and tubing inside a water-filled cave), and instead contented ourselves with a short hike to Tham Jang cave. This vast cave network was used in former times as bunkers. The limestone cave has a smooth ceiling that looks like smooth concrete formed by the action of waves millions of years ago. Laos was a great country to visit; we highly recommend coming here if you enjoy a relaxed pace and rugged beauty.

From Vientiane, we flew to Hanoi, Vietnam. Vietnam is also a communist country like Laos; however, Vietnam has a more developed commercial and industrial infrastructure. Vietnam also opened up to tourism during the past ten years, although on a larger scale than Laos. Vietnam, with a population of almost 80 million, is slightly larger than New Mexico (or approximately forty percent larger than Laos). The United States normalized its diplomatic and trade relations with Vietnam in the mid-1990s.

For most Americans, the word *Vietnam* conjures up memories and images of war. While touring we found few obvious signs of war. When we landed in Hanoi, we met a couple from California. The husband was stationed in Saigon in 1969 and admitted his return was emotional. Before September 11, most tourists in Vietnam were Americans, but now fewer Americans travel here (and everywhere else for that matter). We noticed first-hand how tourist spending directly supports local economies in many places, and in turn, the world economy. Erik asked the couple from California if the events of September 11 made them question their decision to travel, and the wife said she was mad and wanted to travel to support our freedoms. We agree—if we stay home and do not travel the way we normally do, the terrorists win.

Vietnam is a very scenic country with the stunning coastline of the South China Sea, many mountains (not the kind that have snow), and flooded rice paddies with people bent over working in them. Most people wore round, straw-colored, conical hats to protect them from the sun. Outside the Hanoi airport, we saw many corn fields. It reminded Erik of the central valley of California. The Red River Delta near Hanoi provides water to irrigate the numerous fields. The Vietnamese plant two crops of rice on these fields starting with the wet season, and plant a third crop of corn during the dry season. Since we visited at the end of the dry season in the north, the corn was almost ready to harvest. Throughout the countryside and cities, we saw women of all ages carrying what looked like large "justice scales" hanging from a pole that rests on their shoulders. The two large, flat woven baskets are usually filled with fruits and vegetables, but can carry a whole range of other goods.

Our first venture crossing the street in Hanoi was exasperating. About ninety-five percent of the traffic is mopeds, motorcycles, and bicycles, and they travel very fast. To cross a road, you walk slowly into the sea of oncoming two-wheeled traffic and, keeping a steady pace, cross as the traffic veers around you. If you are lucky, a Vietnamese woman with her shoulder baskets is also crossing the street and you walk next to her. Of all of the cities we have been to (including Cairo, Egypt), we found the traffic here the worst. Most store fronts and building fronts have two or three concrete steps leading to the front door with a small 1-foot (30.5-centimeter) concrete ramp in the middle so motorcycles can be driven directly into the home/place of business or hotel and locked up at night. One night as we headed back to our hotel, relieved to be off the street, a motorbike going up one of these ramps almost hit Jennifer as she entered the hotel. Apparently, even walking into the doorway of your hotel in Vietnam can be dangerous!

Throughout the countryside, instead of *wats* or other religious buildings we saw small graveyards. Apparently when someone dies, they are buried for a couple of years in a temporary grave, and later transferred to a larger family grave in their hometown. Living relatives visit and worship the deceased at the family grave. The many unmarked and unknown single graves of men who died in the war frustrate the Vietnamese because the families do not know where to worship them.

Typical Hanoi traffic, Hanoi, Vietnam.

We spent three full days in Hanoi. Other than the traffic, Hanoi is a lovely city with trees, lakes and French-style architecture. We visited the infamous "Hanoi Hilton," the prison that housed American prisoners of war (POWs) from 1967 until 1973. The prison, built by the French in 1896, has only a quarter of it standing today; a high-rise apartment tower occupies the former prison grounds. Most of the displays documented the French imprisonment and torture of Vietnamese Communist "freedom fighters" during the colonial period. One small room was dedicated to the American POWs. Pictures on the wall, including a mug-shot of now Senator John McCain, showed POWs "enjoying" their time at the prison and how "happy and well-treated" they were. The display also included clothing, personal items and a bed used by the POWs. We also saw the mausoleum of Ho Chi Minh, the Communist leader of Vietnam until his death in 1969. His body, displayed in a glass sarcophagus, was in Russia during our visit being taken care of by preservation specialists.

One of the highlights in Hanoi was the water puppet show. Water puppetry has been popular in this part of Vietnam for over a thousand years. Workers in flooded rice fields developed this art to entertain each other and their children. This water puppet troop has performed in cities around the world. In the theater, a large, rectangular pool of murky water is the stage with a screen and decoration at the back. A band and singers sit on a platform to the left of the pool. Behind the screen puppeteers move the puppets using long sticks under the water. The effect is puppets dancing and moving about on the surface of the water and magically popping up from under the water. We saw over a dozen different short scenes, each representing an aspect of life in northern Vietnam including an agriculture scene, a fishing scene, and festival scenes complete with sparklers. It was a treat to watch this unique art form!

From Hanoi, we headed east for a three-day/two-night tour of the stunning Halong Bay on the Gulf of Tonkin. Halong Bay has hundreds of small, rocky islands, mostly covered by thick vegetation. The islands shoot straight up out of the water usually without a coastline. They are the most beautiful group of islands we have ever seen! We traveled with a fascinating group of fifteen tourists—five Americans, three Brits, three Aussies, three Dutch, and one Malaysian. We spent most of the time talking with each other and enjoying each other's company. Our first day on the boat was Thanksgiving, the second Thanksgiving in a row on a tour boat (last year we were in the

Galapagos Islands). We cruised the islands, swam in the warm, murky waters of the bay, and explored caves. We ended our first evening on the deck of the boat, staring at the stars before going to bed.

Our second day on Halong Bay we went to the largest island, Cat Ba Island, and visited a small village a 1.8-mile (3-kilometer) walk from a small dock. Most of the group climbed a very steep hill overlooking the bay, but the two of us and some others decided to forego the difficult climb and enjoy the village instead. Erik drew while Jennifer and two other women walked around the village. Soon a group of seven or eight young schoolchildren with little red scarves surrounded Erik to see what he was drawing. They flipped through the pages of his large drawing pad and wanted Erik to draw something else. Two of them even tried their hand at drawing with some of Erik's artistic crayons. Then they found our Lonely Planet guidebook and enjoyed seeing the pictures of their country. Back on the bay, we motored past a floating village, complete with homes, store and a floating elementary school.

In Hanoi we ate one more meal with our new friends before boarding an overnight train to central Vietnam. We shared our sleeping compartment with an Australian couple who had traveled from London to Australia via Iran, Afghanistan and India in a VW Beetle in 1972. We enjoyed staying up late trading travel stories. In the morning,

Floating village, Halong Bay, Vietnam.

some food vendors on the train opened up our compartment door, set up our table, and started serving a rice soup with chicken. Before we had awakened fully, coffee was poured and the vendors wanted money for food and drink we had not asked for. It turned out to be a good breakfast, but we found it frustrating to have it forced on us.

The Vietnamese are a very enterprising group and want a piece of the tourist action. We encountered con-artists in other countries; but here, that "art" is more out in the open and pervasive. For instance, within an hour of arriving at the Hanoi airport, the airport taxi dropped us off at a hotel with three names on the front door. As it turns out, this hotel "borrowed" the names of other hotels to confuse new tourists into staying there. Many hotel owners and taxi drivers have deals worked out to make this scam happen—we thought we were in the right place, paid for two nights in advance, and once we walked out of the hotel to do our sightseeing, we realized we were nowhere near the center of town and had to walk twenty minutes for the nearest restaurant or shop that sold bottled water. In Hanoi, we also experienced a taxi ride that took us the long way around a lake to visit a museum costing us double what we thought we would pay. We asked the driver why he drove us around this lake and he said taxis cannot go the short way, although the taxi from the airport had taken the short route. The vast majority of Vietnamese are honest and hard-working; it is unfortunate the con-artists operate so frequently here.

We left the train in Dong Ha, just south of the former demilitarized zone (DMZ). The Dong Ha area was home to many American bases during the war. We stayed at a hotel run by the aunt of one of Erik's friends from Kansas City. We took a taxi from the train station to the hotel (the slowest cab ride we have ever taken since the car's transmission was on the brink of collapse). We felt we were the only two tourists staying in this town, and we were the only two people at this particular hotel. We shared our wedding album with the hotel staff using our Vietnamese phrasebook. Everyone on the street was amazed to see us and was very friendly. Our time in Dong Ha was a very positive experience of Vietnam and a total contrast to the hassle at the tourist towns.

The DMZ day tour starts in Dong Ha, although most tourists stay in Hue and take a two-hour bus trip north to join the tour. We met our tour group at the restaurant where they stopped for breakfast. The bus was completely full, so we sat on little, plastic, stool-type seats in the aisle of the bus. We drove west toward the Laos border on a highway built by the American forces in the 1960s. As we entered the country-side, we noticed only short shrubs on the tall hills around us. In other parts of Vietnam, thick forests cover the hillsides. Near Dong Ha however, the heavy use of Agent Orange thirty years ago destroyed the vegetation and still affects the plant life. Our tour guide also told us 225 million unexploded land mines still remain. We are not sure if that is the Dong Ha area or the whole of Vietnam, but it is a lot. Periodically, a cow or farmer is killed or injured when an unexploded mine is hit during farming.

We stopped near a rocky hill called "the Rockpile," where the United States once had a manned surveillance unit stationed, then headed closer to the Laos border to visit Khe Sanh combat base. On the way we passed the famous Ho Chi Minh Trail that the North Vietnamese soldiers used to move troops and equipment. The American base Khe Sanh was overrun and captured by North Vietnamese forces in a bloody battle in 1968. The base opened for tours only five years ago because prior to that the numerous unexploded devices made the place too dangerous. Nothing grows where the airstrip used to be. Various displays of weapons and ammunition left behind include a U.S. tank in decay, an artillery cannon and recon-structions of bunkers. Two local men sold various metal objects recently dug up in the area. Erik bought an intact "dog tag" that looked thirty-plus years old with the name of R.L. Koslowski, an American serving in the U.S. Marine Corps. Erik wants to return it to the person it belongs to or his family when we return to the United States.

From Khe Sanh base, we drove back to Dong Ha for lunch, and then headed north to the Ben Hai River, the former divide between North and South Vietnam. Rice fields now fill the former 3-mile (5-kilometer) no-man's-land on both sides of the river. We crossed the river to visit the famous Vinh Moc tunnels. The town of Vinh Moc was heavily bombed by a nearby U.S. base, so from 1965 to 1966, the residents con-structed 1.7 miles (2.8 kilometers) of underground living tunnels with thirteen entrances (seven facing the sea and six on a hill). Only 1 mile (1.7 kilometers) of the original tunnels remain.

We spent twenty minutes walking through the 5.5-foot- (1.67-meter-) tall tunnels. The tunnels had three different levels and included a conference hall that held from fifty to eighty people. Residents lived for several years in many small "living rooms" off the main tunnel. Families stayed in the tunnels during the day and farmed or fished in the surrounding area at night. The longest continuous time the villagers spent in the tunnels was five days and five nights. Seventeen children were born in the tunnels. The tunnels also housed ammunitions and were used as a base to transport goods to a nearby island. The Americans only successfully bombed the tunnels once, and though the bomb killed many people as it crashed through the tunnels, it never exploded. As an example of the communist rhetoric we encountered periodically in our Vietnamese travels, the back of our tunnel entrance ticket stated in broken English: "Visiting Vinh Moc today, you will feel as you lived back in the glorious time with the historical heroes who made these exploits."

From Dong Ha, we headed to Hue on the DMZ tour bus. After sitting for three hours on the tiny plastic seats, we were extremely happy to arrive in Hue. Not finding Hue particularly interesting, we made our way further south to Hoi An, where we are wrapping up a five-day visit. We heard about a "Full Moon" festival here, so we decided to arrive the day before the full moon. It turns out the festival took place two days before the full moon! We were glad to have extra time in this charming town. Hoi An has many wonderful restaurants, art galleries, and tailoring shops. Hoi An also boasts some of the oldest architecture in Vietnam since the Americans used the town for a rest and relaxation post and did not bomb it. We wandered down narrow streets exploring Chinese-style buildings and temples from the eighteenth century and a quaint covered bridge. At night colorful paper lanterns glowed red and orange outside shops. Several members of our Halong Bay cruise as well as other people we met in Hanoi are also in Hoi An. For the past several days, we have enjoyed sharing meals and sightseeing with them.

Last Sunday, four of us took a day trip to My Son, a world heritage site and the most important religious center of the Kingdom of Champa. The Chams were international coastal traders and practiced Hinduism. They used My Son from the fourth through thirteenth centuries AD. The Americans extensively bombed the site during the war since the North Vietnamese used the area as a military base. Bomb holes are present everywhere. The few remaining structures display incredible brick work. How the Chams laid the brick without mortar still baffles scholars. From My Son we headed north to Danang to visit the Cham museum. This U-shaped building is covered, but large "windows" in the wall are open to the outside air. Numerous carved stone statues from the fourth through fourteenth centuries of Hindu gods and lingas are displayed as they would have appeared as altars. Most statues are at chest level on blocks or slabs of white that sit atop stones that would have formed the base of the altar. Altogether it was a fabulous museum.

In a couple of hours, we fly from Danang to Ho Chi Minh City (formally Saigon). We leave Vietnam on December 10 for Cambodia, and will return to Bangkok on December 17. We wish you all the best during this holiday season!

Love, Jennifer & Erik

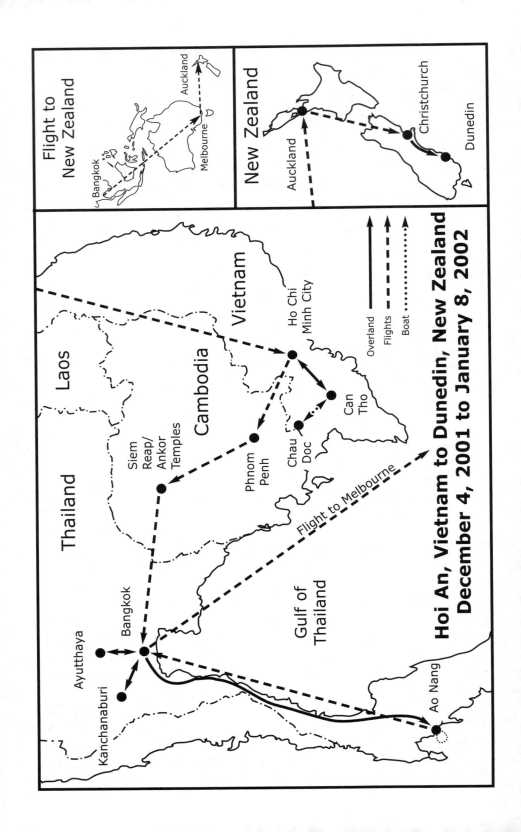

Flight to New Zealand

New Zealand

Hoi An, Vietnam to Dunedin, New Zealand
December 4, 2001 to January 8, 2002

Overland
Flights
Boat

15

Dunedin, New Zealand
Tuesday, January 8, 2002

Dear friends and family,

We hope your holidays were wonderful, and we wish you all the best for a happy, healthy and prosperous 2002! We had quiet holiday celebrations this year, but more on that later.

On December 4, 2001, we flew south from Hoi An, Vietnam to Ho Chi Minh City (formerly Saigon). Saigon is the largest city in Vietnam and more western than Hanoi. The large number of Christmas decorations, including a decorated tree in our hotel lobby, surprised us. We spent two full days exploring the city sights. We visited the War Remnants Museum (formerly the Museum of Chinese and American War Crimes) which is completely one-sided and conveys the impact of the Vietnam War on the civilian population. We both were moved by the special exhibit donated by the State of Kentucky of photographs taken by photographers who lost their lives in the war. These photos, mainly of American and South Vietnamese forces, balanced the other exhibits in the museum. Jennifer visited the reconstructed Cu Chi Tunnels, originally 37 miles (60 kilometers) of tunnels the Viet Cong used to fight the French and Americans. American bombing destroyed the original tunnels; only a small portion, about one-half mile (1 kilometer), has been reconstructed. The reconstructed tunnels are enlarged but still quite small. The entry hole for the original tunnels measured approximately 20 inches by 9 inches (51 centimeters by 23 centimeters). Jennifer also saw a display of the various home-made traps the Viet Cong forces set against the Americans.

On the same tour, Jennifer visited the Coadai Great Temple, which she found very interesting. Coadaism is a religion founded in 1926 AD and with one-third of its 3 million followers in southern Vietnam. The religion is based mostly on Buddhism, with some elements of Taoism, Confucianism, native Vietnamese spiritualism, Christianity and Islam.

The Coadai worship four times a day (at 6 AM, noon, 6 PM and midnight) for a half-hour. Musicians accompany the ceremony of mass silent prayer. Assistants bang a large bell to let worshippers know to proceed to the next part of the service. The exterior of the temple resembles a traditional European Catholic church, while the interior, somewhat art deco in design, is painted in various bright colors and has bubble gum pink pillars with the heads of green and white dragons at the pillar base and the tails winding up around the pillar.

While Jennifer explored the tunnels and temple, Erik explored Saigon from the front of a *cyclo*. A *cyclo* is a type of public transportation common in Vietnam. One or two passengers sit in a seat at the front of a bicycle, and the driver pedals the *cyclo* from a seat behind. In order for the driver to see over the passenger, the passenger seat is low to the ground and tilted back toward the driver. According to Erik, it is the best way to travel on the crowded city streets of Vietnam and see everything going on around you! Most *cyclo* drivers in Saigon are former South Vietnamese Army soldiers and many wear baseball caps of green camouflage. After South Vietnam lost the war, South Vietnamese soldiers attended re-education camps consisting mostly of two years of hard labor in the jungle. Now, they are not allowed to own any land or proper businesses, so many drive *cyclos*.

Ho Chi Minh City sits on the eastern side of the Mekong River Delta, so we took a three-day trip to explore this beautiful area. The Mekong River starts in China and flows nearly 2,800 miles (4,500 kilometers) through Laos, forming part of the borders between Laos and Myanmar (formerly Burma) and Laos and Thailand. The river continues through Cambodia and Vietnam before emptying into the South China Sea. The Mekong Delta is one of the largest delta areas of the world and is densely populated and heavily cultivated. Water is the common transportation means since annual flooding requires all-weather roads to be built on raised embankments. Over the course of our three-day trip we took five different boats and also explored the delta and its many canals by foot, bike and bus. We traveled with interesting Germans, Aussies, Danes, Swedes, Irish and Israelis. We rode on small motorized boats through various canals and took a large boat up and down the mighty Mekong River from Can Tho to Chau Doc near the Cambodian border. We also rode in a small boat powered by a Vietnamese woman in a conical hat rowing in a standing position from the back of the boat with two poles.

On our motorized boat tours, we visited several small family-run factories. Our favorite was the rice candy factory where we saw them pop rice (similar to how we pop popcorn), mix it with a caramelized butter and sugar base, then roll it out in a large rectangular tray and cut it into small squares that resembled big rice crispy treats. The process was timed so enough rice was popped at the same time the butter/sugar mixture finished cooking. While the bars were being rolled out and cut, another butter/sugar mixture was cooked and the whole process started again. Enough young women wrapped the finished rice squares in cellophane bags to keep up with production.

Here, as in most of Vietnam, little separated work and home. The "factory" is an extension of the home, housed in covered areas open to the outside. Small children ran around the work area, and lunch and dinner were cooking in an area near the candy making. The Vietnamese use everything they can and the rice husks that remained after the rice was popped were sifted out and used to fuel the fires for popping the rice and cooking the butter/sugar mixture. Other family-run factories we visited made coconut candy, incense sticks, rice paper and rice noodles. We also visited a mill where rice is separated from the husk and the brown rice polished to make white rice. A single bag of rice brought in for processing is turned into outside husks (used for fuel), rice powder (used to feed pigs and chickens), and white rice (used by the Vietnamese for eating).

Jennifer on small boat with fish farms in the background, Mekong Delta, Vietnam.

The waterways in the Mekong Delta are the highways. We toured a floating market where farmers bring their produce by boat to large boats acting as "middlemen." These boats buy produce in bulk, and then sell it to other people in small boats who take it to the market stall vendors in town. The middlemen advertise the produce they have for sale by hoisting one of each kind of produce on a bamboo pole from the front of their boat. As we floated by, we saw boats with a cabbage, a bunch of bananas, a pineapple, and so forth, strung on a pole in front of the boat!

Boat activity in the market area is quite intense, with the small boats darting in between the large stationary boats avoiding the tourist boats and other boats selling drinks and food. Almost all of the boats we saw on the Mekong Delta were made of wood. As we floated through the various canals, we saw men fishing from small boats and larger boats used for transportation. On the Mekong River, large barges cart loads of rice husks, dirt, sand, and a myriad of other products. We passed rice fields along the shore and small log bridges that cross the various transportation and irrigation canals. With so much traffic and habitation in and along the river, we were amazed no garbage floats in the Mekong Delta waterways. The delta water is a brown color from the silt and dirt carried from upriver, not pollution.

Not surprising, another booming business in the Mekong Delta is fish farming. All along the Mekong River we saw oversized wood houses with a front porch floating on the water. These buildings cover a caged area 20 feet (6 meters) deep stocked with fish. The family lives in the two-roomed house and feed the fish by lifting up the floor panels in the front living room. The house floats to insure the fish farm does not bottom out, since it takes nearly a year of feeding before the fish can be harvested.

We are left with certain unique images of Vietnam. Foremost are high-school girls biking to or from school in *ao dai* uniforms consisting of a white, tight-fitting, long-sleeved, ankle-length tunic slit on each side from the waist to the tunic bottom. The tunic is worn over white trousers and the rider usually wears a conical hat with a ponytail of long black hair hanging down her back. We also have funny memories of "anything and everything" being carried by moto or bicycle. Some of our favorite images include: the bicycle with four school boys—one on the seat pedaling, two behind him on the rear wheel rim, and the fourth seated backward on the handlebars; the moto with a driver and passenger holding onto a large sheet of masonite; and a 5-foot- (1.5-

meter-) tall houseplant tied to the back of a moto. In Vietnam children came up to us in restaurants to sell us things while we ate dinner. Our favorite hawking technique was the girl carrying a banded 4-foot- (1.2-meter-) high stack of pirated, photocopied novels and guidebooks.

From Saigon we flew to Phnom Penh, the capital of Cambodia. Cambodia is slightly smaller than Oklahoma, with a population of 12.5 million. In Southeast Asia, we have traveled through several countries with a recent history of war, but Cambodia's civil war ended just two years ago and the impact on the country is very apparent. Cambodia suffered bombing by the United States as part of the Vietnam War from 1969 to 1973. In addition, the country plunged into a civil war in 1970, which ended with the Khmer Rouge taking Phnom Penh on April 17, 1975. Most Cambodians welcomed the Khmer Rouge as an end to the fighting, but the four years of Khmer Rouge rule tore apart the fabric of Cambodian society.

In early 1979, Vietnam retaliated for incursions of the Khmer Rouge into Vietnamese territory in the Mekong Delta by invading and taking over the country. The Vietnamese stayed until September 1989. When they left, civil war erupted again. The United Nations sponsored elections in 1993, but only in 1999 did the civil war with the Khmer Rouge end. Consequently, Cambodia is visibly recovering from thirty years of civil war and the capital is a blend of modern and less-developed buildings. Recent foreign investment has produced modern gas stations in some parts of Phnom Penh, but many moto riders purchase gas from corner stands selling gasoline from two-liter soda bottles. Also, paved streets in Phnom Penh intersect ones with large potholes or dirt ones waiting to be surfaced for the first time. Visiting here made us more aware of the daunting task that lies ahead for the new government of Afghanistan.

When the Khmer Rouge took over Cambodia in April 1975, they turned the entire country into a rural peasant state by evicting everyone from the cities and towns (including those in hospitals), and relocating them to rural villages. Phnom Penh, with a population of 1 million, was completely deserted and its residents forced to do hard manual labor in the countryside. Anyone associated with power or influence and the educated were killed. Many died from starvation, malnutrition and malaria. The Khmer Rouge sent the vast majority of the food harvested in Cambodia to China in exchange for weapons, so the Cambodians did not eat much of the food they produced. Elderly who could not work were thrown into crocodile-infested ponds.

Gasoline stand for motos, Phnom Penh, Cambodia.

The Cambodians say over 2 million people, approximately thirty percent of the population at that time, died between 1975 and 1979. Some international estimates place the number around 1 million. Almost everyone in Cambodia had some member of his or her family killed during this time. One of our guides, born in 1979, had an uncle killed. Within three minutes of getting in our taxi, the driver for our Angkor Wat excursion told us the Khmer Rouge killed his father because he was a high school teacher and forced the family to live in the countryside and farm rice fields. Cambodia's sealed borders prevented the majority of the world knowing of the events when they happened. It was not until 1980 that mass graves began to be unearthed and stories of the atrocities told.

On our second day in Phnom Penh, we toured the "killing fields," an area where many mass graves were found, just a twenty-minute drive outside of Phnom Penh. We first visited a memorial pagoda filled with the skulls of a fraction of the victims of the Khmer Rouge. The skulls are arranged on different levels by age and sex. We then walked around this site where 129 mass graves were found. About two-thirds of the graves have been unearthed, with the rest untouched. The most eerie thing about walking around the site was seeing on the trail bone fragments and many pieces of clothing from the victims being unearthed as the soil erodes. Our guide even found an intact molar tooth just lying among the leaves on the ground! It was simply unbelievable. In most instances the victims were bludgeoned to death to preserve the limited ammunition.

We also toured the former high school in the center of Phnom Penh that was the holding facility for the victims killed at the killing fields. This center for torture/detention, called S-21 prison, is now the Tuol Sleng Genocide Museum. Our visit was quite depressing. We saw many drawings showing different torture methods. We visited reconstructions of the rooms where the torture took place and the "cells" where the prisoners were kept. We also saw hundreds of "mug shots" of people of all ages and sexes held at this prison; every person was eventually murdered. Cambodia preserves this place to insure something like this does not happen again.

In addition to clearing the people from Phnom Penh, the Khmer Rouge also destroyed much of the city during their reign. One of the few buildings they preserved was the royal palace complex, built between the mid-1800s and the early twentieth century. We toured the large coronation hall and attached *wat* complex. The *wat* buildings resembled the *wats* and palaces of southern Thailand, with steep, tiered roofs. The main temple of the *wat* is the Silver Pagoda built in 1892 and rebuilt in 1962. The pagoda is named for the over 5,000 silver floor tiles, each weighing approximately 2.2 pounds (1 kilogram).

From Phnom Penh we flew to Siem Reap, the tourist town next to the Angkor sites. Angkor was the capital of the Khmer empire during its heyday from 802 AD to 1432 AD. The empire had numerous periods of decline and revival, and most of the temples stem from certain revival periods. Overall, the temples of Angkor are the only surviving buildings of the former capital because they were the only buildings made of stone. However, surviving is a misnomer, since the majority of temples stand today due to extensive restoration in the twentieth century. The Khmer kings were primarily Hindu, so most temples are dedicated to Siva, although Angkor Wat is dedicated to Vishnu and the Angkor Thom temples are Buddhist.

We started our three-day visit to the various temple sites by watching the sunrise over Angkor Wat. Angkor Wat is the world's largest religious monument and was built mainly during the early- to mid-twelfth century, with some later additions. Angkor Wat, extensively renovated, is the most complete of the temples we visited. The complex is designed as a microcosm of the Hindu universe with the top main temple representing the five peaks of Mount Meru. We entered the complex through a causeway over a moat that surrounds rectangular-shaped grounds. A large, walled compound with grass and two pools lead to the next higher walled compound. Carved scenes from the two main Hindu epics, the *Ramayana* and *Mahabharata*, decorate the outside walls of this complex. A covered, colonnaded walkway protects the carvings from the elements. Inside this enclosure the main temple sits atop a yet higher platform. The steps to this temple are steep and very narrow. The main temple has four Khmer-style, beehive-like towers on each corner. Another similar-style single tower sits in the center at an even higher elevation. Carved stone blocks about 12 inches by 18 inches (30 centimeters by 46 centimeters) form the buildings. In the innermost temple of Angkor Wat, carved dancing figures called *apsaras* decorate the walls. All in all, it was quite impressive!

From Angkor Wat we visited the nearby remains of Angkor Thom, a 5.6 square-mile (9 square-kilometer), enclosed Khmer city built in the late twelfth century. We entered through one of the five gates that breach a moat surrounding the city. Each gate approach is lined with two sets of large figures holding a serpent. The figures to the right of the approach are identical and represent gods; the figures on the left are identical and represent demons. The gate is topped with four faces facing the cardinal directions. The main temple, Bayon, sits in the center of the city. Beautifully carved, narrative bas-reliefs detailing daily

Entry to Angkor Thom, Cambodia.

life and Khmer history surround the temple base. The reliefs depict battles with commanders on elephants, a woman playing with her children, people grilling skewered meat over an open fire, people cooking a deer carcass in a large pot, women selling fruit, and people observing a cock fight. The battle narratives show the defeat of the Khmers by the Chams (from Vietnam) in 1177, and the retaking of Angkor by the Khmers in 1181. The main temple has many face towers, similar to those at the gate. These serene faces are quite large (approximately 6 feet (1.8 meters) tall) and face each of the cardinal directions in most instances. The temple itself is constructed in three-tiered levels, like Angkor Wat. We thoroughly explored this temple and the ruins of the palace and other temples on the grounds.

We had two favorite temples after Angkor Wat. The first was Ta Prohm, built in the late twelfth century to early thirteenth century and in a similar style to Bayon. We liked this temple because it has been left in a fairly "natural" state. Large silk-cotton trees intertwined with the ruins. These trees start to grow on the tops of the ruins and run their root systems down to the ground over the stone walls. The roots push out the walls, in some instances toppling them over, and in other instances merely displacing them. This temple is left in this state so visitors can appreciate how the temples were first found and the amount of work needed to reconstruct the temples.

We also liked Banteay Srei, situated 12 miles (20 kilometers) north of Angkor Thom and originally constructed in the second half of the tenth century. This temple was only recently opened to visitors due to Khmer Rouge activity in the area. This small temple complex, set in beautiful, sparsely-wooded surroundings, is built of pink sandstone, a harder rock than the stone used at other Angkor temples. Consequently, the beautifully intricate carvings of three-dimensional figures and floral decorations have survived virtually intact and are simply breathtaking.

We finally pulled ourselves away from the Angkor temples and flew back to Bangkok on December 17. We were greeted by non-stop Christmas music at the airport and in the shopping malls in this predominantly Buddhist country. It turns out the Thais will incorporate any excuse for festivities and have adopted Christmas as yet another of their holidays. The Thais like to party so much they even celebrate three New Years each year! After spending a day getting our fix of Hollywood movies and western shopping centers, we hopped on the overhead skytrain to another part of the city and had dinner with some of Erik's relatives we met in Sweden last summer. The family was in Thailand for three weeks and recovering from jet lag before heading to the beaches in the south. We also headed there, but took two excursions near Bangkok first.

Our first excursion was to the town of Kanchanaburi, a ninety-minute drive northwest from Bangkok, and the start of the famous "death railway." When the Japanese occupied Thailand during World War II, they built a railway linking Thailand and Burma to reduce the number of supply ships sailing to Burma. Work on the railway began in June 1942 and finished in October 1943. The Japanese used a peak work force of 61,000 prisoners of war (mainly British and Australian) and 250,000 Asians as forced labor to build the 258-mile (415-kilometer) railway.

Commencing with the bridge over the River Kwai, the prisoners and forced laborers constructed 688 bridges, mostly of lumber. The combination of primarily manual work and low rations was difficult and dangerous, and led to the loss of 16,000 prisoners and 75,000 Asians. The original bridge over the River Kwai was destroyed during Allied bombing at the end of World War II, so we walked on a reproduction then rode a ninety-minute train along part of the perilous death railway, gazing at the beautiful scenery.

The next day we traveled due north from Bangkok to the former Thai capital of Ayutthaya. The city, founded in 1350 AD, was the capital of a kingdom that ultimately stretched from Angkor in the east to Burma in the west. Rivers on three sides and a linking canal on the fourth fortified the city. During the 400 years Ayutthaya was the capital, the Burmese attacked the kingdom twenty-four times. The last attack in 1767 resulted in the sacking of Ayutthaya and the complete destruction of its wooden buildings and brick temples. At the height of its prosperity in the sixteenth century, Ayutthaya allegedly had more than forty different nationalities living in and around the city walls and a population larger than London at that time. Today we could still see the remains of the extensive canal system throughout the city plus the remains of the numerous Buddhist temples from its heyday. We found the remains as interesting for the extensive kingdom they represented as for the depiction of the underlying construction of the various *wats*, stupas, and statues we have seen in other parts of Thailand.

Having had enough culture, we headed far south to join other tourists enjoying the white, sandy beaches of Thailand. We boarded an overnight bus packed with backpacker travelers heading for the east coast beaches (where there was rain, but much partying). Fortunately, we chose to stay on the west coast and had beautiful weather for our Christmas on the beaches of Thailand. Christmas Day we treated our-selves to a full day of snorkeling and cruising around the beautiful islands near Ao Nang where we stayed. We sailed for ninety minutes before jumping into the water to snorkel off Bamboo Island. We then boarded small boats to that island where we swam, dried off on the beach and had a wonderful lunch on the grounds of a beautiful national park. We cruised for another hour (interrupted by a couple of stops to fix the broken boat engine) to another snorkeling spot and then boarded a "rescue" speedboat for a return to Ao Nang. We feasted that night on local seafood at a restaurant overlooking the bay. It was a much more relaxing Christmas than last year on the Inca Trail in Peru! The next day Jennifer kayaked through limestone caves on a nearby river, enjoying the beautiful scenery.

We spent December 27 flying from Thailand to Australia. We arrived in Melbourne at 6 AM on the morning of December 28 and pro-ceeded through the strict Australia customs. Australia and New Zealand are extremely cautious about the foot-and-mouth disease plaguing Great Britain and wanted to know where we had been in the last three months, so we told them—India, Nepal, Thailand, Laos, Vietnam and Cambodia. Well, that raised some red flags! We took our luggage through the "red zone" and once there, were asked to produce all of our footwear. The inspector took all our shoes to be disinfected. We sat for ten minutes in our stocking feet waiting for our clean shoes to arrive. The hiking boots we were wearing were fine, but each pair of sandals was in its own plastic bag and completely soaked with whatever disinfectant they used. With that little ordeal behind us, we found our way to our friend's apartment in the city. One of our fellow passengers from the Halong Bay cruise graciously lent us her flat for our short time in Melbourne, as she was away at the beach. (We were only in Melbourne for twenty-seven hours before flying off to New Zealand; we will be back in March for a much longer stay.)

We instantly became big fans of Melbourne—a big yet personable city near the southeastern coast of Australia. We hear Melbourne has more of a European flavor to it than other Australian cities. In Melbourne, we spent the day with a former colleague of Jennifer's (who lives in Seattle) and her boyfriend (who lives in Melbourne). We wandered around various parts of the city, and took a short boat ride to the Williamstown area of Melbourne. From Williamstown we had a great view of the whole city, and enjoyed ice cream and fish and chips! Apparently the ozone layer is almost non-existent over much of Australia, and we believe it. We ended up sunburned even though we are tan from over one year in continuous summer and wore sunhats.

The next morning we flew to Auckland, New Zealand, the country's largest city. New Zealand is comprised of two large islands known as the "North Island" and the "South Island" and many tiny islands around the coast. The total land area is about the size of Colorado. Approximately 3.8 million people live in New Zealand, of which eighty percent are of European descent, ten percent Maori (the native indigenous people), and the rest Pacific Islander and Asian. New Zealanders are commonly referred to as "Kiwis." Because of its physical distance from most other countries, New Zealand depends highly on exports to keep competitive economically.

A friend from our Egypt/Jordan trip met us at the Auckland airport. We stayed with her and her husband for several days at their lovely home in the hills near Auckland. On New Year's Eve, we wandered into downtown Auckland to have a look at art galleries and found most of them closed. (We did end up seeing lots of great art at the contemporary art museum.) Since Kiwis have January 1 and 2 off as a public holiday and Christmas and New Year fall in the middle of their summer, most head for a beach somewhere in the country for a two- or three-week holiday and large cities like Auckland are very quiet. We also wandered around the waterfront area to see the large sheds where the different America's Cup racing boats are constructed. New Zealand won the last two America's Cup races, so the next race takes place here. The last race was in 2000 and the next challenge will be in 2003. Millions of dollars are invested to construct and race these boats as teams from many different countries come to compete.

On January 2, we boarded a ferry in Auckland for a short thirty-minute ride to nearby Waiheke Island, visiting another friend from our Egypt/Jordan trip and her family, who were vacationing on the island. We spent a wonderful twenty-four hours on the island where we swam in the ocean, relaxed on a deck overlooking spectacular scenery, and enjoyed delicious barbecued food. One thing we noticed about the Kiwis is that they love to barbecue. They will barbecue any food, even their breakfast! We have learned many delicious new ways to cook food in our short stay here.

After our short visit in Auckland, we flew early on January 4 to

Christchurch, the third largest city in New Zealand and the largest city on the South Island, and picked up our new touring vehicle—a campervan! Campervanning is a common way to tour New Zealand, and since we have not traveled this way before, we decided to "give it a go," as they say in New Zealand. For six weeks, we rented a two-berth campervan, the size of a regular van with a raised ceiling so even Erik can stand upright inside. We have a small refrigerator, sink, two-burner gas stove, and a table that converts into a double bed for sleeping at night. The campervan came fully equipped with bedding, towels, dishes and cookware. Like England, Australia, India, Nepal, Thailand, Malaysia, Singapore, and sub-Saharan Africa, New Zealand drives on the "left-hand side" of the road. It took about an hour before Erik, our primary driver, was comfortable operating the manual gearshift with his left hand and driving on the left side. The best part is we have plenty of storage space and have unpacked our luggage for the first time in months. We are definitely enjoying this type of travel!

After stocking up on food supplies (our first joint grocery shopping experience in fourteen months of marriage), we set off south down the east coast of the South Island. The scenery in New Zealand is stunning. We have mountains in sight inland and beautiful coastal scenery on the other side. We stopped at Moeraki Beach where about thirty large naturally-created, spherical boulders sit on the beach in various states of decay. Millions of years ago under the sea, calcium and carbonate deposits hardened around a small organic object, similar to how pearls are created. These deposits grew for four million years until they reached 6.5 feet (2 meters) in diameter and resembled a large marble. Over time the exterior shell cracked and filled in with a crystallized substance, so the boulders are solid with rough veins running through them. As the ancient seabed is eroded away, these large boulders are unearthed, exposed to the elements and break into large pieces along the lines of the crystallized veins.

For the last few days we have been in Dunedin, the second largest city on the South Island with a population of 190,000. Last Sunday afternoon we rode a train up the Taieri River gorge through beautiful, rugged scenery. The track gradually ascends up the wide gorge along one side for 28.5 miles (46 kilometers). The engineers blasted through rock, carved tight tunnels, and traversed deep depressions to build the railroad. Since it stopped raining that morning, we had a lovely ride.

Yesterday we toured the nearby Otago Peninsula, home to New Zealand's only castle and two bird sanctuaries—one for nesting royal

Rocks at Moeraki Beach,
New Zealand.

albatross and one for yellow-eyed penguins. We explored Larnach Castle, built by banker and politician William Larnach in the early 1870s, and admired the stunning view of the rolling hills and coastline from the tower at the top. The castle, completely renovated starting in the 1960s, has beautiful gardens and restored original woodwork.

We were fortunate to see nesting royal albatross on land. The royal albatross spends eighty percent of its life at sea, traveling westward completely around Antarctica before returning to New Zealand every other year to breed. A royal albatross can travel up to 311 miles (500 kilometers) in one day. It spends the first year of its life on land, the next five years at sea, and then comes back to land to breed once every two years. When the birds are breeding, the parents take turns spending two or three days on the nest while the other hunts for food. The royal albatross has a wingspan of 10 feet (3 meters) and uses its wings to glide with the wind current. We were fortunate to see one of these beautiful birds in flight while on a wildlife boat cruise around the tip of the peninsula.

The sanctuary for the yellow-eyed penguins is designed carefully to minimize human interaction with the birds. Yellow-eyed penguins, the third largest in the world, stand about 16 inches (41 centimeters) tall. The adults have yellow eyes (hence the name) and a horizontal yellow band that wraps around their head at eye level. Because this particular species is very shy, visitors view the penguins from underground bunkers with an 8-inch (20-centimeter) slot just above ground level. Camouflage-covered trenches connect the viewing bunkers. Because we were in bunkers, we stood 6 inches (15 centimeters) from two young chicks and 6 feet (1.8 meters) from an adult.

From here we travel along the south coast to the west coast of the South Island, and then head north. We have another three weeks on this island and two weeks on the North Island before we head back to Australia in mid-February.

Love, Jennifer & Erik

Dunedin to Auckland, New Zealand
January 8 to February 14, 2002

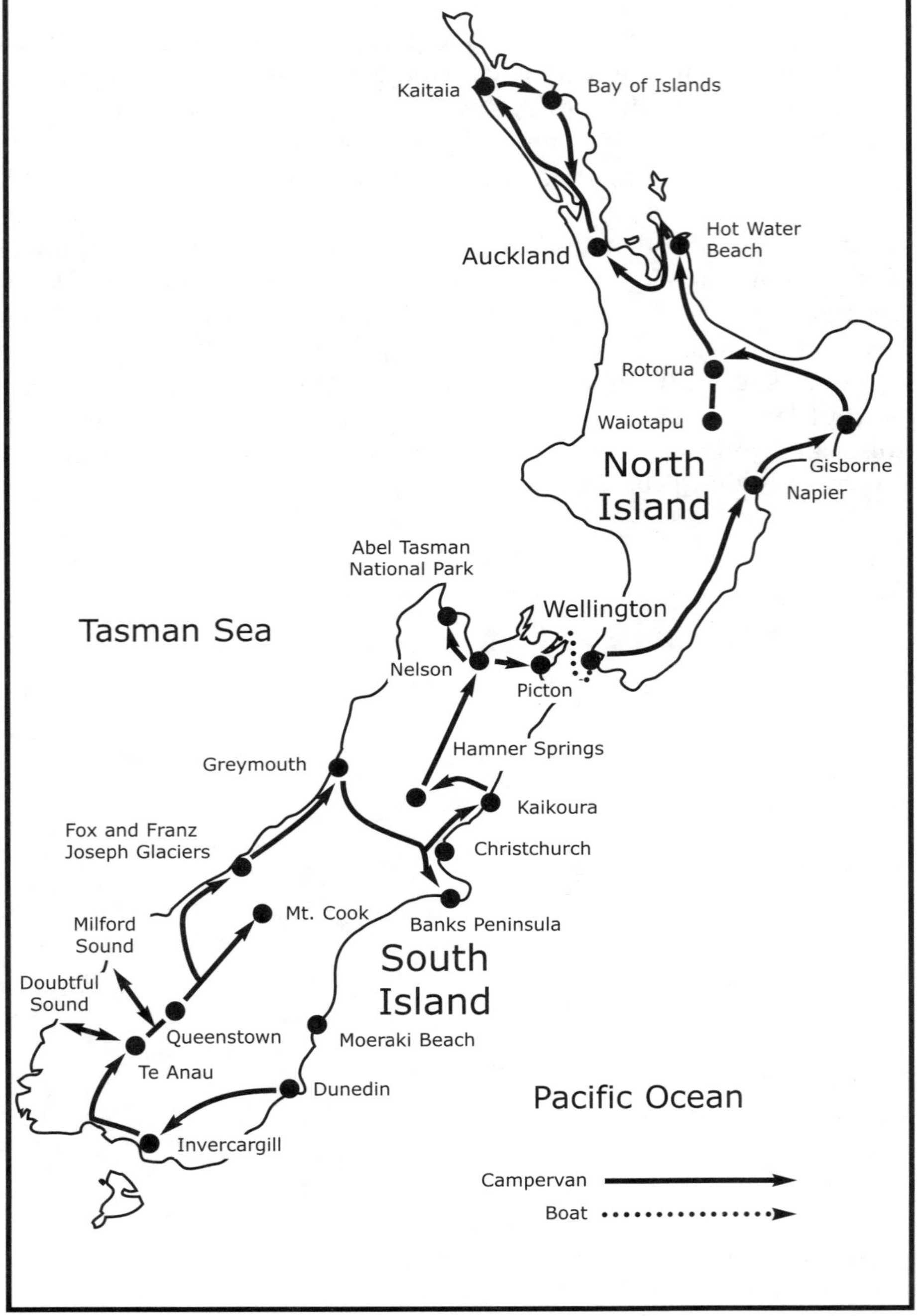

Kaitaia

Bay of Islands

Auckland

Hot Water
Beach

Rotorua

Waiotapu

**North
Island**

Gisborne

Napier

Wellington

Tasman Sea

Abel Tasman
National Park

Nelson

Picton

Hamner Springs

Greymouth

Kaikoura

Christchurch

Fox and Franz
Joseph Glaciers

Mt. Cook

Banks Peninsula

Milford
Sound

**South
Island**

Doubtful
Sound

Queenstown

Moeraki Beach

Te Anau

Dunedin

Pacific Ocean

Invercargill

Campervan

Boat

16

Auckland, New Zealand
Thursday, February 14, 2002

Dear friends and family,

Since we last wrote, we drove all over the South and North Islands of New Zealand. We found the scenery altered every thirty or so miles (50 or so kilometers), with the scenery in the South Island of New Zealand being some of the most stunning either of us has ever seen. In New Zealand we drove past numerous sheep pastures, dairy farms, and the occasional deer farm set in wide, glacier-carved river valleys with mountain ranges rising in the distance. We also passed through wonderful forested areas, hugged twisting mountain pass roads, and drove through active geothermal areas and along beautiful coastline.

From Dunedin, we headed southwest through rolling hills with many grazing sheep to Invercargill, a quiet town on the south coast of the South Island. Invercargill is the southernmost city in New Zealand. We drove along the rugged, rocky coastline stopping to visit a 180 million-year-old, fossilized forest at Curio Bay (where we saw petrified tree trunks on the beach) and walk across sheep pastures to visit Slope Point, the southernmost point of land of the South Island. This was the furthest "south" we have ever been on planet Earth! The scenery was quite stunning, although you are never quite sure what is ahead of you on the road. At one point, we rounded a corner to see two dogs and a farmer in a small tractor herding sheep from one pasture to another. Sheep filled the road as far as the eye could see! It was fascinating to watch the dogs herd the sheep, watch the odd oncoming car slowly weave its way through the sheep, and drive into this sea of sheep ourselves.

We headed north along the eastern side of the area known as Fiordland. This area in the southwest corner of the South Island consists of fourteen different fiords. We explored two—Doubtful Sound and Milford Sound. Milford Sound was the most dramatic—the equi-

Erik at the southernmost point of our trip, Slope Point, New Zealand.

valent of a Yosemite Valley you explore by boat (we chose a three-hour tour on a large sailing ship). Milford Sound is probably the single-most "must see" sight of the South Island. Milford Sound is 13.6 miles (22 kilometers) long with sheer peaks rising out of the water. We happened upon a rare clear day (the annual rainfall in this area is 18 feet (5.5 meters)); in fact the locals feared a drought since it had not rained in three days! The scenery is simply jaw-dropping with snow-capped mountains just behind the rocky peaks lining the sound. We even saw a penguin that had arrived early for the February breeding season.

Milford Sound is very different from the less touristy, larger Doubtful Sound. It takes a boat ride across a lake and a bus ride over a pass to reach Doubtful Sound. But the trip is well worth it to tour this 24.8-mile- (40-kilometer-) long sound with tree-lined hills. Every now and again a large bare spot on the hills or an area of lower growth indicates where a tree slide occurred and the large trees have not yet taken over. The large pine trees cling to the rocky sides of the sound in very little soil, so water rushing down the hillsides periodically uproots them and takes out a large section of plant life.

In the area, we also visited the "glow worm caves" along Lake Te Anau. New Zealand is full of these natural wonders. Water seeping down between the rocks erodes the limestone and forms an underground cave complex with a flowing river, underground waterfalls and rapids. We walked along platforms over the rushing underground river and traveled by flat-bottomed square boats pulled along by over-head rope to a dark grotto lit by glow worms. It was like staring up at the Milky Way on a clear moonless night! The glow worms, larvae of a small fly, feed on small insects attracted to the glowing blue light of a chemical reaction in their stomachs. The larvae can turn the light on and off and the hungrier the larvae, the brighter the glow, so the "stars" had different levels of intensity. It was an incredible and magical sight!

From Te Anau we traveled north through Queenstown to Mt. Cook. Queenstown is a very popular, quaint tourist town on the shores of a lake surrounded by mountains and home to many high adrenaline sports (it is where bungee jumping was invented). We enjoyed a won-derful three-hour hike to the base of the Hooker Glacier at the bottom of Mt. Cook. Mt. Cook is the tallest peak in New Zealand and stands 12,316 feet (3,754 meters) high. We hiked through fields surrounded by glacier-topped mountains and across two swing bridges to the lake at the base of Hooker Glacier. We had a lovely, clear day and periodi-cally heard glaciers breaking off in the distance. We were almost back to the trailhead when we heard the distinctive sounds of Indian music. At first we thought a group of Indian tourists were carrying a stereo with them as they hiked, but instead we walked into a crew of a dozen people filming an Indian movie! Indian movies, known as "Bollywood" films, are very distinctive and each have the exact same format—basically a long series of "music videos" with a man and a woman embracing and singing to each other with fantastic scenery (in this case the glaciers) behind them.

The South Island of New Zealand is sparsely populated and has lit-tle traffic outside of the main cities. Many of the bridges are one-lane since usually only one car is in an area at a time. (We only waited for other traffic about one out of every twenty one-lane bridges we crossed). We quickly learned to read the right-of-way signs: a small red arrow pointing up and a large black arrow pointing down means to "give way" to the oncoming traffic; a large black arrow pointing up and a small red arrow pointing down means they must give way to you. Our favorite bridge was the 1.5-mile- (2.5-kilometer-) long one heading to the glaciers with three turn out bays where you could give way to cars headed toward you. We crossed a handful of single-lane bridges that are also railway bridges with some apprehension, and were relieved to reach the other side with no trains coming toward us!

New Zealand is a perfect country for the adventurous. We passed up the numerous opportunities to throw ourselves off of bridges (bungee jumping) or out of airplanes (sky diving), jet boat or white-water raft down rivers, hike glaciers, kayak, or inner-tube through dark caves. We could even go wine tasting via jet boats! We contented ourselves with driving through the spectacular scenery and enjoying an occasional walk to break up the driving. One of our favorite walks was at Ship Creek on our way to Fox Glacier. Despite contending with the numerous biting sand flies, this area had two fascinating short walks. (Sand flies are small gnat-like insects that bite without too much notice, with the bite itching incessantly for twenty-four to sev-enty-two hours afterward. Invariably we felt bites one day, and had a whole new set of itches a day later!)

Jennifer with our campervan near Mt. Cook in New Zealand.

We walked along the dunes through wind-stunted forest. The trees stood only about 6 feet (1.8 meters) high along the dune, and the trail wound through lush vegetation inland. Once we arrived in the forested part of the track, the sand flies left us alone. We also explored a swampy rainforest said to resemble swamp forests that existed 100 million years ago! We marveled at the tall fern trees and the lush greenery drooping with moss.

We spent two rainy days exploring the Fox and Franz Joseph Glaciers. These glaciers sit on the western side of the Mt. Cook range and terminate just 984 feet (300 meters) above sea level. Because that side of the mountains is a temperate rainforest, the glaciers receive enormous amounts of water and are presently growing. We took an hour-long hike along the glacier moraine to the base of the Fox Glacier. Glaciers are a very thick river of ice that slowly moves down a mountainside, grinding away at the rock underneath. Usually water runs underneath the surface of the glacier, and that water empties into a lake or river. The moraine is the ground up dirt and rocks left when a glacier recedes.

In areas without landslides, trees and other vegetation have started to grow, so we walked over bare rocky areas and through new forest on our way to the glacier face. The face of Fox Glacier is an impressive wall about 100 feet (30 meters) high of compacted ice with large cracks running through it. The ice looks dirty from the ground up rock.

From the glaciers we drove up the coast to Greymouth and used that town to explore the Punakaiki pancake rocks. On our way to the pancake rocks, we passed a cordoned-off police area that was part of a murder investigation. We knew all about this "police action" from the radio news as we did about the derailed train we saw on the side of the road and other important New Zealand news. Erik is a news-junkie so we listened to the hourly radio newscast just about every waking hour in our one and one-half months in New Zealand (only a little exaggerated).

Since New Zealand has a small population, the national news reports every car fatality, murder, drowning, and so on in the country. Just about every day without fail, we heard about someone drowning, which gave the impression more people drown in New Zealand than anywhere else in the world. World news on New Zealand radio and television is not very extensive (similar to the United States). The hourly news might include one, maybe two world news stories (many times about Australia), so we relied on the Internet and newspapers to keep up to date with the never-ending fighting in Israel and the war on terrorism.

Weather reports in New Zealand are also important since the weather changes quite frequently. We arrived during an unusually wet summer. For the most part, we missed the majority of the severe weather but did spend a few eight-hour days driving on curvy roads in the rain. We seemed to be just ahead of some major flood, as we would hear news reports about different highways closed due to torrential flooding a couple of days after we drove on those roads. New Zealand weather terminology differs from what we hear in America. We soon discovered the word "fine" actually meant "sunny," and the weather forecasters used the word "odd" often as in "the odd light shower" or "the odd heavy shower, then turning fine" or "Auckland mainly fine, Christchurch mainly fine." Once we counted the word "fine" being used around twelve times in a two-minute forecast for the country. But back to the pancake rocks...

The pancake rocks are a unique natural formation consisting of layers of compressed ancient seabed thrust out of the water millions of years ago. These mostly limestone rock formations look like stacks of Swedish pancakes (according to Erik who has much experience eating them). The continual tidal action of the Tasman Sea against the rocks erodes them at varying rates, resulting in several channels and small holes for the ocean water to spray up in dramatic fashion. We visited the rocks at high tide on a calm day, so the show was not at its spectacular best. We hear the blowholes are quite impressive during a raging storm.

From Greymouth we drove back across the South Island over the very beautiful Arthur's Pass to explore more of Christchurch and take in a whale watching adventure up the coast. We spent a couple of days visiting Banks Peninsula (just east of Christchurch) and the fabulous International Antarctic Center. Christchurch is the airport many countries use to support their research bases on Antarctica. For example, across the street from the center was the "United States Antarctic Program" that houses many U.S. Air Force transport planes and personnel. The Antarctic center includes a fabulous exhibit showing how the New Zealand researchers live year-round on the continent, a small room where you can experience what a spring day in Antarctica feels like, and videos and information on the animal life. We especially enjoyed the videos showing the penguin antics. All in all, it was a fun and informative place.

We also visited a wildlife park on our way north and saw live kiwi birds for the first time. Kiwis are about the size of a chicken with brown hair-like feathers. In an amazing feat, a female kiwi lays an egg one-fourth her size and one-fifth her body weight! Kiwis are nocturnal and, being flightless, have a hard time defending themselves against the introduced animals in New Zealand. The park we visited had a wonderful nocturnal house where the birds were active, walking along the ground with their long, pointed beaks.

Sticking with the wildlife theme, we stopped in the small town of Kaikoura to go whale watching. We sailed 6.6-foot- (2-meter-) high ocean swells on a catamaran outfitted with sonar devices and satellite navigation equipment to assist in the location and tracking of the whales. Our guide sat at the front of the boat behind a laptop computer with a flat screen monitor above him that mapped our location and all the recent whale sightings. All of this equipment permitted us to see five sperm whales within an hour or so. Sperm whales dive to eat for about forty-five minutes at a time, resurface at about the same point they dove, swim around for about fifteen minutes releasing toxins that built up in their blood during their dive and taking in oxygen before their next feeding dive. The dive is the best part, since you only see about a fifth of the whale as it swims around releasing toxins, but as it dives it comes out of the water a little more and then you see the tail disappearing under the water—very cool!

Having had our fill of wildlife for the time being, we headed back across the South Island stopping at a couple of hot springs (Erik's favorite places), including the famous Hamner Springs hot pools. Hamner Springs is a spa town surrounded by mountains with wonderful natural and more modern hot pools. Tourists have visited this beautiful area since the 1860s. We then headed north to Nelson, a wonderful town surrounded by wineries and wonderful galleries. We celebrated Jennifer's 38th birthday with a quiet seafood dinner overlooking the bay. Dinner was quite a treat since we usually cooked in the campervan and this was our first dinner in a sit-down restaurant since early January. (Mind you, up until New Zealand we had eaten nearly every meal for the last fourteen months in a restaurant, so cooking in the campervan was a treat!)

We drove north from Nelson to Kaiteriteri, a town near the Abel Tasman National Park. We stayed for four nights at a campervan park with over 400 powered sites on the edge of a beautiful beach. Many New Zealanders vacation/holiday by traveling to a campervan park and setting up their home away from home. Most people at the Kaiteriteri Park lived in Christchurch (an eight-hour drive away) and stayed for a fortnight ("two weeks" for those who speak American-English). We visited during one of the last big weekends before school started; so many families were enjoying the sunny weather and wonderful national park environs.

What surprised us was the extent people moved their homes to this park. Most people had a camper they towed behind their car, and then a tent area that expanded from the camper in roughly the same dimensions as the camper. Other people just set up huge tents roughly 20 feet by 15 feet (6 meters by 4.6 meters) and filled it up with the essentials from home—full-size refrigerators, book shelves, large television sets, and dining-room size tables and chairs. We inquired at reception about the rental of the refrigerators and were told many families return annually for two weeks, so they buy a refrigerator and leave it in storage at the park when they are not using it.

Abel Tasman is New Zealand's smallest national park, but has the highest number of visitors. New Zealand has numerous three- to five-day walking tracks, and one of them is in this park. The Abel Tasman Coastal Track is a well-maintained 18-inch- (46-centimeter-) wide track that climbs and dips in some places, but mostly winds along the hillside with forest on one side and periodic views of blue water and

Jennifer hiking in Abel Tasman National Park, New Zealand.

golden beaches on the other. We enjoyed parts of this track on two separate day trips. Much of Abel Tasman is a forest with a coastline of alternating golden beaches and rocky outcrops. During low tide over ninety different beaches dot the shore. The best access to the park is via "water taxis" which are speed boats that drop you off near a beach and then you wade to the beach. Anything and everything is carried on these boats—at one point Jennifer had to crawl under several kayaks loaded on a water taxi when she boarded at the end of a walk!

From Abel Tasman we headed back through the lovely town of Nelson to Picton at the northeastern side of the South Island. Picton, located at the edge of the Queen Charlotte Sound, is the southern port for the ferry to the North Island. The day before we left the South Island, we went wine tasting in and around the city of Blenheim. New Zealand has fabulous wines and many small wineries in various pockets of both islands. These wines were previously unknown to us since New Zealand exports its wines mainly to Australia, the United Kingdom and Europe. The Marlborough area near Blenheim and Picton is known for its sauvignon blancs. Much to our surprise, these wines are fruitier and more robust than California sauvignon blancs, and the chardonnays of the region are generally not oaky and are fruitier than the ones we are used to from California. We loved tasting these wonderful wines.

On January 29, we took a three-hour vehicle ferry across the Cook Straits to Wellington, New Zealand's capital and second largest city. The first hour we traveled through the narrow, tree-lined Queen Charlotte Sound, then an hour across the rough, open strait, and the final hour through the Wellington Harbor. In Wellington we had dinner with fellow travelers from our South America trip and explored the beautiful botanical gardens. We took the short cable car/trolley ride to the top of the gardens and wandered back to town admiring the flora and breathtaking views over the city and harbor. Interestingly, the gardens incorporate some of the first cemeteries of Wellington, so we found ourselves ambling past old grave markers during this beautiful walk. We also spent the good part of a day in the national museum called Te Papa. The museum is well-designed architecturally and has fabulous exhibits. We learned about New Zealand's geology, ecological systems, explored the history and culture of the Maoris who discovered New Zealand around 1000 AD, and saw exhibits about the European settlement that started around 1840.

The highlight of our Wellington visit was seeing "Fellowship of the

Ring." As you may or may not know, the landscapes in the Lord of the Rings trilogies were filmed in New Zealand. Many Kiwis were excited a Kiwi film was sweeping the globe in popularity. We planned to see this movie at some point and decided the best place to see it was at the Embassy Theatre in downtown Wellington where the movie made its worldwide premiere. The theater was still decked out with statues of different characters from the movie. When driving around the North Island after seeing the movie, we frequently commented how the scenery looked like what we saw in that movie.

New Zealand has many international tourists traveling around like us. We met mainly Dutch, Germans, Canadians, Japanese and Australians. The first couple of times we met Canadians we asked where in "the States" they were from. They inevitably said they were Canadians. Later when we heard people with nearly the same accent as us, we could not assume they were from the United States (unless we clearly heard a Texan or Southern accent). The same goes with the Australian tourist in New Zealand. We could not tell whether they were from New Zealand or Australia (as so many Kiwis tour their own country). Growing up in the United States, it was hard for us to imagine we might have an "accent" to other people. One day when we were in the supermarket checkout line, the clerk said, "Love your accent, where are you from?" We really got a kick out of that comment!

From Wellington we drove northeast to the town of Napier. Napier sits in the middle of Hawke's Bay, another famous New Zealand wine region. However the town is best known for its art deco architecture. Geologically, New Zealand sits where the Pacific Plate is sliding underneath the Indo-Australian Plate, so the North Island has a lot of volcanic and earthquake activity. One such earthquake (measuring 7.9 on the Richter scale) occurred in Napier and the surrounding area in 1931. The earthquake was so large it pushed a 25-square-mile (40-square-kilometer) chunk of seabed above sea level! The subsequent rebuilding of Napier left one of the largest concentrations of art deco architecture anywhere on the planet. We both enjoyed strolling along the main shopping streets of town admiring the unique facades.

We headed north along Hawke's Bay to the seaside town of Gisborne (where we found out that Erik's sister gave birth to twin boys on Jan. 31), then west to the geothermal area near Rotorua. We took a Monday afternoon off to watch the Super Bowl, the championship game for American football. Most Americans tune in to see the game, pageantry of the half-time show and new multi-million dollar television commercials that debut. Since New Zealand is nineteen hours ahead of where the game was being played (on a Sunday evening in New Orleans this year), we watched it live on a Monday afternoon in New Zealand! As a side note, to figure out what time it was in California from New Zealand, we would add three hours and take away one day.

After our American sporting fix, we visited the remains of a town buried by a volcanic eruption in 1886 AD that covered 580 square miles (1,500 square kilometers) in mud and ash. The area still has diverse geothermal activity, and we especially enjoyed visiting Waiotapu to see the bubbling mud, hissing fumaroles and the beautiful champagne pool. This very large pool, covering approximately one acre, is the color of ginger-ale and bubbles just like a glass of champagne. Erik also enjoyed thermal pools at each campsite in the area; but the best thermal water experience was further north on the popular Coromandel Peninsula east of Auckland.

One of the most popular sites in the North Island, and definitely on the Coromandel, is "Hot Water Beach." We stayed overnight near the beach to experience it fully. For the two hours before and after low tide, dozens and dozens of people, with shovels in hand, head out to a small section of beach to create their own thermal pool. Low tide exposes a particular section of beach with boiling hot thermal springs just under the sand, so when you dig a hole in the sand, it fills up with hot water. People usually spend twenty to forty minutes digging their hole (big enough for several people to lay down in it). We first tried this around 10 PM, when it was quite dark out. Some people who were leaving graciously let us use their hot water holes. It was an amazing experience to lay down in shallow hot water looking up at the cosmos watching satellites pass overhead and the odd shooting star—the perfect way to end the day! We tried it again the next morning but had a difficult time finding a spot that wasn't too hot or too cold. Suddenly most of the people lying in the hot pools jumped up and ran toward the beach to watch about two dozen dolphins swimming and jumping in the shallow surf, a spectacular sight!

Having thoroughly enjoyed Hot Water Beach, we drove around the remainder of the Coromandel Peninsula, through Auckland, and north to the top of the North Island. We drove along the west coast through the wonderful Kauri forests. The Kauri tree is a large conifer found only in the North Island of New Zealand that grows to a height of 100 feet (30 meters) and can live for up to 2,000 years. The root sys-

Jennifer enjoying Hot Water Beach, New Zealand.

tem and grain of Kauri trees is beautifully patterned. In the late nine-teenth and early twentieth centuries, Kauri trees were extensively logged for their beautiful and hard timber and tapped for their resin to make varnish. Few of the very old trees survived the logging era, although we did see one tall Kauri tree reputed to be 1,400 years old. Kauri trees have existed for tens of thousands of years and many ancient trees can be found preserved in swamps in the Northland. That wood is used today to make Kauri wood products. In one store, an internal staircase was carved inside the tree trunk of an 8-foot- (2.4-meter-) wide ancient Kauri tree found in a swamp.

To see these lovely trees, we traveled on the scenic secondary roads. At one point we had to cross a river via ferry. The ferry crossed once an hour on the hour. We neared the ferry landing as the clock approached 6 PM. At 5:59 PM, we headed down the last hill to see the ferry with one place left. We drove onto the ferry just as the gate closed behind us. The ferry started across the river before we even had a chance to turn off the engine and pay for our crossing.

We also toured the top of the North Island to see where the Tasman Sea meets the South Pacific Ocean, but we could hardly see the light-house in the rainy weather. We traveled down Ninety Mile Beach (which is actually 60 miles (96.5 kilometers) long), a hard-packed beach best known for its lack of vegetation and a great road at low tide. Unfortunately for us, the rain continued in the Northland so we did not see the beautiful coastal scenery on the east coast, including the Bay of Islands.

Tomorrow we fly to Australia and spend two weeks in Tasmania visiting a family we met in South America. On March 1, we fly to Alice Springs in the center of Australia where we start an eight-day tour south to Adelaide. We will update you further from Adelaide!

Love, Jennifer & Erik

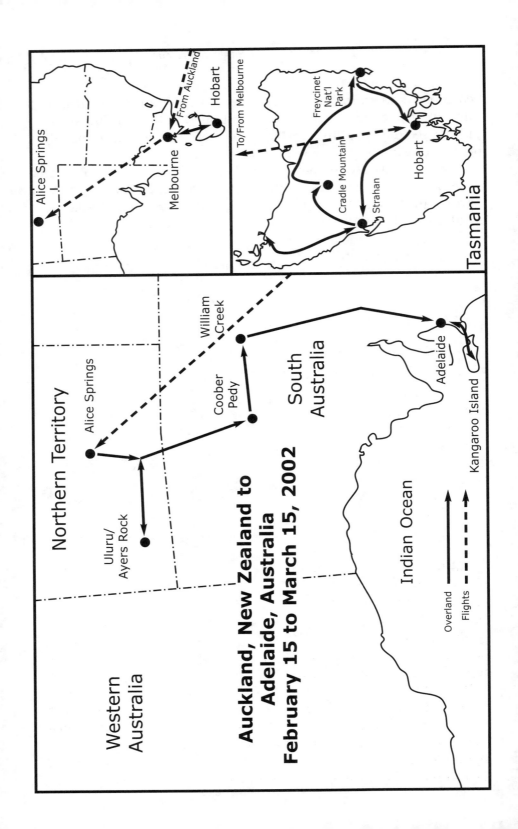

**Auckland, New Zealand to
Adelaide, Australia
February 15 to March 15, 2002**

Northern Territory

Western Australia

South Australia

Indian Ocean

Alice Springs

Uluru/
Ayers Rock

Coober Pedy

William Creek

Adelaide

Kangaroo Island

Overland
Flights

Alice Springs

Melbourne

Hobart

From Auckland

Tasmania

To/From Melbourne

Freycinet Nat'l Park

Cradle Mountain

Strahan

Hobart

17

Adelaide, Australia
Friday, March 15, 2002

Dear friends and family,

On February 15, we departed New Zealand and returned to Australia. Australia is approximately the size of the continental United States with a population of 19.3 million. The Australians are very proud of the two gold medals they won this year at the Winter Olympics in Salt Lake City. Before their two gold medals, Australian winter athletes had only won two bronze medals in their participation in the winter games.

Australia has excellent international news coverage and usually devotes a good ten minutes on the radio to world news each hour. In Australia we were pleasantly surprised to hear some programs from National Public Radio in the United States. One Australian television station devotes twelve hours a day to televising national news from a dozen countries. On Australian television you can also watch some American network news programs from PBS and NBC, and also catch "The Late Show with David Letterman" and the "Today" show.

We flew into Melbourne to change planes and then onto Hobart, Tasmania. We once again passed through the rigid Australian customs since we had still been in third world countries during the past three months. The "red zone" line zigzagged its way through the baggage claim area. It looked as if passengers from ten flights originating in Asia also waited in line. Jennifer stood in line even before we had any of our bags, as the line tripled in length five minutes after we arrived.

With little time to spare to catch our flight to Hobart, we unpacked our bags in front of the inspector showing him our "wood products" (handles on Erik's painting tools, a back massager, and stand for an art piece) and our shoes. The inspector saw dirt on the bottom of Jennifer's sandals and wanted to disinfect them. Jennifer had bought the sandals in New Delhi, India and they were already in a sorry state after the first time the Australian customs officials disinfected them (it took several days for the leather to dry). We told the official to just throw them away because we were about to miss our flight and disinfecting them again would destroy them altogether. The surprised inspector tried to convince us to keep them and have them disinfected, but we left the sandals and headed for our plane.

We barely caught our flight to Australia's southernmost state, an island state known for its rugged beauty and the "Tasmanian devil." Tasmania is slightly larger than West Virginia with a population of 473,000. Tasmania had a land link to Australia until approximately 13,000 years ago when the melting of the last Ice Age covered that link. We flew into Hobart, the capital and largest city of Tasmania located on the southeast coast. The father of the Tasmanian family we met on our South American tour and another fellow South American traveler from London (whom we also saw in London back in August) met us at the airport. We spent a couple days with the rest of the family in Hobart before the four of us took a week-long road trip of the state.

Before we explored the rest of Tasmania, we explored some of the convict history. In the late eighteenth century, Great Britain emptied her prisons by transporting her convicts to her colonies. Once the American colonies became independent, Great Britain needed another place to send her convicts. The relatively empty Australia seemed the perfect place; far enough so the convicts would probably never come back to England. The first convict transport ships arrived in what is now Sydney in 1788. Needing a place to punish transported convicts that committed further offenses in Australia, Tasmania became the penal colony for Australia. Penal settlements operated on an island in Macquarie Harbor from 1821 to 1833 and at Port Arthur from 1830 to 1877. (The policy of transporting convicts from Great Britain ended in 1853 and led to the gradual decline of convicts at Port Arthur.) In Tasmania, convict forced labor cut down timber, mined coal, built ships, quarried stone, and constructed numerous bridges, homes and government buildings, including those at Port Arthur.

Port Arthur was selected as a penal settlement due to its remoteness. A narrow strip of land called Eaglehawk Neck links Port Arthur, located southeast of Hobart at the end of a peninsula, to the main island. To prevent the prisoners from escaping, a 33-foot (10-meter) ditch was dug across Eaglehawk Neck and vicious dogs chained in close intervals to guard the land link. Today Port Arthur is a grassy area with the remains of the penitentiary, church, hospital, and military barracks. Full reconstructions of a "test" model prison (where prisoners could make no noise and never saw any other human being), a two-story commandant's house, a junior medical officer's house and a house for the clergy are also on the site. In 1996, a crazed gunman killed thirty-five people in and around the Port Arthur site before surrendering. A memorial reflecting pool and the stone foundation of the cafeteria where many victims were killed honor the dead.

We drove from Hobart over to the west coast, a four-hour drive away. Along the way we stopped to see a large pipeline for the transport of water made of wood, one of the few of its type left in the world. We stopped in Strahan and took a half-day boat cruise up the Macquarie Harbor and Gordon River to see the Huon pine and the remains on Sarah Island where they housed the convicts. One of the most famous trees in Tasmania is the Huon pine, a prized tree for shipbuilding because a substance in its bark prevents it from rotting in water. The penal settlement on Sarah Island was created to log the pine. After the settlement was abandoned, loggers followed and jeopardized these trees. The remaining forests are now part of a vast world heritage site created to preserve these beautiful and slow-growing trees. A Huon pine can grow for 4,000 years, and a 500-year-old tree is about 19 inches (50 centimeters) in diameter.

We traveled on the Wild Way Highway, a gravel two-lane (some-

The port at Strahan, Tasmania.

times one-lane) road through beautiful forests, to the northwest coast. We passed only four cars in two hours on the isolated road. While driving we saw a few Tasmanian devils. (At first we thought we saw a black cat, but later realized that it was indeed the Tasmanian devil.) These fierce creatures are about the size of a large cat with a 2-inch (6-centimeter) snout and very strong jaws/teeth. These scavengers eat road kill which can transform them into road kill themselves.

At a small, private wildlife park, we watched six Tassie devils at feeding time. When devils eat, they eat as fast as possible and eat everything (meat, bone, fur, and so on) which makes for very humorous observation. At one point, four of the six devils pulled simultaneously on one large piece of meat. They growled loudly and chased the others once one of the devils broke free with a piece of meat. Their pen had a small covered area where the devils would hide. When three or more of these little creatures were under there, they fought ferociously and nearly knocked the entire structure over! The Warner Brothers cartoon of the Tasmanian devil is not too far off the actual behavior, except the live animals do not spin around like a tornado. Also at the wildlife park, we saw numerous wallabies and kangaroos jumping around, and a couple koala bears hanging out on trees.

From the west coast we traveled toward the center of the state to Cradle Mountain. Unfortunately it rained for most of our visit, so we walked around a beautiful lake with low clouds blanketing the nearby hills. The weather cleared up for our hike a couple days later in Freycinet National Park on the east coast of Tasmania. We climbed over beautiful, pink granite rocks to lookout over Wineglass Bay with its blue water and white sandy beach. Tasmania can experience four types of weather in one day (cold, rainy, hot and sunny), and that creates diverse forests in a small area. At times on the west coast we were in temperate rainforest, then less dense vegetation near Cradle Mountain. In Freycinet National Park we saw five different eco-systems during a four-hour hike!

On March 1, we flew from Hobart, Tasmania to Alice Springs in the center of mainland Australia. Alice Springs is the largest town for 620 miles (1,000 kilometers) in any direction. We stayed here overnight to meet our tour group for an eight-day overland trip through the Outback to Adelaide. In Australia, many companies operate one-way tours between major cities and we opted to travel this way much of the time. The transportation of choice is a twenty-one-passenger van with a trailer for luggage attached to the back. We found the various driver/guides very knowledgeable and enjoyed stopping at unique sights off the beaten track and going for short walks in the bush. We also enjoyed meeting fellow travelers from all over the globe, including France, England, Japan, Korea, and Denmark.

Alice Springs is a unique Australian town as it sits in the part of the country with the highest proportion of Aborigines. The Aboriginal people are perhaps the world's oldest, most intact culture. They have lived on the Australian continent for about 40,000 years and led an uninterrupted stone-age, nomadic life until the British came to Australia in 1788. When the British landed in Australia, groups of Aborigines lived in every part of the country and had over a thousand languages. Their common unifying belief is the earth is their "mother" and the sun is "father." As the Europeans settled the coastal areas of Australia, Aborigines were gradually pushed into the drier center of the country and deprived of the abundant coastal lands.

The history between the Aborigines and the white European-descended Australians is filled with violence and discrimination. In certain cases, Aborigines were pushed off of cliffs into the ocean, forcibly removed from land, and treated as non-citizens for many years. The clash of cultures produced an attitude that Aborigines needed to be "saved from themselves," as their lifestyle was completely unacceptable to European Australians. It was an affront to predominantly Victorian sensibilities that Aboriginal children did not go to school or wear clothing, and of course, did not practice Christianity. From the 1900s to the 1970s, a governmental policy removed Aboriginal children not of "pure" Aboriginal blood from their families and placed them in orphanages. Thousands of children systematically removed from their families are known as the "stolen generation."

The dramatic difference in the lifestyles of Europeans and Aborigines is obvious in Alice Springs. When walking in the town we noticed many Aboriginal people walking in groups of two to four people, some barefooted, and many sitting in the shade in small groups not doing much. Some Aborigines openly drank alcohol and appeared to be homeless. Unfortunately, many times this is the only image tourists have of Aborigines when visiting Australia. Today, many Aborigines live on large areas of land in the center of the country called reservations and rarely come to town. Australia is working with the Aboriginal communities to balance the clash between lifestyles, preserve the Aboriginal culture, and reverse the effects of various government policies against the Aborigines. There is criticism and debate about the extent of integration and the means to do so.

Having visited both New Zealand and Australia, we noticed a striking difference between the integration of white European settlers and the Maoris or Aborigines. In New Zealand, Maori customs and beliefs permeate modern New Zealand culture and the Maori people are seen all over the country. For example, the national museum in Wellington has a Maori name and an extensive exhibit of Maori culture and traditions, including a full-sized, carved meeting house. Maoris are featured with pride in New Zealand tourism commercials and many white New Zealanders know many Maori words and sayings. In contrast, most Aboriginal beliefs are distinctly separate from modern Australian culture, and the majority of Aborigines keep to themselves in communities in the interior of the country. There is very little tourist access to Aboriginal culture and communities in Australia.

Our first surprise upon leaving Alice Springs was the abundance of vegetation in the center of Australia. While many people think of central Australia as a vast desert, it actually has large areas of semi-arid zones with grass and trees. This scenery was very green during our visit since Alice Springs has had above average rainfall the last two years. We were also surprised by the large number of red-brown rock formations that dot the land. Large tracts of flat land separate these formations since the center of Australia was once a large inland sea. As we traveled further south toward Adelaide, the land became more arid with fewer trees and grass. Trees indicate underground water tables or creeks and streams that form during flash floods.

We were truly amazed while driving in the Outback to turn off the sealed road onto a dirt track, travel about 6.2 miles (10 kilometers) and find a huge lake in the middle of the arid region! These sudden water sources and underground water tables permit cattle ranching in this rugged environment. These cattle ranches are quite large as it takes approximately 3.8 square miles (10 square kilometers) of land to feed one cow. The largest ranch we saw was 11,583 square miles (30,000 square kilometers), or approximately the size of Belgium, and that would only support 3,000 head of cattle!

Our favorite sight on the trip to Adelaide was the monolithic red rock rising out of the desert known as Uluru, or Ayers Rock. This single piece of rock stands 1,142 feet (348 meters) tall and has a circumference of 5.8 miles (9.4 kilometers). Geologists estimate Uluru is buried to a depth of 3.7 miles (6 kilometers), so the visible rock is only six percent of the total rock! While the rock is a monolith, erosion and falling water have created numerous caves and overhangs. Uluru is a sacred site to the Aborigines who used the overhangs for various gatherings and ceremonies. Aborigines believe they communicate with people on the opposite side of the country through similar dreams, and they hold Uluru sacred as the "heart" of their country and an important part of their "dreaming" communications. For a number of years a conflict existed between the Aborigines who wanted to use this site privately for sacred ceremonies and the Australian government who operated the area around the rock as a national park. In 1985, the Australian government returned the national park to the Aborigines, who continue to operate the park for visitors with assistance from government park rangers. We hiked around the rock admiring the caves and overhangs and the waterfall cascading down the vertical sides. Heavy rainfalls in recent weeks caused full streams and pools around the base of the rock and green vegetation. Paintings created during the sacred Aboriginal gatherings are still visible in many overhangs. We especially enjoyed seeing a beautiful sunset and sunrise (with accompanying pancake breakfast on the side of the road) dramatically color the rock.

From Ayers Rock we drove nearly 500 miles (800 kilometers) south to the opal mining capital of the world, Coober Pedy. The drive to

The monolith Uluru in Australia.

Coober Pedy was long, hot and dusty, although we were still on paved roads. The landscape reminded us of driving through the desert in southwest America. Having such a long sealed road is a treat in the Outback. Due to the small population and the long distances in the Outback, few roads are sealed—only those necessary for truck travel or tourists. We passed several "road trains" which are semi trucks with three trailers. Very massive indeed! These long trucks are the main cargo transportation along the north/south and east/west axis of Australia. The road trains tend to travel at night when it is cooler and can reach great speeds, as the roads through the Outback are perfectly straight for hundreds of miles. Unfortunately, these vehicles need plenty of time to stop and the nocturnal kangaroo is a frequent victim of road trains when it crosses the road during its nightly grazing. Our Outback guide told us when he passes a road train coming toward him, he moves over as far as possible to counter the wind turbulence the trucks create when passing.

Coober Pedy is an Aboriginal word meaning "white man's holes," acknowledging one of the unique features of this town—underground buildings. In 1915 opal was discovered in this area and, after World War I, this barren, empty land became a bustling town of several thousand miners (former veterans who learned to dig trenches in France) hoping to strike it rich. Miners are still here today and Coober Pedy is a bustling, dusty town that survives in the harshest of conditions.

Water is the first concern in this barren landscape, so the town has a desalinization facility to provide drinking water. In addition, to cope with the immense heat (daytime temperatures in the summer can reach 122°F (50°C)), most of the population lives underground. (We stayed in an underground bunkhouse that stayed a constant 72°F (22°C).) Underground homes are quite comfortable. Interior walls are coated with a substance to reduce the amount of dust, and former mine shafts provide light to the interior. Today mining is banned in the city limit; so many people now apply to "extend" their underground homes in the unspoken hopes of finding more opal. Many times a house for two people will have ten "bedrooms"!

For large portions of our trip from Coober Pedy to Adelaide, we saw a few poles with original telegraph wire still hanging from them and the remains of train supply stations, old tracks, and abandoned towns that once supported the Old Ghan Railway. The center of Australia was settled in large part to assist communication and train transport. In the nineteenth century, camels from Afghanistan transported goods across the barren center. As communication and the country developed, telegraph stations were set up in the Outback in 1822 and a railway finally linked Alice Springs to Adelaide in 1929. Construction and operation of the railway proved quite difficult because the steam trains needed a reliable supply of fresh water and the tracks frequently washed out during flash floods stranding trains and passengers for weeks on end. The Ghan Railway ceased operating in 1980 when the new railway track moved next to the new sealed highway and standard gauge tracks replaced the narrow gauge ones.

From Coober Pedy we headed east into the Outback toward a tiny town called William Creek. Our guide told us upon our arrival our group of ten would double the population and it would have but for the other two tour groups in town that night! The town is actually just a pub, campground, and a radio transmitter that broadcasts a weak FM signal from Coober Pedy. When you drive about 20 feet (6 meters) outside of town, the signal goes away! This outpost, however, is very important for passersby as there is not much else for nearly 100 miles (160 kilometers). We set up our tents and fought off the pesky flies that wanted to land on our eyes, nose, and mouth looking for moisture. Once the sun set, the flies left, but the mosquitoes hit in full force!

We were relieved to reach Adelaide and leave the tents, dust and flies of the Outback behind us. Adelaide, like most Australian towns, is laid out on a grid pattern so it is easy to find your way around town. Australian cities inevitably have lovely Victorian architecture, many parks, a botanical garden and a river that initially provided drinking water for the settlement.

We happened upon a fascinating exhibit of animals that became extinct in the last 500 years around the world. The exhibition included life-size drawings of animals from specimens gathered before the animals became extinct. In most cases the animals were birds or small mammals that became extinct due to the introduction of foreign animals (mostly rats and cats) from ships and by settlers. It made us wonder about the impact of introduced plants to native flora in various parts of the world.

Adelaide boasts fabulous restaurants and we enjoyed eating delicious Indian and Thai food. The valleys around Adelaide are also home to fantastic wineries and we spent a day tasting at the wineries in the famous Barossa Valley and eating lunch in an old railway diner car. The highlight of our visit to Adelaide, however, was our trip to Kangaroo Island.

Kangaroo Island is a small island (93 miles by 31 miles (150 kilo-meters by 50 kilometers)) with tons of wildlife located a two-hour drive and forty-five minute ferry ride south of Adelaide. We opted for a quick overnight wildlife tour with Daniel's Tours and had a wonderful and fun time. Our guide, Daniel himself, met us at the ferry and drove us ten minutes to a place where a short walk away, wild wallabies hopped around in the dusk eating dinner. So many wallabies surrounded us that if you stood in one place, they hopped right by you.

After watching the wallabies and a beautiful sunset, it was off to a barbecue dinner. We ate kangaroo and marinated shark. Both were incredibly delicious! Kangaroo meat is very healthy, tasty, has almost no fat, and is in ample supply here. After dinner we headed to Daniel's sheep farm for more animal watching.

Wild koala bear in tree,
Kangaroo Island, Australia.

Many Australian animals are active from dusk to dawn, so that is the best time to see them. We saw kangaroos and opossums on the drive to the farm and then climbed a ladder for an eye-level look at a koala bear eating eucalyptus leaves 4 feet (1.2 meters) away! The next morning, we woke up early to see more koalas and kangaroos and fur seals. After exploring wonderful rock formations and eating lunch, we sat on the beach and watched Australian sea lions at play. Unfortunately, the resident fairy penguins (the smallest of the penguins standing only 10 inches (25.4 centimeters) high) were at another island until later in the year. All in all, it was a wonderful place to visit!

Tomorrow we head to Melbourne and then travel up the east coast of Australia to Cairns via Sydney and Brisbane over the next month before we return to the United States at the end of April. We will next catch you up on our adventures from somewhere on the east coast of Australia!

Love, Jennifer & Erik

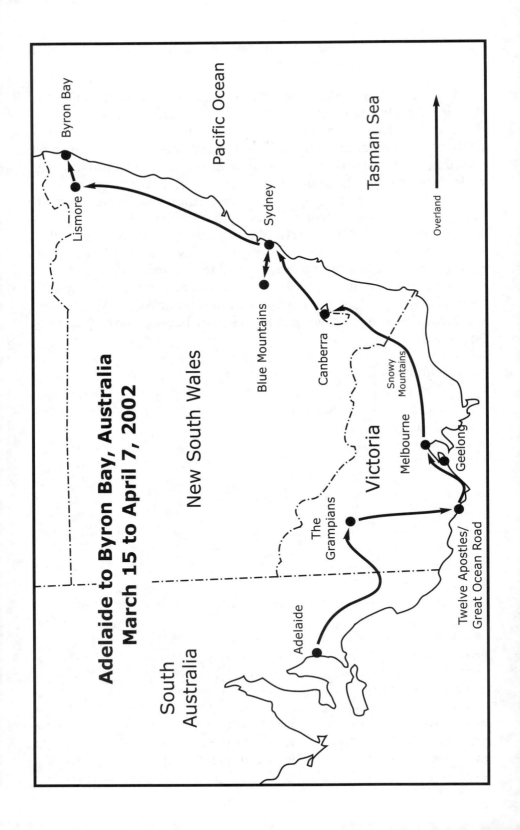

Adelaide to Byron Bay, Australia
March 15 to April 7, 2002

Byron Bay

Lismore

Pacific Ocean

Tasman Sea

Sydney

Overland

Blue Mountains

New South Wales

Canberra

Snowy Mountains

Victoria

Melbourne

Geelong

The Grampians

Twelve Apostles/
Great Ocean Road

Adelaide

South
Australia

18

Byron Bay, Australia
Sunday, April 7, 2002

Dear friends and family,

From Adelaide we took a three-day tour to Australia's second largest city, Melbourne, via the Grampian Mountains and the Great Ocean Road. The Grampians are very old sandstone mountains, approximately 300 million years old, so are quite worn. Today the tallest mountain in the Grampians is 3,832 feet (1,168 meters), with most mountains measuring around 2,625 feet (800 meters). Millions of years ago these mountains stood taller than Mt. Everest is today and were islands in the inland sea. Erosion and the large deposit of sediment left when the sea retreated reduced these mountains to their current height. One of the best vistas of our entire trip was looking out over the forested valley next to a gray rock formation called "Jaws of Death" (so named because it resembles an open mouth of a lizard).

We also enjoyed our time on the Great Ocean Road, a coastal road built in the early twentieth century and inspired by an Australian's visit to the Pacific Coast Highway in California. The Great Ocean Road hugs the coast in some areas, travels through sheep pastures in others, and overlooks fabulous sandstone outcrops in the water. Most of the coastline is sandstone cliffs eroded by the ocean. In several places the wave action erodes the lower rock faster than the upper part, creating wonderful sandstone islands, bridges and pillars. The most famous formation is the "Twelve Apostles"—nine pillars standing offshore near the coast. We watched a picture-perfect ocean sunset backdrop this magnificent formation. Spectacular!

Once in Melbourne we alternated sightseeing with visits to the numerous friends we met in our travels. The young, energetic couple we met in Diakofto, Greece showed us the natural beauty of Geelong (a city to the southwest of Melbourne) and surrounding coasts. We explored Melbourne with friends we met in South America and

Jennifer with the "Twelve Apostles," Great Ocean Road, Australia.

Vietnam, and shared dinner with fellow travelers from our Africa and Egypt/Jordan tours.

Jennifer enjoyed her trip to the Immigration Museum, which was especially enlightening. Australia, like America, is populated largely by immigrants. The first immigrants to Australia came in the convict fleet, arriving in Sydney in 1788. Over the years the countries of emigration have shifted from primarily England, Ireland and Wales during the nineteenth century, to Greece and the Baltic countries post-World War II, and Vietnam and Cambodia in the 1970s and 1980s. The form of transportation has also changed from sailing ship to steam ship to airplane.

We also enjoyed our tour of the Old Melbourne Gaol ("jail" for Americans), now a museum. The jail was built in 1841 to house short-term prisoners and those awaiting execution (135 individuals were hung at the jail). However, the discovery of gold in 1851 increased the prison population and a new wing was completed in 1864. This three-story building with solitary cells and a requirement of silence by the prisoners operated until 1929. The museum also had an excellent exhibit on Australia's famous bushranger (outlaw), Ned Kelly. Ned Kelly was born in Australia to a former convict. He took to bank robbing in the 1870s and is best known for fashioning armor from plates of metal for himself and his gang. The armor is on display in the museum. Ned Kelly was eventually captured and executed at the jail, but remains a popular character, like Jesse James.

One sight which we did not see in Melbourne was an "Aussie Rules Football" or "footy" match. In Australia, three main sports dominate the public's attention/gossip and television schedules: Aussie Rules football, cricket and rugby. To an American, Aussie Rules football might appear to be similar to rugby, but come to find out is nothing like rugby, and has four goal posts at either end of the rounded field. Cricket, well... we are still trying to figure that game out! On the television news each night, sports seem to be the most dominate feature next to rumors about different athletes. Australians love their sports and everything related to it.

One errand we ran in Melbourne was the purchase of a fifth camera for our trip. The camera we brought from the United States stopped working after getting wet in the Iguacu Falls, so we bought a second camera in Curitiba, Brazil. That camera died moments before the sun rose on the Himalayas. The third camera we purchased was a manual 35-mm one we bought in Agra, India because, when we went to take pictures at the fort, we realized Erik had left our camera in Amritsar. (Because of our wonderful friends, the camera was returned to us before we left India). We purchased another Advanced Photo System camera in Kathmandu, and that is the one that quit working in Melbourne. The Melbourne camera shop employee commented that we must have worn our cameras out with the large amount of film we shot. He was right!

We left Melbourne early on a Sunday morning and headed inland toward Australia's largest city, Sydney, via the Snowy Mountains and Australia's capital city, Canberra. The Snowy Mountains contain the highest mountain in mainland Australia, Mt. Kosciuszko, measuring 7,310 feet (2,228 meters). As the mountains are below the permanent snow line, the Snowy Mountains only have snow in winter (roughly June through October here in the Southern Hemisphere). The Snowy Mountains are part of the series of mountains ranges that sit roughly 90 miles (150 kilometers) west of the eastern seaboard of Australia. This Great Dividing Range creates the arid center of Australia, a stark contrast to the forested hillsides of the Snowy Mountains and other mountain ranges. The majority of Australia's population resides in and around the mountains and along the land between the mountains and the coast. Driving in this part of Australia is like driving in the United States, with towns and cities close together. When we traveled through the Outback, we could drive for several hours without seeing any signs of civilization besides the occasional road sign.

Unknown to many Americans, the capital of Australia is Canberra, an inland town approximately halfway between Sydney and Melbourne. Australia became a federation in 1901. At that time, Sydney and Melbourne vied to be the capital city—Sydney being the first settlement and Melbourne being the financial capital since the gold rush in 1851. It was decided a new town should be the capital and Canberra was created. Like Washington D.C., Canberra is a planned city. It has a lovely lake in the middle with the Parliament buildings in a line on one axis and the national war monuments and memorial on another. We really enjoyed touring the Australian War Memorial (museum), especially the dioramas and exhibits about World War I. Being part of the British Empire, Australia fought in both world wars (among others). Australia fought in the forces that occupied the Turkish Gallipoli Peninsula in the early part of World War I (at great loss of life) and were subsequently evacuated to fight at the European front. Australia's World War I exhibit was started in 1928 and relied on first-hand accounts from soldiers in designing the dioramas. Consequently, the dioramas depicting the battles are some of the most accurate in the world.

We also toured the new Parliament Building opened in 1988. The lobby is decorated with beautiful marble columns of rust, white and green. Similar to the United States, Australia has a House of Representatives and a Senate since the smaller states of Western Australia and Tasmania objected to population representation only. Australia, the size of the continental United States, has only a fraction of the population (19.3 million vs. 278 million) and only six states and two territories. Consequently, to have a large senate, each state has twelve senators and each territory has two. Also, Parliament is set up along the British party system, so the party in the majority sets up the government, and the other parties are the opposition, rather than having only two political parties. Interestingly, Australians are required by law to vote. In several countries we traveled to, the right to vote is a requirement (such as Peru) and registered voters who do not cast a ballot in elections are fined. This was a new concept for us as voting in America is an option, and not a requirement.

On our first day in Sydney we took a day tour to the nearby Blue Mountains. This is the area that suffered devastating bush fires during Christmas week 2001, although we saw little evidence of that in the areas we visited. The Blue Mountains are named for the blue haze that hangs over the forested valleys after it rains. Again, the rocks are made of sandstone, and the edges of the hillsides are vertical sandstone cliffs like those we saw along the Great Ocean Road. Our favorite part of the Blue Mountains was the scenic railway ride down the side of a mountain. This rail system used to haul coal up from the mines in the middle of the mountain. Thinking we were boarding a quiet "scenic" railway, we were very surprised this "train" resembled a roller coaster ride with several cars attached to the track. No problem, this would be an adventure! Just when we thought the railway could not be steeper, it dropped to an almost vertical descent (a fifty-two-degree incline) through a tunnel in the mountain! The fantastic ride was over all too soon (although just in time for the four Korean girls sitting in front of us who were quite distressed during the ride). We explored trails to the Katoomba waterfall and through the rainforests before boarding a large cable car for a scenic (and more sedate) ride back to the top.

In Sydney we again alternated sightseeing with visiting friends. The first stop was of course Sydney's architectural icon—the Sydney Opera House. Just about any image of Sydney seen overseas includes this building. It was completed in 1973 after a long and controversial design and construction period. Jorn Utzon, a young Danish architect, won the design competition in the late 1950s. His design consisted of

Sydney Opera House, Sydney, Australia.

a series of unique white shell-looking forms facing the Sydney Harbor. Utzon's design was so revolutionary even he did not know how to build it at first. He completed the exterior shells at an enormous cost and lengthy construction time. Due to the cost and time delays, after completing the exterior of the building, Utzon was forced to resign as the architect (the state government stopped paying him) and his unique interior features were never constructed. Work on the building's interior stopped for two and one-half years until a local Sydney architect revised the interior design, much to the chagrin of many international architects. Utzon has never seen the completed Opera House and the question remains whether future renovations will incorporate any of his original interior plans.

We enjoyed wandering around "The Rocks" area (the area of the original convict settlement, now an upscale restaurant/hotel area), visiting the Museum of Contemporary Art, and visiting the Sydney Aquarium. The aquarium was great since we saw the elusive platypus (very hard to see in the wild) and fairy penguins. We most enjoyed walking through glass tunnels at the bottom of the shark tank and having the sharks and massive (8-foot- (2.4-meter-) wide) stingrays swim directly overhead! We finished our aquarium visit with the Great Barrier Reef exhibit, whetting us for our visit to the actual Great Barrier Reef less than three weeks from now. We also enjoyed a personal tour of the coast north of Sydney by a friend we met in South America. Sydney sits inside a well-protected circular harbor that has a small opening to the open seas. We walked along the beach in Manly (unique because a one-half-mile (800-meter) strip of land separates the harbor shore from the ocean) and climbed to the lighthouse near Palm Beach to overlook the coastline and the harbor.

Australia is the first country we visited where we stayed in hostels rather than hotels. In the majority of countries we traveled in, we found comfortable hotel rooms for about US $15 per night. In India, we often used room service since we were certain our room was air conditioned (not a sure thing with the restaurants) and it cost no more than the restaurant prices. Erik also preferred watching television news during dinner, especially around September 11. In Australia, we stayed in backpacker-type hostels in individual rooms. Bathrooms were down the hall and most hostels have kitchen facilities. It is more difficult to cook for ourselves than in New Zealand, since we have to carry our extra food with us and in New Zealand we had our own refrigerator and pantry.

On Saturday, March 30 we boarded a comfortable twelve-hour night coach bus north to Lismore to visit yet another friend from our travels. Traveling by bus in Australia was quite a treat, much like traveling on overnight buses in Chile and Argentina. We mostly traveled with British women between twenty-two and twenty-six. Australia allows young Brits a work visa where the young people can work and travel in Australia for up to a year. Aussies can live and work in England for up to two years. When we stopped around 3 AM for breakfast, our bus driver informed us that Britain's Queen Mother had died. For the next week, Australian newspapers and television had many remembrances of her life. We learned much about the Queen Mum's life (and that of her daughter Margaret who died in February) due to the strong ties between Britain and Australia.

Lismore is an inland town half an hour drive west of Byron Bay (where we are now) and a three-hour drive south of Brisbane (where we head tomorrow). We spent two rainy but wonderful days with our friend exploring the beautiful beaches on the coast and the inland-forested areas. We are now in Byron Bay enjoying the beach and vistas, and staying out of the rain by learning Zen Shiatsu massage techniques, painting (Erik created five new paintings), and wandering around this lively community. Byron Bay and the surrounding area are known for their "hippie" lifestyles. The area reminds us of a cross between a Florida surfer city and Berkeley, California.

We have less than three weeks remaining on the overseas part of our Grand Adventure. From Brisbane we continue north to Cairns with stops to explore Fraser Island (the largest sand island in the world) and cruise the Whitsunday Islands. On April 25 we leave from Cairns for Tokyo, Japan where we will spend one night before flying to San Francisco on April 26. We will write again when we have returned to America. Until then!

Love, Jennifer & Erik

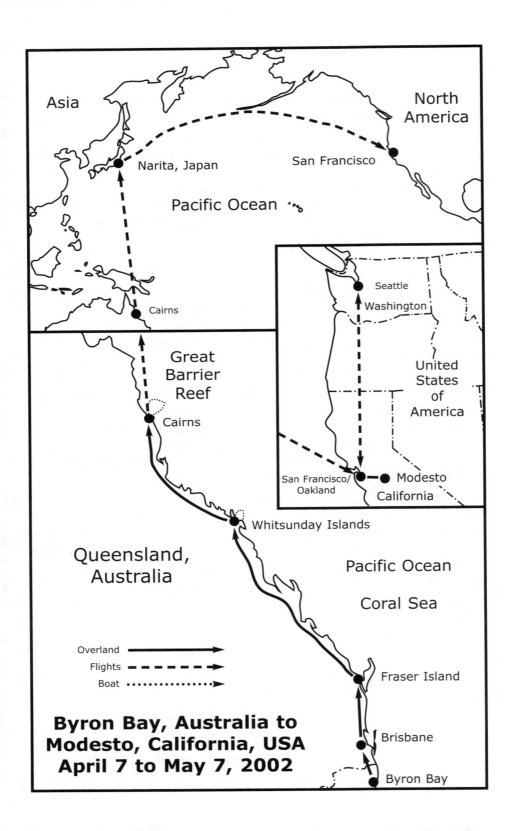

Asia

Narita, Japan

San Francisco

North America

Pacific Ocean

Cairns

Great Barrier Reef

Cairns

Seattle

Washington

United States of America

San Francisco/ Oakland

Modesto

California

Whitsunday Islands

Queensland, Australia

Pacific Ocean

Coral Sea

Overland
Flights
Boat

Fraser Island

Brisbane

Byron Bay, Australia to Modesto, California, USA April 7 to May 7, 2002

Byron Bay

19

Modesto, California, USA
Tuesday, May 7, 2002

Dear friends and family,

Greetings from America! On May 1, 2002, we returned to Oakland International Airport eighteen months to the day from when we departed on this grand adventure of ours.

From Byron Bay, Australia, we took a short bus ride to Brisbane, the capital of Queensland. Arriving at the Brisbane bus station reminded us how easy it is to travel in Australia. The bus station had a helpful tourist desk, numerous fast food options, clean bathrooms with western-style toilets, and elevators. We realized we take many things for granted in Australia since it is very similar to America.

Brisbane is a beautiful city with a compact city center and quaint suburbs that sprawl up the hillsides and along the banks of the winding Brisbane River. One evening we rode one of the city ferries that zigzag across the river for a beautiful view of the night cityscape. We stayed with an Australian friend we met on our Egypt/Jordan tour who took us to a lookout point and lovely botanical garden near her home. We also toured the South Bank of the city. This historical wharf area of Brisbane has a wonderful cultural complex including a history museum and art gallery. The highlight of the museum was seeing the only surviving German tank in the world from World War I. The Germans built only twenty tanks during that war, and most were destroyed in battle. This particular tank became bogged down during a German offensive and a group of soldiers from Queensland recovered it and brought the tank home with them at the end of the war.

From Brisbane we headed north to Hervey Bay, the base for trips to Fraser Island, the largest sand island in the world. We opted for a three-day/two-night camping adventure to explore this world heritage area. The experience was one of the best we had in Australia. Fraser Island is a long, narrow island that stretches for 74.5 miles (120 kilometers) and is only 12.5 miles (20 kilometers) across at its widest point. Because the roads are all sand, only four-wheel drive vehicles are allowed on the island. You can hire a vehicle yourself, but since we had no experience driving in sand, we opted for a guided tour. We were quite happy with our choice, especially when we passed rented vehicles stuck in the sand!

On the first morning we boarded the vehicle ferry at Hervey Bay for the island. To our surprise the ferry landed on one of the numerous beaches on the island and our island adventure started with a drive over the beach to the road. We expected an island of large sand dunes, but in reality the island is mostly forested, including pockets of rain-forest. We drove through these forests until we reached the other side of the island. Here the state highway is Seventy-Five Mile Beach and is a wide or narrow highway depending upon the tide. At low tide, the vehicles drive along a large area of packed sand that becomes increasingly smaller as the tide comes in. The highway also functions as a landing strip for aircraft coming to the island, so traffic can be quite busy at times.

We spent the afternoon exploring some of the sights along this beach. We enjoyed seeing the multi-colored sand formations and the rusted remains of the *Maheno*, shipwrecked on the island in 1935. This passenger ship was built in 1908, operated as a hospital ship during

Wreck of the *Maheno*, Fraser Island, Australia.

World War I, and was sold to Japan for scrap metal in 1935. When being towed to Japan, the boat disconnected in a storm and lodged on Fraser Island. The sand has slowly buried the ship, and the wind and seas eroded the exposed frame leaving a beautiful rusted skeleton along Seventy-Five Mile Beach. The highlight of the afternoon was swimming down Eli Creek. This fresh water creek flows from the center of the island toward the sea. Fraser Island receives large amounts of rain, so the excess in the sand wells up and runs to the sea. The creek is fairly shallow, so we floated on our backs and were pushed along by the current. We spent a very fun hour floating many times down the fast-moving, crystal-clear water looking up at the tree branches as we passed underneath.

The next morning we headed in the opposite direction along Seventy-Five Mile Beach to climb one of three rocky outcrops on the island. Sand caught at the bottom of these three rocky outcrops grew into Fraser Island. The rock we climbed was named Indian Head, as this is the point Captain Cook saw Aboriginal people during his initial voyages around Australia. After descending from the rock, we swam in the nearby Champagne Pools. These pools fill with water during high tide, and as the waves roll in, the water foams over the side of the rocks, just like in a champagne glass.

Australia has some of the most poisonous animals in the world and we encountered one of them—a death adder—in our campsite. Fortunately, a fellow traveler saw the snake before she stepped on it. Our guide quickly captured it and released it in an unpopulated area the next morning. Australian snakes, insects and jellyfish are frequently harmful to humans. In almost all places along the east coast, we could not swim in the ocean from the gorgeous beaches due to the danger of poisonous jellyfish. We even had to watch out for the jellyfish washed up onto the beach during low tide. It was a new experience to be on guard while taking a "relaxing" stroll along the beach!

On our last day on Fraser Island, we climbed over large sand dunes to see Lake Wabby, the deepest lake on the island. This particular lake was created by a sand dune blocking the exit of the freshwater creek to the sea. The lake is actually getting smaller as the sand continually blows in and fills in the lake. The blowing sand fills in uneven swirls, so it buries previous forests, leaving bare treetops sticking up out of the sand.

After returning to the mainland, we continued north along the Queensland coast to Airlie Beach. Queensland has a tropical climate and sugar cane fields stretch to the foothills of the various coastal ranges that line the highways. The contrast of the light green sugar cane fields with the darker greens of the foothill rainforests is quite beautiful. Sugar cane takes a year to grow and is planted continuously so the fields are in various stages of growth, with one field ready to be harvested each month. Before using machines to harvest the cane, farmers set fire to the cane fields the night before harvest to rid the fields of the snakes and rats that live in the cane.

Airlie Beach is the jump off point for sailing tours of the Whitsunday Islands. We had extra time before our sailing adventure, so we spent a half-day touring the nearby rainforests. Our guide had quite a sense of humor and planted rubber snakes and insects in the forest to surprise his guests. We saw numerous strangler fig trees that grow by wrapping themselves around a host tree. The coolest one we saw was where the host tree was no longer standing, so the strangler tree looked like it was hugging a void. We learned many plants in the rainforest are quite poisonous, so we walked carefully on the path trying not to touch any plants. This was fine until a fallen tree that had taken several other trees and plants down with it blocked our path. We were almost done with our tour, so we plunged into the blocked path, traversing some 200 feet (60 meters) with trepidation. Fortunately, we did not contact any poisonous plants in our plunge through the bush!

The highlight of our Queensland adventure was the three-night/three-day cruise aboard a 100-year-old tall ship, the *Solway Lass*. We boarded the ship at night, so we fully appreciated her beauty the next day. The ship was built in Holland in 1902 and used by the British in World War I and the Germans in World War II. For most of her life, she was a coastal trader in the Baltic and North Seas. In the 1970s, she carried cargo in the South Pacific. In the mid-1980s, *Solway Lass* was rebuilt and sailed in Sydney Harbor as a floating restaurant for ten years. In early 1999, the ship was refit as an overnight cruise ship with private sleeping quarters and transferred to the Whitsunday Islands. We sailed with twenty-nine passengers and six crew on our three-day adventure. Yet again, we were the only Americans on our tour. The majority of the passengers were from Britain with a few from Holland and Germany.

On our trip we snorkeled four different times, walked on the beach, hiked to a vantage point overlooking the Whitsunday Islands, and relaxed and conversed with our fellow passengers. Food was served buffet-style on the deck and was simply awesome. We even had an

Our 100-year-old tall ship, *Solway Lass*,
in the Whitsunday Islands, Australia.

Aussie barbecue on the main deck! The Whitsunday Islands are rocky and forested with beautiful white sand beaches. They are the tops of a mountain range submerged when the seas rose six thousand years ago. Sailing the Whitsundays is a popular tourist attraction and we were constantly surrounded by numerous sailing boats, mostly refitted racing boats. One of these boats accidentally left two of their passengers stranded after an island excursion and we had to fetch them and ferry them to their boat!

The best part of the trip was the snorkeling. The Whitsundays sit between the coast and the Great Barrier Reef. The graduation of the beaches and the water temperature create a beautiful environment of soft coral and fabulous tropical fish. The coral is many different shapes and colors and waves with the tidal flow. We saw many small, colorful fish and several 3-foot- (1-meter-) long Maori Wrasse. The white stripes on the face of the wrasse resemble the facial tattooing of upper class Maoris. As the Maori Wrasse swam below us, they would stir up all of the other fish and we suddenly found ourselves surrounded by swimming fish. It was very cool! Because dangerous jellyfish swim in these waters at this time of year, we wore full body wetsuits when snorkeling. It took a little time to get used to them, but we soon appreciated their protection from the sun and buoyancy, as well as their protection from jellyfish.

Upon our return to an Internet cafe in Airlie Beach, we found out Jennifer's sister in Chicago gave birth to a healthy baby boy while we were on the *Solway Lass*. We now had three new nephews to visit upon our return to the States!

After a wonderful time in the Whitsundays, we were off to our last destination in Australia—Cairns (pronounced "cans"). Erik found a wonderful hotel with a swimming pool, free Internet, free continental breakfast, and a very friendly staff. It was quite a treat and difficult to leave after our five-night stay. Cairns is a small town teeming with Japanese tourists. Australia is relatively close to Japan and offers very inexpensive prices (compared to those in Japan), so it is a popular vacation destination. We enjoyed excellent food, including a dinner made with native Australian ingredients at the "Red Ochre" and a Greek feast that reminded us of our visit to that country eleven months ago. The tourist trail in Australia is rather defined and we continually bumped into fellow travelers from our *Solway Lass* trip.

In Cairns, we took three one-day excursions, including snorkeling in the Great Barrier Reef! We opted to sail on *Falla*, a boat recommended to us by a fellow traveler in New Zealand. We sailed for two hours to the part of the reef closest to Cairns. The entire reef is massive, a chain of reefs and islands that extends from the Whitsunday Islands north to Papua New Guinea. We snorkeled three times there. Jennifer used a prescription facemask, so finally she could see with clarity the smaller fish and details of the coral. At times we snorkeled near crashing surf, so we had to be careful where we swam. No dangerous jellyfish were in the reef area so we did not need a stinger suit. All and all, the best snorkeling we experienced was at the Whitsunday Islands, a few days earlier. The reef was still wonderful, but lacked the intense color of the Whitsundays. Each boat goes to a different spot on the reef, so we expect people have different experiences.

After lunch on the boat, we swam out to a small sand island, a bit larger than a tennis court. Many people from other boats laid in the sun and swam near this sandy outcrop. Our skipper, who was from the Florida Keys, explained how coral is formed. As we swam back to the *Falla*, we followed a crewmember for a "swimming tour" of the area. We saw giant sea clams that were 4 feet (1.2 meters) wide! Some snorkelers put their hand inside its "mouth" and you could see the entire clam essentially closing around the hands (we were told it was quite safe). We saw a sea turtle swimming around, squishy dark green sea cucumbers, and some incredible dark blue starfish. We had a wonderful day on the reef. The only downside was without the stinger suits, we ended up with small areas of sunburned skin where we missed putting sunscreen on!

Another day we visited a large section of rainforest to the east of Cairns. We started the day with a visit to an Aboriginal cultural park called "Tjapukai." Here, we were exposed to various aspects of the Aboriginal culture of northern Australia. We saw a depressing film describing the horrors these people faced when the European settlers arrived, and their eventual triumph to reestablish their heritage and dying language. Then we saw a very cool play where people in traditional dress and body paint acted out aspects of their creation stories. This live acting was combined with computer-enhanced, three-dimensional graphics for an incredible visual presentation. We also saw traditional dancing, heard a *didgeridoo* (a long, wooden musical instrument) demonstration, and tried our hand at throwing boomerangs and spears. The boomerang was fairly easy to throw, but the spear was a completely different story! We then took the Skyrail up the side of a mountain and over the rainforest toward the town of Kuranda. We stopped twice to walk around elevated walkways and view the waterfalls. After a quick walk around Kuranda, we rode the Kuranda Scenic Railway back to Cairns. We passed through fifteen tunnels and hugged the mountainside as we descended to Cairns.

Our final day trip of our grand adventure was up the coast on the Captain Cook highway, north of Cairns to Cape Tribulation. Captain Cook discovered Australia for the British in 1770. After leading a scientific expedition to Tahiti, Captain Cook sighted the southeast coast of Australia and followed the land north naming a variety of rivers, inlets and points along the way. At Cape Tribulation, Cook's ship struck a reef and required six week of repairs before it was seaworthy once again. We rode in a 4-wheel drive truck similar to our Africa and Fraser Island trucks. We enjoyed beautiful vistas, a guided walk in a rainforest (on a nice boardwalk, unlike the Airlie Beach rainforest walk where we walked among the mud and foliage), and a swim in a lovely salt-water swimming pool at the place we ate lunch. We finished the tour with an hour-long boat ride looking for crocodiles on the Daintree River. We saw a baby crocodile and also a large male one swimming peacefully along the edge of the river.

On April 25, we packed up and flew from Cairns to Tokyo's Narita International Airport in Japan. From the plane we saw some of the Great Barrier Reef islands and Papua New Guinea. We landed in

Tokyo in the evening and proceeded to the hotel arranged for us as part of our flight to San Francisco. Surprisingly, we found no automatic teller machines at the main arrival terminal and the money exchangers in the terminal dealt in cash only. We thought that Japan, as technologically advanced as it is, would have several ATMs at the main airport!

The next day, April 26, was a forty-hour day for us, meaning we spent a full April 26 in Japan, and then another April 26 in America, after our flight! During our twenty-three hours in Japan we took the hotel bus to the nearby market town of Narita. We wandered down narrow streets enjoying a new culture. We visited food markets and grocery stores and watched a man skinning eel in a fish shop. We wandered into a large temple complex in the heart of town and meandered along the forested pathways admiring the various statues, ponds, and gardens. We watched schoolchildren playing games at lunch and noticed each child wears a reversible baseball-type cap so one team had one color hat and the other team another. We saw another group of schoolchildren finishing lunch around a fountain near a temple. We noticed their lunchboxes contained individual plastic containers for the different parts of their lunch and each child sat on a mat without their shoes on. Their mats folded up and were part of their lunchbox pack. Jennifer looks forward to a longer visit to Japan next time.

Jennifer and Japanese market street, Narita, Japan.

We then returned to the airport where we flew to San Francisco. One nice feature with our flight starting in Australia was that we checked our luggage all the way to San Francisco, so in Japan, we only had our carry-on bags. We felt we were missing things with only a day pack and a bag of Erik's paintings with us! At the departure gate, we were told that due to added security measures in the States we had to show our passports once more at the gate area (this was a prelude to what we have experienced back here in the States).

On a very funny note, the "economy class" lined up to board the flight with the first class and business class people lined up next to us. In Japan, it is typical for people to apologize for keeping you waiting. After standing in line for five minutes, someone from the airline said over the public address system, "Sorry for the delay, we are waiting for all the 'rich people' to line up so they can board first." We asked each other whether we had just heard them say "rich" people? Too funny!

Our 747 flight was uneventful. A cool feature was the video camera located near the front nose of the plane, so we could watch what was in front of the plane as it took off down the runway. Erik thought it was especially cool to see the San Francisco runway lights on the monitors as we landed. Jennifer did not care for it, as it contributed to her being a bit queasy. During the nine-hour flight, we each had our own video monitor and remote control for channel surfing and game playing. The first part of America we flew over was Mendocino, California.

Once at the San Francisco International Airport, we proceeded to immigration and customs. We thought for certain that we would have to pay duty as about eighty percent of our belongings were purchased overseas. The customs officer did some quick calculations and eventually told us we did not have to pay anything. Erik's parents met us at the airport and we went to lunch near the airport before our flight to Seattle, Washington later that afternoon. When we returned to the airport for our domestic flight, we noticed that we were definitely back in the States as the security lines were long, and we had to show our driver's licenses about four times during the boarding process.

We spent a few days in Seattle, visiting Erik's sister, her husband, and their three-month old twin boys. We also did a bit of Seattle sightseeing and visited a couple of friends living there. While sitting at a seafood restaurant, Erik ran into a friend he knew from the School of Architecture at the University of Kansas!

We have been back in Northern California, specifically Modesto and various parts of the San Francisco Bay Area for the past week and are busier now than traveling around to various countries! We are gathering and repacking our belongings to move to St. Louis, Missouri. We look forward to visiting with friends and family in this area. Erik's paintings arrived in the mail from Australia (minus the miscellaneous books and souvenirs also in that box!). Erik met with an art gallery in Tiburon (across the bay from San Francisco) and three of his paintings were chosen to be in a July/August exhibition on abstract art! In early September, we will move to St. Louis, Missouri. We chose St. Louis because of its proximity to family, its lower cost of living, and as a place for Erik to build his art career as it is only a day's drive away from cities like Chicago, Kansas City, Minneapolis, Cleveland, Indianapolis, and Memphis. Our move to St. Louis is not a permanent one, as we are planning to live in Europe for a couple of years starting in October 2004 and continue our travels.

We wish all of you well and THANK YOU for reading (or skimming) these e-mails!

Love, Jennifer & Erik

Closing Thoughts

Returning to the United States was easier than either of us anticipated. We expect having spent the last four months of our trip in New
Zealand and Australia helped our transition. Also, we are both working for ourselves (Erik painting and Jennifer writing), so the structure
of our day and flexibility of our time remain similar to when we traveled around the world.

There are certain things we do not miss from our travels. Gone are
the days we needed to carry a roll of toilet paper with us because the
locals in the country do not use toilet paper. Gone are the Indian days
of slabs of floor with a small trough at the back that function as a toilet. Gone are the days in South America where you toss toilet paper
into a small wastebasket next to the toilet because the plumbing cannot handle toilet paper flushed down the toilets.

We have discovered a decreased need for material things. Having
lived without extra things for eighteen months and needing to make
creative use of what we had, we still make do with the things we
stored while we traveled and purchased a limited amount of new
things for our apartment. That being said, in the United States we
usually drive to visit people and now travel with far more things than
before. Jennifer sometimes wonders how we managed to travel
around the world carrying just five bags when we hardly ever travel
to see friends and family without the back of our GMC Jimmy packed
full of things!

In describing our travels and adventures, we are usually asked one
of five questions. First, what was your favorite place? Second, what
did you pack? Third, were you scared for your safety anywhere?
Fourth, what was it like to travel with each other for so long? Fifth, did
you get sick anywhere? Since most people want to know the answers
to these questions, we answer them below.

What was your favorite place?

We loved all aspects of New Zealand and our entire visit there is the highlight of our eighteen months abroad. A simply enchanting, magical country, New Zealand has incredibly friendly people, stunning scenery and is relatively inexpensive to travel in (once you are there). In terms of other highlights, we could give you a list of our top two hundred, but we will limit ourselves to our top twenty-five.

1. The Galapagos Islands, Ecuador—An incredible week-long cruise to interesting islands with an abundance of fascinating and accessible wildlife.

2. The province of Rajasthan, India—Beautiful desert palaces and delicious food, plus an air-conditioned car with driver!

3. Santorini Island, Greece—A gorgeous Greek island in the Aegean Sea with amazing architecture and scrumptious food.

4. Petra, Jordan—A fascinating complex of facades carved into sandstone.

5. The Inca Trail and Machu Picchu in Peru—A four-day/three-night hiking odyssey with the magical lost city of the Inca civilization at the trail's end.

6. Uyuni Salt Flats, Bolivia—While driving through the largest salt flats on Earth, it seemed like we were on the very edge of the world.

7. Egyptian temples—Vast complexes with beautiful, tall columns decorated with hieroglyphics and carvings.

8. Iceland—Just breathtaking, awesome and peaceful!

9. Fraser Island, Australia—The largest sand island in the world, full of spectacular vistas and an amazing fresh-water creek we swam and floated down.

10. Whitsunday Islands, Australia—Three days and nights aboard a one-hundred-year-old refurbished tall ship sailing and snorkeling in beautiful waters.

11. Monemvasia, Greece—A small, wall-enclosed, pedestrian-only city on the Peloponnese peninsula.

12. The Australian Outback—A whole different world: rugged, isolated and mysterious.

13. Kangaroo Island, Australia—Twenty-four very fun hours touring a wildlife-filled island with an energetic guide.

14. Halong Bay, Vietnam—A three-day/three-night boat tour with a fun group of people viewing small, beautiful, green islands.

15. Annapurna Range, Nepal—A five-day trek in the foothills of the Himalayas with our guide.

16. Our felucca ride up the Nile River, Egypt—By day, reading and relaxing on our sleeping bags watching the banks of the Nile River pass us; by night, gazing at the stars.

17. Serengeti Plains and Ngorogoro Crater in Tanzania—Three days of jeep riding, mile after mile of animal herds, and fabulous animal sightings.

18. Luang Prabang, Laos—An enchanting town along the Mekong River with beautiful *wats* and a peaceful way of life.

19. Angkor temple complex, Cambodia—Wonderful old temples spread over a huge area just recently popularized by tourists around the world.

20. Tasmania, Australia—A fun time driving all over this island state, hiking, eating and enjoying its history.

21. Hoi An, Vietnam—Our favorite town in Vietnam; full of great shops and restaurants and lit up at night with hundreds of paper lamps.

22. Mekong Delta, Vietnam—A fascinating complex of waterways with an even more fascinating way of life.

23. Istanbul, Turkey—An architectural and cultural wonderland.

24. Bayt El Suhaymi merchant house and Bazaar, Cairo, Egypt—A large, restored, sixteenth-century merchant house—an architectural joy—and a bustling, crowded bazaar with wonderful sights and smells.

25. Iguacu Falls, Brazil—Our favorite waterfalls by far; the views never end!

What did you pack?

We had enough clothes for five days at a time in terms of lightweight shirts, underwear and pairs of socks. We each had two pairs of shorts; a warm, long-sleeved shirt; swimsuit; jacket; pair of gloves; roll-up sunhat and warm hat; and a pair of hiking boots and sandals. We also had a pair of pants for Erik and two for Jennifer. We scaled our toiletries down to the essentials and had no electrical appliances with us. We packed a plastic box full of Chinese and herbal remedies for various ailments and a small, but powerful, water filter. We packed small flashlights, duct tape (indispensable for mending tears in clothes), a handful of books (guidebooks and others), one compact Advanced Photo System camera with panoramic capabilities, fifteen rolls of new film in a lead bag, and a small album of color copies of our wedding pictures. We had a few other things, like passports, money belts, robe, sarong and small quick-drying towels, but definitely tried to keep the amount of things limited.

We used about ninety-five percent of the things we brought. We exchanged guidebooks and other books along the way. We shipped things home once every four months or so (mostly used film). We replaced clothes as they wore out and found that, for the most part, we could buy what we needed wherever we traveled. We purchased sleeping bags in Cape Town and we had Jennifer's sister bring American cash to us in London.

Were you scared for your safety anywhere?

Cape Town, South Africa was the place we were most concerned for our physical safety. We had no specific incidents, but were told not to walk around in the downtown area alone after dark or on the weekends. Also, for Erik, India and Nepal were not safe places in terms of public transportation. He found bus travel on these roads scary, as buses passed car after car and truck after truck, turning back into the lane at the last moment. Otherwise, we took the regular precautions we would in the United States, but generally found that we felt safer in most parts of the world than in our home country.

What was it like to travel with each other for so long?

It took a month or so to ease into traveling with each other. This was the first time the two of us had lived with each other or spent a full twenty-four hours with each other day after day, so it was not so much about the travel as just getting to know each other. By the end of South America, packing up and moving every three days became routine. We passed another hurdle when we slept together in tents during our African safari. By that point, traveling together was routine, so it was a matter of adjusting to the close quarters of a tent. (The fact that Erik was not fond of sleeping in tents did not help the matter.)

Traveling with tour groups early on was a bonus since we did not have the stress of figuring out what to see, how to get there, where to eat, and where to stay added to our learning to live with each other. By the time we reached Greece and were traveling on our own, we were comfortable with the continuous traveling life and really enjoyed creating our own itinerary and emphasizing our interests. We did tire of eating in restaurants for every meal and welcomed cooking in our campervan in New Zealand. Actually, traveling in the campervan was ideal since we unpacked our bags for six weeks straight and could eat what we wanted whenever we wanted without having to hunt down a particular type of food. That was heaven!

Did you get sick anywhere?

For the most part we stayed healthy and we never saw a doctor on our trip. Jennifer had an upset stomach from the water on our Galapagos Island cruise and used the water filter after the third day. She also had a bout with food poisoning in Bolivia and recovered in four days. This was the most ill Jennifer was on our trip. We both experienced mild cases of diarrhea for the first few days in most countries.

We also both had a stomach virus in Cambodia that lasted three days. This was the most ill Erik was on our trip.

We would do the trip all over again in a heartbeat; it was worth the time and money to explore the world, chasing summer. We plan another three-year trip in the end of 2004. We plan on living in various parts of Europe, using Europe as a base to return to places we enjoyed, travel through northwest Asia and the Baltic states, and extensively tour Europe. Until then!

Acknowledgments

We wish to thank all those who made our trip easier, richer and more enjoyable. To list you all by name would take an entire book. In addition, we thank the following people who provided exceptional encouragement and support in creating this book.

We thank Dayla Soul, who encouraged us to "write a book now" after our third e-mail installment.

We thank Linda Duringer, who graciously gave up her kitchen table so we could send out our first draft manuscript for review.

We thank Alison Cleaver, Alesia Foster and Bill May for reading and commenting on our first draft manuscript.

We thank Kathy Rooney for reading and commenting on our second draft manuscript.

We thank our wonderful editor, Hollie Keith.

We thank Kristi Whitfield for assisting in formatting the book.

About the Authors

Jennifer and Erik Niemann left careers in law and architecture to travel the world between November 2000 and May 2002. Jennifer graduated from Harvard Law School and is now a writer. Erik is a graduate of the School of Architecture and Urban Design at the University of Kansas and is now an abstract painter. *Chasing Summer* is their first book. They currently reside in St. Louis, Missouri.

Share a Grand Adventure

CHECK YOUR LEADING BOOKSTORE OR ORDER FROM JSL PUBLISHING

- Fax this form to 314-754-9191

- Call toll-free 1-877-255-5749. Have your credit card ready. International toll-free calls also accepted.

- Send this form to: JSL Publishing
  6614 Clayton Road #333
  St. Louis, MO 63117 USA

  Telephone: 314-537-1049

Send me _____ copies of *Chasing Summer* at $14.95 each.
** Missouri residents add 7.325% sales tax**

Within the United States:

☐ Send by priority mail—add $4.00 for 1 or 2 books. (Call for larger orders.)

☐ Send by first class mail—add $3.00 shipping and handling for the first book and $1.00 for each additional book.

Outside the United States, add $5.00 shipping and handling for the first book and $2.00 for each additional book.

Please print clearly

Name _____

Address _____

City/State/Zip _____

Phone _____ E-mail _____

☐ My check or money order payable to "JSL Publishing" for $_____ is enclosed. All check or money orders must be in U.S. funds.

☐ Please charge my   ☐ VISA   ☐ MasterCard

Card # _____ Expiration Date: _____

Signature _____
(as it appears on the card)